HOW THIS BOOK CAN HELP YOU EXERCISE YOUR FREEDOM TO CHOOSE

- It helps you learn more about yourself and what your location needs and interests really are, and gives you the means to compile your personal Prospering Profile.
- It gives you a chance to review the most important facts and predictions about each potentially excellent place to live well and happily.
- It provides a simple but effective system for rating the areas so that you can record your assessments and make judgments.
- It offers a simple procedure for integrating your ratings with your own Prospering Profile so that you can make an intelligent final analysis.

The authors of this book have worked together for many years as co-directors of a major educational corporation, as university deans and professors, as researchers, and as psychotherapists. In *Finding Your Best Place To Live in America,* they have combined their talents and experience to help you make the best possible choices for the happiest, fullest life.

About the Authors

The authors have filled many professional roles and lived many places. We have worked together for many years as co-directors of a major educational corporation, as university deans and professors, as researchers, and as psychotherapists.

In all our efforts to help others, we have become increasingly aware of the *urgent need for a method* for helping people find their best places to live.

We have been shocked at how difficult it has been for our clients and students to search out the vital information they need to identify the places in which they will prosper and be happy.

This book, then, integrates our interests in therapy, research, and helping others live life to the fullest.

Finding Your Best Place to Live in America

Dr. Thomas F. Bowman • Dr. George A. Giuliani
Dr. M. Ronald Mingé

WARNER BOOKS

A Warner Communications Company

Dedication

Marilyn Mingé, Carol Giuliani, and Marie Bowman
have helped so many others to find happier and more
exhilarating ways to live. Their encouragement, example,
and inspiration have helped countless friends, family members,
and three lucky husbands.

This book is, of course, dedicated to them.

Table of Contents

Acknowledgments

Mark McCoy has been responsible for research coordination and, as usual, has accomplished wonders.

The information in this book has come in large part from the tireless, inspired, and creative research efforts of Mrs. Ronnie Gold. She has maintained her excellent wit and enthusiasm throughout this major project. And not incidentally, she introduced us to her lawyer husband, Bruce Gold, whose help and insights are very much appreciated.

Dr. Marilyn Oser contributed mightily to the successful completion of our project.

Several wonderful librarians have made significant contributions; their consideration and research assistance were invaluable. They are:

Joanna Barton, U.S. Dept of Commerce, Bureau of the Census

David Clemens, Huntington Public Library, Huntington, N.Y.

Anne McCormack, C.W. Post College Library

Masako Yukawa, C.W. Post College Library

Reference librarians at Plainview-Old Bethpage Public Library, N.Y.
Reference librarians at Syosset Public Library, N.Y.

Additional appreciation is expressed for the invaluable assistance of the National Climatic Center, Ashville, North Carolina.

Dr. Leon Taub, Vice President of Chase Econometrics, was generous with his time and expertise.

Father Patrick Shanahan, Ph.D., assisted in the formulation of the project and provided encouragement throughout.

To all of the above, our heartfelt thanks.

Preface

One of the greatest gifts you can give, to others or to yourself, is that most precious of commodities: special knowledge for living more happily and successfully.

The purpose of this book is to share special information with you. It offers this knowledge on two levels:

(1) It will help you, as an individual, to identify the best place for you to live in America. Your decision will be based on *improved self-awareness* and an *easy-to-follow system* for deciding which of all the wonderful options really fits you best.

(2) The book also describes and compares 82 *different areas* across the United States. Five vital factors are discussed and presented in detail, with more than 60 charts and maps, with in-depth discussions. Predictions and trends are outlined as well.

As you learn about what is happening and likely to happen throughout America, you will gain exciting new insights into the real stories behind the newspaper headlines.

In our therapeutic and consulting practices, we have discovered that *the place where a person lives dramatically affects his happiness and success in life*.

Putting it another way, there are places which are really right for you. Living in the right place will increase your income, improve your enthusiasm and mental outlook, and do so much more to help you live a fuller and more complete life.

Your best place could be where you are right now, or it could be a genuine surprise. You will find out when you have completed the Prospering Inventory and have learned so much about the amazing opportunities America has to offer. The result will be your own list of the best places in America for you.

1

Finding Your Place to Prosper

"Why, you haven't changed a bit," we reassured each other. Next we swapped a few stories about our various children and asked the obligatory questions about each other's relatives. And then our old friend began to moan about the misfortunes which had befallen the town where he lived.

"Oh, we've had a lot of problems. Our soap business went down the drain. The limestone quarry is in the pits. And the skiing is going downhill fast. Pollution is peeling our paint and turning everyone's hair a light green. And when the sewage treatment plant exploded...it just changed the atmosphere of the whole place."

"Good grief! Why don't you move, Filbert!"

"Move??!! Are you crazy? I couldn't move. It's my home!"

Have you noticed how proud most people are of whatever place they call home? The man eating a pork tenderloin sandwich in Missouri is just as convinced as the woman crunching through a soft-shelled crab in Maryland or the girl sipping an egg cream in New York that there is no place like where they live.

We will agree that each region, whether urban or rural, sunbelt or frostbelt, has much of which to be proud. But the premise of this book is that the area you call home should be, and can be, selected on the basis of accurate information.

Our Plan for You

What kind of information do you need? We have found that most people need three types:

1. You need to know more about your own values and interests in order to make the best location decisions for yourself and your family.
2. You also should have vital information about all of the wonderful locations throughout America . . . including predictions about what is likely to happen to them in the years ahead.
3. And then you need a system for choosing the best place for you to prosper.

All of these are provided in this book.

Your Freedom to Choose

Finding the right place to live can make you happier, wealthier, safer, and more comfortable. It can bring you opportunities you never dreamed of.

Where you live can make an incredible difference in your future career, your cost of living and purchasing power, your health, and the quality of life you will enjoy. For example, did you know that more than *five times as many jobs* will be available in those many parts of the country which are booming? Or that *property taxes are six times higher* in some states than others?

Can you name the regions considered by climatologists to be so hot and humid that it's *extremely difficult to function* several months of the year . . . and yet the regions are thriving?

Like millions of other Americans you may have had the

2

feeling that you should make a move, but didn't know which areas would be most appropriate. There are so many choices, with so many variations. The good news is that all that variety offers marvelous opportunities to find the places which are practically tailor-made for you to thrive and prosper.

We have written this book to help you identify your own best places to live happily and well, given your individual needs and interests.

Our concern, frankly, is that a large part of our American population has not realized that the concept of freedom includes the freedom to choose the best place to thrive. Far too many of us have been programmed by experience to accept passively whatever life has handed out. How many times have you heard a friend or relative say something like, "Oh, gollywhiz. I couldn't move there. That's not for me. I was born here, and . . . ."

Many Americans move frequently. In fact, 20% of our population moves in any given year, although most stay in the same general area. Over a five year period, however, approximately 20% moves to another county or another state. The question is, are they making the right moves?

In the past, Americans have moved mainly for economic reasons. Now they are beginning to relocate for sunnier weather, less crime, improved quality of life, less pollution, lower humidity, and a host of other important and legitimate reasons. All of these are discussed in detail later in this book.

But please keep in mind that there is another, very personal, reason for considering a change of location. It was, in fact, one of the motivating forces behind our writing this book: Much of *how* you are and *who* you are is determined by your environment. Why not select a new place to prosper with the intention of becoming an improved, happier, more prosperous you?

John Oliver's Story

John Oliver, an acquaintance for many years, is a terrific example of an individual taking control of his own destiny and moving to a better place to prosper.

He had inherited the family cement business in a midwestern state, and managed it extremely well. He clearly was on his way to becoming very wealthy and enjoyed the advantages of growing power and respect in the area. Still, he was not entirely happy. As a college student in Florida he had discovered that he enjoyed the water and sand of beaches much more than water and sand mixed into concrete. He continually longed for the ocean and the sailing he had grown to love. What to do? In John's own words:

"I decided that I didn't want to be locked into a place where I wasn't happy, even if I was successful. I was lucky, because I knew where I wanted to live, but I didn't know how to make a living being on the beach. For my family's sake I couldn't just be a full-time beachbum, but I was willing to trade my high income for a chance to live where I wanted to be."

John's solution took some nerve and confidence, because he sold the concrete business and bought a part-ownership in a Florida yacht building firm with an ex-college buddy. Few yachts are made of concrete, so his previous experience didn't help all that much. But he learned fast and soon the new company was thriving. As John explained it:

"I got my wish! We opened new plants in South America and in Connecticut. I always get to live and work in summer weather, and I am on the beach or sailing every day. Even if the company didn't make a lot of money, I am a much happier man."

And now John is a yachting millionaire instead of a concrete millionaire. The money is the same . . . but he's having a lot more fun.

How This Book Can Help You Find Your Best Place to Prosper

The decisions you make regarding the most appropriate place to live and thrive depend upon four essential procedures.

First, a special chapter has been devoted to helping you *learn more about yourself* and what your location needs and interests really are. In our extensive experience in helping others make appropriate decisions, we have learned that values and interests are not easily sorted out without some objective processes. We have developed a self-evaluation test, called the Prospering Inventory, to aid you in determining your own values and their relative importance in selecting a best place to prosper.

After completing the Prospering Inventory, which takes only about 30 minutes, your scores are easily translated into your own Prospering Profile. The profile graphically shows the relative importance of your needs and interests. It will help you make the crucial decisions about whether to relocate, and if so, where.

It should be most interesting to compare your own Prospering Profile with those of family members and friends.

Second, you need to have a chance to *review the most important facts and predictions* about each potentially excellent place to live well and happily. To help you do this, we have gathered the most useful information available which is essential to the best decision-making process.

Information has been collected and analyzed relating to five decision-making factors. Each of the five factors is treated in detail, with easy-to-interpret charts and discussions, in separate chapters. The five decision-making factors are:

(1) Economic facts and predictions
(2) Essential weather information
(3) Population characteristics and trends
(4) Area risks and hazards
(5) Quality of life considerations

Third, as you learn about the wonderful variety of places in which you potentially could prosper, a simple but effective *system for rating the areas* is provided. The Locations Rating System which we have developed should be invaluable in helping you make the best judgments about the various areas. In addition, it helps you to keep an easy-to-follow record of your assessments.

Fourth, a simple procedure for *integrating your ratings*

5

with your own Prospering Profile is provided for you. This procedure, which we have dubbed "The Final Analysis," will give you a list of the best places for you to prosper. The list will be based on your own needs, interests, and values and on the best information and predictions available.

82 Places You Might Like

This book is chockablock full of exciting information about 82 areas throughout the United States. We have selected these 82 places because they are spread across the map and represent very well the options which are available. In addition, a great deal of information about them was obtainable, although usually with an enormous amount of digging and research.

State-by-state comparisons also are provided as supplemental information to help you gain an excellent understanding of the areas you are giving consideration.

In most instances we have presented the areas and states in rank order, to make your comparisons easy and your decisions less complicated. You will find, for example, that the regions are ranked from most to least, highest to lowest, warmest to coldest, and so forth, depending upon the factor being described.

The areas are designated by the cities in them, but they are not restricted to the cities themselves. In most cases the places include surrounding areas as well, encompassing suburban and even rural regions.

The federal government has designated these and other areas in the United States as "Standard Metropolitan Statistical Areas." For a description of what is included in the statistical areas, see Appendix A. If you are not particularly interested in Appendix A, then take our word for it: the areas we have selected are representative of a good cross-section of America.

In some charts in later chapters you will find that a few of the 82 areas are not included. The reason for this is simple: information was not available. However, in most cases, the same areas are not consistently missing from the charts. You should find abundant information for making your decisions.

A map showing our 82 areas is provided on the next page.

What About Rural Areas and the Suburbs?

Even though we have designated our 82 areas by the city most prominent in them, most of them do include surrounding suburban areas and many include rural countryside as well.

If you are interested in rural living, you no doubt are aware that housing costs usually are lower than in more developed neighborhoods. And even if you like living "down on the farm," the cultural advantages of the nearby city likely will be important to you.

Some interesting statistics from the 1980 census show a higher percentage of Americans are moving to rural areas than into cities. The last time this happened was in 1820!

A major reason for this shift to country living is the ability of Americans to live in rural areas and still work, shop, and play in nearby suburbs and cities.

When making judgments about an area's rural living possibilities, you should be able to anticipate lower taxes and other living costs, higher commuting expenses, less convenience, and, of course, fewer crowds. We suggest you use the charts as guidelines but adjust for rural lifestyles.

Don't Trust the Grapevine

Much of what we Americans think we know about our country's regions is based on hearsay and second-hand impressions. Many friends on the west coast have told us that they never could live on Long Island because, "It's too crowded for us! All those skyscrapers, and people cheek-to-jowl . . . how do you tolerate it?"

The fact is that long-standing zoning laws have made most Long Island towns much less crowded than most western towns. But most of us gain our knowledge of other places by the grapevine, and as a result we can miss out on wonderful

7

Our Eighty-Two
Areas in America

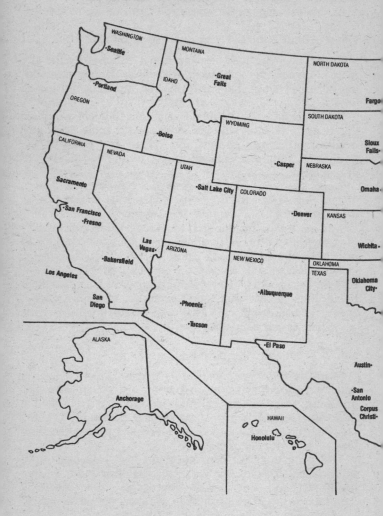

opportunities. Here is an example of how the grapevine works:

"Well, guess what! We're thinking of moving to Houston. I heard that things are really percolating in Texas."

"Holy coyotes, Barbie! Are you really thinking of going down south? I don't think you're cut out for life on the lone prairie. I heard the bugs there are bigger than the Cadillacs. And the humidity . . . forget it!"

"That's not what my cousin Gridlock said. Would you pass the peanuts, please? She said you can find a job there without any problem at all. And you know how long I've been looking for a teaching position here."

"I don't know. My sister-in-law's best friend just came back from Dallas, or was it Phoenix . . . anyway, she didn't like it at all. And the prices are out of sight. Want some coffee?"

"No thanks. I'm decaffeinated. I thought prices were much lower in the south. Do you know what the schools are like?"

"Listen, my friends. Forget Houston. I heard Colorado is where it's at. In fact, my brother's hair dresser told him . . . ."

Minnesota or Mississippi? Arkansas or Alaska? Exciting options, but your decision about where to locate is too important to your future to make based only on grapevine information.

What Prospering Means

A pocket full of virgin credit cards and a wheelbarrow full of cash are not necessary for one to live prosperously. Being richer than a whiskey baron is one way of prospering, but there are several others, and they are given careful attention in this book too.

Some of them will be extremely valuable to you, and the others will be important but not as vital. Our intention is to help you identify the dimensions of prospering which are of the greatest benefit to your life. Here are the prospering factors which are featured in this book.

10

Living
Where You Fit

Your own personal interests and needs are different from those of other people. You are a unique individual, and as such deserve the right to live in a place which is consistent with what you want out of life.

For example, the authors have found that many people like a mellow and relatively serene lifestyle. At the other extreme, there are those who crave excitement, change, adventure, high stimulation, and flirtation with danger. The point is that no one should have to live where he does not fit in, or where the environment is not going to support and nurture him and contribute to his greatest satisfaction in life.

But, you might ask, isn't there a place, a Shangri-la, which is wonderful and appropriate for everyone? The answer is yes! It's called Heaven. But here in America we have to compromise a little. We have to find the best place to meet our own individual needs.

Sometimes you may run across an article or book touting some spot or another as the answer to everyone's dreams. It may be a small undiscovered town just six miles south of Flatrock, Arizona. It could be a major city hailed as the cleanest, or safest, or cheapest place in the nation, and therefore the place we all should rush to prosper.

But the differences among us make such an approach simplistic and even harmful. Uncounted numbers of people have charged off to one place or another because it has been described as "the best place in America," only to be disappointed because it wasn't right for them.

We provide all kinds of lists and rankings in this book, but also give you a simple system for deciding which places are best for you, based on your individual characteristics. Our message is that there are a great many terrific places to live, and some of them will fit you much better than will others.

Making More Money

No doubt about it. This is an important prospering factor. You can increase your income dramatically by relocating to

11

where money is being made in prodigious amounts, where people are being hired instead of being laid off, and where incomes are predicted to continue to rise over the next ten years.

The money facts and predictions we provide in this book are based on several sources. However, we have been extremely fortunate to be able to use data generously provided by one of America's foremost economic think tanks and consulting services, Chase Econometrics. Their consideration is greatly appreciated, and we know that you will benefit from our application of their findings to your search for the best place to prosper.

So, thanks to their help, if making lots of money is your bag, have we got a chapter for you!

Improving Your Career

You've heard it said that climbing the career ladder often depends on being in the right place at the right time. There is more truth than fiction in that point of view. Our effort here is to help you find the right place before the right time has passed you by. Or as a favorite uncle might say, "You don't want to be the last gold miner to arrive at Sutter's Mill!"

The career information contained in this book can be very valuable if you are concerned with this prospering factor.

Lowering Costs of Living

You can improve your standard of living, whether or not you make more money. How? By increasing your buying power through reducing costs and expenses. If your approach to prospering involves saving money, the information provided in this book can save you a bundle.

You will be happy to discover that living expenses are really pretty reasonable in some areas of the country. An appropriate relocation could make a wonderful difference in your standard of living. And keep in mind that lowered costs of living save you after-tax dollars . . . the most precious kind of bucks you can own.

Improving Quality of Life

If you could live in a beautiful environment, with an abundance of cultural and educational opportunities, and a plethora of public services, wouldn't you likely be prospering? For many of us, this variable is the most important of the prospering factors. We probably could not be satisfied with a town whose greatest cultural boast is the state's largest flag twirling team.

Recently a friend considered moving to a rural region in upstate New York, but after enjoying (perhaps, for him, "enduring" is more appropriate) a tractor pull, the once-a-year fair, and the gossip in the village coffee shops, he recognized that for all its charm, the rural life has a brand of culture which may not be appealing to those used to metropolitan living.

Finding the Best Weather

Oh, America has it all! From fantastic fall festivals of fiery color to misty mornings by the bay, desert landscapes, to snow up to our armpits ... America is a kaleidoscope of weather variety and opportunity. And living in the right weather is another important prospering factor.

If you are a weather-reactive person, as we shall find out in Chapter 2, you will be particularly interested in the climate and weather information we have included. Even if you are not all that weather-reactive, you will find it helpful when you are deciding whether to pack your old galoshes or your longjohns.

Avoiding Risks and Hazards

To paraphrase the Bible, for what does it profit a man to gain anything if he is whirled off in a tornado, falls into an earthquake canyon, or over breakfast reads that he's been living for nineteen years next to a chemical dump site?

To many of us, prospering means being able to live in a healthy and safe place. Risk and hazard factors described in this book include crime, pollution, hurricanes, thunderstorms, earthquakes, tornadoes, nuclear installations . . . if we mention any more you might have nightmares! Suffice it to say that with this information you can identify the places in America which are relatively free of risks and hazards to your health.

Choosing Your Neighbors

America's citizens are stirring, and many are on the move again. Hordes of northeast and north central residents are moving south and west, and a sizable number are moving in the opposite directions. As they relocate, they are changing the nature of many of the populations across the nation. One of your main prospering factors may be living in an area with certain population characteristics. For example, you may be looking for places with rapidly growing numbers of people, or you may prefer to avoid the crowds.

Predictions for the next ten years also are provided, so that the population winners and losers can be identified. Such factors as religion, ethnic, sex and age characteristics for each region are included in the chapter on population.

In sum, then, our aim is to help you to find the best place to prosper based on the factors which are of greatest importance to you.

This is not to say that you have to move thousands of miles or even hundreds of blocks to find the best place. The spot in which you live right now could be superb for you. It is quite possible that after considering the wonderful options discussed in this book you might choose to remain where you are.

If you do decide that your present home is your own best place to live and thrive, you will do so knowing it was an informed, educated selection. Moreover, you will be even more aware of the benefits and the drawbacks of the area you have chosen to call home. Your review of both the 82 locations and your own preferences will help you become more aware of the opportunities which surround you today. And you will certainly get some terrific vacation ideas along the way!

Managing Your Own Future

Prospering has another meaning which deserves special consideration here. It means being in control of your own destiny, with freedom to choose and to be your own person. This lifestyle need not be the sole province of the very rich, who can live where they want. If you will try to be more open to the possibilities which exist both elsewhere and where you live now, you can become a more fulfilled person.

Actors and Reactors

In our practice of psychotherapy and through research, we have discovered that effective, successful people are willing to make the kinds of changes which will enhance their prospering. People who prosper have something very important in common. They are not passive. They are not content to simply accept what circumstances have dictated for their lives.

Instead, people who prosper are those who make things happen. They view life as manageable, as at least partly under their control. And they are not likely to blindly go along with the accidents of inheritance, birthplace, or name. They are the Actors, because they act on life.

Reactors, on the other hand, are much more apt to wait and see what develops for them. They react to events rather than try to manage them. Often they are discontented with life, hemmed in by situations and expectations, and believe what they have been told about themselves.

In effect, they have been trapped by their surroundings, both physical and social, and cannot envision a way out. Even more unfortunate, most Reactors do not realize that they are in a trap.

Most of us, if the truth be known, have more Reactor tendencies than Actor. We usually have given little thought or organized planning to where we should live. We have grown up in various towns, cities, or the countryside, stayed in one place or moved due to circumstances mostly not of our own making . . . but it's been aimless for the most part, or due to chance.

We have identified ourselves as southerners, New Englanders, Hoosiers, Texans, suburbanites, westerners, city dwellers, from South Hill or Lincoln Avenue. Much too often we have become a *part* of the locale, identifying with it, living it. And mindlessly staying in it, whether it is good for us or not.

Where you live now could be a satisfactory place. It could even be an ideal place for you. On the other hand, life is far too important to live in a place determined by luck or your grandparents.

Remember that what was right for your ancestors may not be at all correct for you. Not only have the things which attracted them to a location probably changed enormously over the years, but you are your own person. You deserve the right to make your own informed decisions about where you will live and prosper.

Now, before you quickly try a disclaimer, "Oh gosh, this is only little old me, from the second reading group and not too great a neighborhood," we must insist that others have made the moves and the changes. It is more than just possible. With planning, it is even easy.

Leave Some Baggage Behind

In our efforts to help people find more satisfying lives, our clinical experience has led us to sometimes make a suggestion which some other practitioners tend to view with horror. We frequently suggest to people that they try another location in order to improve their chances of personality change.

What?? But aren't personalities formed by the age of five? Doesn't sibling rivalry or a difficult birth cause the anal retentiveness which make Lester into a grouchy bookkeeper? After all, doesn't one take his personality along wherever he might move?

Not if you don't want to take all the baggage along with you! One of our clients moved three times in two years, each time with several purposes. Jane wanted to climb the corporate ladder, live in various places for the fun of it, and she wanted to get married.

Jane also had made a decision that each time she relocated

16

she was going to try to take along the best features of her personality and leave behind those attitudes she did not like in herself.

But wouldn't this make Jane a phony? What about her authenticity?

In our professional view, no one should have to passively accept all of the personality tendencies molded into us by our experiences, whether recent or long past. In fact, once we become old enough or wise enough to recognize the impact of our environments on us, both social and physical, we have the right to select the surroundings which will help us become the persons we wish to be.

In many instances, moving to another location can be most conducive to beneficial personality change. That is, if we are insightful enough to leave some baggage behind.

What happened to Jane? It wasn't easy for her. One of her problems was a deep distrust of men, and she compensated with sarcasm and assertiveness. But when she moved to an area where people tend to be extremely courteous, she was able to relax her defenses and become a someone others could love more completely.

Did she meet the man of her dreams? Yes, a most courtly fellow, and they developed a passionate love affair. Unfortunately, he didn't tell her he was already married and not about to leave his very wealthy wife.

All of which tells you that you can change yourself by changing your environment . . . but you should never mistake courtliness for sincerity.

2

The Prospering Test and Location Rating System

Recently one of the authors took his family to an expensive restaurant, and as young children always seem to do as soon as the family is settled, his two-year-old son loudly announced to the world that he "had to go potty." Daddy took him to the men's room, and apparently Bobby was unfamiliar with the urinals he saw being used there. He was wide-eyed when they returned to the table, and he couldn't wait to announce for all the restaurant to hear, "Hey Mom! Guess what Dad did in the sink!"

What made it even worse is that he didn't know his money values either, and as Dad later tried to quietly herd the children out of the restaurant, the two-year-old's voice again piped over the murmur of the crowd, "Hey Daddy! You left a nickel! You left a nickel under your plate!"

It's not easy to know what's going on when you're two, or even eighty-two. Our perceptions of ourselves are often not as accurate as we like to think. Usually we greatly underestimate our potential for growth and change. Often we are not sure of what we want or need in life. This can be especially true when we are trying to decide which place meets our individual needs and interests.

Not all places touted as terrific or ideal can even come close to ideal for most people. We are too different from one another to justify pointing out any spot, whether in the sunbelt or the frostbelt, as being THE PLACE for everyone. Your best place is a personal place, depending on your interests, needs, and values. We have developed the Prospering Test to help you clarify those personal interests on which your location decision depends.

The Prospering Test

The Prospering Test has been specially designed for this book to help you identify your own personal interests and needs when it comes to finding the best place to thrive in America. You will not find the Prospering Test anywhere else, because we developed it specifically to provide a simple but effective system for choosing the most likely place for you to live and thrive.

The Prospering Test takes about 30 minutes to complete, and the scoring is easy. The scores that you achieve are then converted into your Prospering Profile, showing which of your location needs and interests are highest and which are less important to you.

The scores on your Prospering Profile will be extremely helpful. Not only do they help you learn and clarify more about yourself, but they are designed to be part of the easy system we have developed.

As you discover amazing things about the various areas in America, and what will likely happen to them in the next ten years, your Prospering Profile will help you make the most beneficial judgments in each of the following chapters.

After all, it will be much easier for you to understand the implications of job predictions, the cost of living, weather information, etc., provided in this book when you have a better idea of what your individual Prospering Profile looks like.

Another benefit of the Prospering Test comes in the last

chapter. A simple procedure has been developed for combining your Prospering Test scores with your reviews of the most likely places to prosper. The results of this process, which we call The Final Analysis, will give you a rating for each of the places you have given consideration. In short, you will end up with a score sheet which will indicate the places best suited for *you* to thrive in America.

Directions

The Prospering Test consists of 90 matched pairs of descriptive statements. Your mission, should you choose to accept it, is to select the statement from each pair of items which is more important to you personally as you look for the best place to prosper.

Place an x, or √, or whatever symbol turns you on, in the box next to the statement you have selected for each item. In each case, try to choose the statement which is more important to you. Even if both are about equally important, or if neither is very important to you, please select one anyway. If you cannot make a choice fairly quickly, pass the item and come back to it after completing the rest of the test.

It is not necessary for you to attempt to be consistent with your responses. Pairings are not repeated in the test. As you make choices, try to imagine the implications of each statement for the place you might select to live. Answer as honestly as you can, because it's what YOU value that counts. There are no right or wrong answers; there are only choices which are best for you.

The Prospering Test should take about 30 minutes to complete, although there is no time limit. Work at a pace which is comfortable for you.

Good luck. The chair you are sitting in will self-destruct in 12 seconds.

Prospering Inventory

For each item, choose the alternative which is more important to you when selecting a place to live. Be sure to make a choice for all items.

1. ☐ C. The density of population in an area,
        or
   ☐ B. The amount of heat and humidity to be found there.

2. ☐ A. Employment opportunites in an area,
        or
   ☐ E. The type and quality of health care facilities available there.

3. ☐ B. How long and severe the winters become,
        or
   ☐ D. The amount of violent crime in an area.

4. ☐ C. The percentage of people by various religions,
        or
   ☐ E. The quality of transportation to be found there.

5. ☐ A. Property taxes in an area,
        or
   ☐ D. The amount of crime found there.

6. ☐ A. The cost of living,
        or
   ☐ C. The ethnic composition of an area.

7. ☐ D. The risk of tornadoes and hurricanes in an area,
        or
   ☐ E. The quality of newspapers, television and radio stations.

8. ☐ A. The amount of money you will earn in an area,
        or
   ☐ B. The heat and humidity there.

9. ☐ C. Predicted population growth in an area in the next ten years,
        or
   ☐ D. The presence of nuclear power installations.

10. ☐ B. The average temperature during each month in an area,

               or

    ☐ E. The chance to attend major sporting events there.

11. ☐ C. The number of single people in an area,

               or

    ☐ B. The number of rainy days there.

12. ☐ A. The growth of your income over the next ten years,

               or

    ☐ E. The quality of transportation available.

13. ☐ B. The number of months with freezing temperatures,

               or

    ☐ D. The amount of violent or property crime in an area.

14. ☐ C. The racial characteristics of the population in an area,

               or

    ☐ E. Cultural opportunities, such as theater, opera, etc.

15. ☐ A. How much it will cost to buy a house in an area,

               or

    ☐ D. The incidence of thunderstorms there.

16. ☐ A. The amount of money you will be able to save,

               or

    ☐ C. The religious composition of the population.

17. ☐ D. The incidence of such natural hazards as earthquakes, floods, hurricanes, etc.

               or

    ☐ E. The number of excellent hospitals and clinics.

18. ☐ A. The rate at which new houses are being built in an area,
    or
    ☐ B. The number of days with snow there.

19. ☐ C. The political makeup of an area—Republican, Democrat, Independent, etc.,
    or
    ☐ D. The likelihood of tornadoes or hurricanes.

20. ☐ B. How warm and humid it becomes during the summer,
    or
    ☐ E. The scenic beauty of an area including lakes, forests, flowers, hills, etc.

21. ☐ B. The weather on a typical winter day in an area,
    or
    ☐ C. The growth in population of an area over the next decade.

22. ☐ A. The amount of property taxes one must pay,
    or
    ☐ E. The general cleanliness of an area.

23. ☐ B. The amount of heat and humidity in an area,
    or
    ☐ D. The incidence of floods or earthquakes.

24. ☐ C. The composition of the population by religion,
    or
    ☐ E. The quality of schools in an area.

25. ☐ A. The growth in employment over the next ten years,
    or
    ☐ D. The amount of pollution in an area.

26. ☐ C. The racial composition of an area,
   or
   ☐ A. The general economic conditions to be found there.

27. ☐ D. The presence of nuclear power installations,
   or
   ☐ E. The quality of education available in local schools.

28. ☐ A. How much it costs to live in an area,
   or
   ☐ B. The number of days with sunshine.

29. ☐ C. The size of the population,
   or
   ☐ D. The amount of crime to be found there.

30. ☐ B. The amount of precipitation each year,
   or
   ☐ E. The quality of news media in an area.

31. ☐ B. The number of days the sun shines in a year,
   or
   ☐ C. The number of aliens in an area.

32. ☐ A. The cost of buying or renting a house,
   or
   ☐ E. The quality of museums, operas, philharmonics, etc.

33. ☐ B. The number of rainy days,
   or
   ☐ D. The amount of pollution in an area.

34. ☐ C. The ratio of young people to older people in an area,
   or
   ☐ E. The number and quality of health care facilities.

35. ☐ A. The cost of living in an area,
       or
    ☐ D. The presence of nuclear power installations.

36. ☐ A. The growth in your income over the next ten years in an area,
       or
    ☐ C. The growth in population in an area during the eighties.

37. ☐ D. The risks of natural hazards, such as hurricanes, tornadoes, etc.,
       or
    ☐ E. The quality of major sports teams to be found there.

38. ☐ A. How much it costs to buy a house,
       or
    ☐ B. The amount of snow which falls each year.

39. ☐ C. The percentage of single people in an area,
       or
    ☐ D. The risks and hazards from tornadoes and hurricanes.

40. ☐ B. The level of heat and humidity in an area,
       or
    ☐ E. The presence of cultural opportunities such as theaters, operas, etc.

41. ☐ C. The percentage of retired people in an area,
       or
    ☐ B. The first and last days that frost normally occurs.

42. ☐ A. The extent of unemployment in an area,
       or
    ☐ E. The quality of newspapers, television stations, etc.

25

Rock Valley College - ERC

43. ☐ B. How hot and humid it gets in the summer,
       or
   ☐ D. The presence of a nuclear reactor within fifty miles.

44. ☐ C. The density of the population in an area,
       or
   ☐ E. The quality of major sports teams there.

45. ☐ A. Anticipated job opportunities during the next decade,
       or
   ☐ D. The incidence of criminal violence in an area.

46. ☐ A. The property taxes one must pay in an area,
       or
   ☐ C. The ethnic composition of the population.

47. ☐ D. The incidence of criminal violence in an area,
       or
   ☐ E. Cultural dimensions such as museums, opera, etc.

48. ☐ A. The amount of money you will earn in an area,
       or
   ☐ B. The first and last day of frost.

49. ☐ C. The racial characteristics of an area,
       or
   ☐ D. The general quality of the air and water.

50. ☐ B. How comfortable the weather will be during the year,
       or
   ☐ E. Recreational opportunities such as beaches, hiking trails, skiing facilities, etc.

51. ☐ B. The normal daily temperature,
       or
   ☐ C. The ratio of men to women in an area.

52. ☐ A.   The amount of your personal income,
          or
    ☐ E.   The quality of professional sports teams.

53. ☐ B.   The number of days that it rains during the year,
          or
    ☐ D.   The incidence of natural hazards such as hurri-
          canes or tornadoes.

54. ☐ C.   The growth in population in an area during the
          next decade,
          or
    ☐ E.   The quality of education available in the local
          schools.

55. ☐ A.   The amount of your personal income,
          or
    ☐ D.   The presence of nuclear power installations.

56. ☐ A.   The amount of money you will pay for state and
          local taxes,
          or
    ☐ C.   The number of people per square mile in an area.

57. ☐ D.   Risks or hazards such as tornadoes, hurricanes,
          etc.,
          or
    ☐ E.   The quality of education available in local schools.

58. ☐ A.   The growth rate of new jobs during the next
          decade,
          or
    ☐ B.   The amount of heat and humidity during the
          summer.

59. ☐ C.   The composition of the population by religion,
          or
    ☐ D.   The amount of pollution in an area.

60. ☐ B. How comfortable the weather will be during the year,
     or
    ☐ E. The number and quality of universities in an area.

61. ☐ B. The number of bright, sunny days,
     or
    ☐ D. The general quality of air and water.

62. ☐ A. How much it will cost to live in an area,
     or
    ☐ E. The quality of education available in the schools.

63. ☐ B. How comfortable the weather will be over the year,
     or
    ☐ C. The number of people living in an area.

64. ☐ C. The composition of the population by race,
     or
    ☐ E. The general scenic attributes of an area.

65. ☐ A. Property taxes on a house,
     or
    ☐ D. Natural hazards such as hurricanes or tornadoes.

66. ☐ C. The ratio of males to females,
     or
    ☐ A. Increases in personal income during the present decade.

67. ☐ D. The level of pollution in an area,
     or
    ☐ E. The quality of medical facilities to be found there.

68. ☐ A. How expensive it is to live in an area,
     or
    ☐ B. How comfortable the weather will be during the year.

69. ☐ C. The number of people living in an area,
    or
   ☐ D. Risks and hazards such as floods, earthquakes, etc.

70. ☐ B. The number of frost-free days,
    or
   ☐ E. The quality of health care facilities.

71. ☐ B. The number of cloudy and rainy days each year,
    or
   ☐ E. The quality of newspapers, television stations, etc.

72. ☐ C. The composition of the population by religion,
    or
   ☐ D. The general quality of the air and water.

73. ☐ A. The tax rate for state and local taxes,
    or
   ☐ B. The number of days with sunshine.

74. ☐ D. The amount of crime in an area,
    or
   ☐ E. The availability of quality transportation.

75. ☐ C. The population density of an area,
    or
   ☐ A. Desirable job opportunities there.

76. ☐ A. State and local taxes to which you will be subject,
    or
   ☐ D. The exent of natural hazards, such as hurricanes or tornadoes.

77. ☐ C. The growth of the population in an area during the next ten years,
    or
   ☐ E. The availability and quality of public transportation.

78. ☐ B. The number of snow storms each winter,
    or
    ☐ D. The presence of nuclear power installations.

79. ☐ A. The extent of unemployment in an area,
    or
    ☐ E. The availability of quality medical services.

80. ☐ B. The number of days it rains each year in an area,
    or
    ☐ C. How highly populated an area will become during
    the next decade.

81. ☐ B. The number of days it snows each year in an area,
    or
    ☐ C. Population characteristics of an area such as age,
    race, sex, etc.

82. ☐ A. How much of your income will go toward property
    taxes,
    or
    ☐ E. The quality of newspapers, television, etc.

83. ☐ B. How cold it normally gets during the winter,
    or
    ☐ D. The possibility of natural disasters such as floods,
    earthquakes, etc.

84. ☐ C. The growth in population in an area during the
    eighties,
    or
    ☐ E. The number and quality of universities to be found
    there.

85. ☐ A. The annual growth rate in personal income in an
    area,
    or
    ☐ D. The general quality of air and water.

86. ☐ A. How much it costs to buy a house,
           or
    ☐ C. Population characteristics of an area by religion.

87. ☐ D. The amount of crime in an area,
           or
    ☐ E. The beauty of the scenery to be found there.

88. ☐ A. The annual growth in your personal income,
           or
    ☐ B. The number of days with below-freezing temperatures.

89. ☐ C. Characteristics of the population of an area by race,
           or
    ☐ D. The presence of a nuclear reactor within fifty miles.

90. ☐ B. The amount of snow which falls each year,
           or
    ☐ E. The general scenic qualities of an area.

Developing Your Prospering Profile

Check again to see if you have left any items blank. It is important to make a choice for each of the 90 items.

Count all the marks you have made in the boxes next to the letter A, and then enter the number of "A" statements at the top of Your Prospering Profile. In the same way, count the number of times you selected "B" statements, "C" statements, "D" statements, and "E" statements. Enter these totals in the appropriate places at the top of Your Prospering Profile also.

Your next step, and a simple one it is, is to plot the totals on the chart itself. A sample Prospering Profile is provided as an example.

SAMPLE PROSPERING PROFILE

A.	Economics	28
B.	Weather	10
C.	Population	14
D.	Risks & Hazards	26
E.	Quality of Life	12

A. Economics Chapter 3	B. Weather Chapter 4	C. Population Factors Chapter 5	D. Risks & Hazards Chapter 6	E. Quality of Life Chapter 7
36				
35				
34				
33				
32				
31				
30				
29				
28				
27				
26				
25				
24				
23				
22				
21				
20				
19				
18				
17				
16				
15				
14				
13				
12				
11				
10				
9				
8				
7				
6				
5				
4				
3				
2				
1				
0				

YOUR PROSPERING PROFILE

A. Economics
B. Weather
C. Population
D. Risks & Hazards
E. Quality of Life

	A. Economics Chapter 3	B. Weather Chapter 4	C. Population Factors Chapter 5	D. Risks & Hazards Chapter 6	E. Quality of Life Chapter 7
36					
35					
34					
33					
32					
31					
30					
29					
28					
27					
26					
25					
24					
23					
22					
21					
20					
19					
18					
17					
16					
15					
14					
13					
12					
11					
10					
9					
8					
7					
6					
5					
4					
3					
2					
1					
0					

Using Your Prospering Profile to Make Decisions

Each of the five factors (Economy, Weather, Population, Hazards, Quality of Life) in the Prospering Profile is the subject of a special chapter in this book. The purpose of the Prospering Inventory is to help you determine the *relative* importance of each of the factors to you personally.

Obviously, if your scores are quite high for one or two factors, you will want to give extra consideration to them in making location decisions. To help you do this in a systematic way, we have developed a bonus point procedure, but this can wait until the last chapter when you make your Final Analysis.

In like manner, if your scores are very low for certain variables, you probably will not give as much consideration to those factors when making your choices. However, please keep in mind that the Prospering Inventory is intended to help you decide the *order* of importance that the factors hold for you. It is possible that even a factor which you did not select as often as others can still be important to you. In brief, we do not suggest that you should ignore the factors which you have scored as relatively less important, because they can still have some genuine decision-making value.

It can be both interesting and informative to compare your profile with that of others you know. If your profile is very different from that of your spouse, for instance, you may have a wonderful opportunity to demonstrate your capacity for compromise. Or it could be just the excuse you have been needing to dump the old fool. We are sure that everyone will understand when you explain that "It was no one's fault, actually. Our profiles were just not compatible."

What Comes Next?
Using the Location Rating System

We have packed a tremendous amount of information into the following chapters about our 82 different areas in the United States. However, we do not want the information to be overwhelming or too bulky for you to assimilate or apply in your decision-making process.

In other words, we don't want you to say about this book what the third-grader wrote in his first book report: "This book tells more about fish than I care to know."

To help you make the best use of the facts and discussions provided, we have developed the Location Rating System. It is a highly useful and easy-to-follow procedure which involves three simple steps:

Step 1

On page 37 we have provided a Tentative Interest List of all 82 areas reviewed in this book. As you look over the list, we suggest that you select a minimum of <u>five</u> and a maximum of <u>fifteen</u> areas in which you have a tentative interest.

As you work with this list later, you undoubtedly will add some other regions to it and probably will remove some of your original possibilities. You need not be concerned that your original tentative list will limit you in any way. Its purpose is to reduce the number of possible places to prosper to a size which is readily manageable, with additions and subtractions easily accomplished.

After you place a check by the areas on the list, write their names on a separate piece of paper. This will serve as a handy reference guide as you review charts in the next five chapters.

Again, as you discover other regions which are of interest to you, please add their names to your list of possible places to prosper.

Step 2

In the next five chapters we provide approximately 60 charts and maps. Each chart includes a Reaction Column. Do you need to review each chart and make a decision about each city? No, it is not necessary, although some readers may enjoy doing so. We *would recommend* that you review every chart for the cities you have tentatively selected, and stay on the lookout for other promising regions.

Charts have been especially designed to be easy and pleasant to review, because they present useful information in rank order. You should be able to quickly determine how a region compares to others and interpret information and its implications without difficulty.

If the information in a chart makes a city look like a winner for you, place a (+) next to the city in the Reaction Column. If the information reduces your interest in the region, place a (–) in the Reaction Column. We have left space for additional comments and notes if you would like to add them.

Remember to add to your list those cities which look promising, and consider removing those names from the Tentative Interest List when the negative information becomes significant to you.

Step 3

You will find Summary Grids at the end of Chapters 3, 4, 5, 6, and 7. It is important that you fill in each Summary Grid as soon as you have finished each chapter.

The procedure is a simple one. We have found it easiest to work with one city from your Tentative Interest List at a time. As you look back over the (+) and (–) ratings in the Reaction Columns for each city on your list, give a score of 5 on the Summary Grid to those cities which have a predominance of (+) ratings. Give a score of 3 to the areas with enough (+) ratings to be a distinct possibility, although not a sure winner. If a city has only a few (+) ratings and is only an outside chance, give it a score of 1.

If a city has no appeal based on the chapter's information, consider removing it from your Tentative Interest List.

After you have gone over each city on your Tentative Interest List, for each of the charts, for each of the chapters, you will no longer have a Tentative Interest List. Using the procedure in Chapter 8 called The Final Analysis, you will have completed the exciting process of **Finding Your Best Place to Live in America.**

TENTATIVE INTEREST LIST

Directions: Place a check mark by five to fifteen areas in which you have a tentative interest. On a separate piece of paper write these names so that you will be able to refer to them as you review charts in the following chapters. As you identify additional areas of interest, check those areas. You may remove areas from your list as you lose interest in them.

	Areas	Check Tentative Interest Areas	Initial Comments
1	Akron, Ohio		
2	Albany, New York		
3	Albuquerque, New Mexico		
4	Anchorage, Alaska		
5	Atlanta, Georgia		
6	Austin, Texas		
7	Bakersfield, California		
8	Baltimore, Maryland		
9	Baton Rouge, Louisiana		
10	Beaumont, Texas		
11	Biloxi, Mississippi		
12	Birmingham, Alabama		
13	Boise, Idaho		
14	Boston, Massachusetts		
15	Buffalo, New York		
16	Burlington, Vermont		
17	Casper, Wyoming		
18	Charleston, South Carolina		
19	Charleston, West Virginia		

	Areas	Check Tentative Interest Areas	Initial Comments
20	Chicago, Illinois		
21	Cincinnati, Ohio		
22	Cleveland, Ohio		
23	Columbia, South Carolina		
24	Columbus, Ohio		
25	Corpus Christi, Texas		
26	Dallas, Texas		
27	Denver, Colorado		
28	Des Moines, Iowa		
29	Detroit, Michigan		
30	El Paso, Texas		
31	Fresno, California		
32	Fargo, North Dakota		
33	Grand Rapids, Michigan		
34	Great Falls, Montana		
35	Hartford, Connecticut		
36	Honolulu, Hawaii		
37	Houston, Texas		
38	Indianapolis, Indiana		
39	Kansas City, Missouri		
40	Las Vegas, Nevada		
41	Little Rock, Arkansas		
42	Los Angeles, California		
43	Louisville, Kentucky		
44	Manchester, New Hampshire		
45	Memphis, Tennessee		

	Areas	Check Tentative Interest Areas	Initial Comments
46	Miami, Florida		
47	Milwaukee, Wisconsin		
48	Minneapolis, Minnesota		
49	Mobile, Alabama		
50	Nashville, Tennessee		
51	Nassau-Suffolk, New York		
52	Newark, New Jersey		
53	New Orleans, Louisiana		
54	New York, New York		
55	Norfolk, Virginia		
56	Oklahoma City, Oklahoma		
57	Omaha, Nebraska		
58	Orlando, Florida		
59	Philadelphia, Pennsylvania		
60	Phoenix, Arizona		
61	Pittsburgh, Pennsylvania		
62	Portland, Maine		
63	Portland, Oregon		
64	Providence, Rhode Island		
65	Raleigh, North Carolina		
66	Richmond, Virginia		
67	Rochester, New York		
68	Sacramento, California		
69	Salt Lake City, Utah		
70	San Antonio, Texas		
71	San Diego, California		

	Areas	Check Tentative Interest Areas	Initial Comments
72	San Francisco, California		
73	Seattle, Washington		
74	Shreveport, Louisiana		
75	Sioux Falls, South Dakota		
76	St. Louis, Missouri		
77	Tampa, Florida		
78	Tucson, Arizona		
79	Tulsa, Oklahoma		
80	Washington, D.C.		
81	Wichita, Kansas		
82	Wilmington, Delaware		

3

Where the Money Trees Bloom

Do you think you might need a change of location? Your wallet may need a change even more than you do! Because where you live can make a world of difference to your bank account, your career outlook, and your security in life. Consider these examples:

In those areas which are thriving, personal *income growth* is *six times greater* than in sluggish regions.

More than seventy times as many *jobs* will be available in booming areas.

Costs for *electricity* are *six times higher* in some regions than in others.

Ten times as many *houses* will be built in growing areas as in regions with dwindling populations.

House prices in some areas average more than *twice as much* as in others. Regardless of prices, houses and condominiums are *jumping in value* some places, and not even keeping up with inflation in others.

State and local *taxes* in some areas are nearly *twice as high* as in some other places.

Property taxes in some states are as much as *six times as high* as in other states.

For most people, the main reason for moving to another place is financial. This usually implies the possibility of earning more money, making better investments, or reducing living expenses. With careful planning, you might even be able to relocate to a place offering all three of these financial advantages.

In order to earn a higher salary or discover skyrocketing investment opportunities, one usually should consider moving to areas which are thriving and in an expansion phase. Your own fortunes are likely to rise dramatically when you are in the right place at the right time for growth. Consider the example of Shari and Roger, when they transported their small business to one of the burgeoning cities of Texas:

"Unbelievable! This place is a gold mine compared to where we were living. We were breaking our backs trying to earn a living selling enough antiques, watching taxes shoot upward, and some of our customers were terrible . . . they would haggle and complain. They were used to buying, or should I say stealing, at garage sales. They didn't realize what quality was. When we found that professional buyers from the west and south were scooping up the best antiques for resale there, we looked into moving our business.

"Now that we're here in Texas, our customers have sufficient income that they can afford quality and don't bicker about a few dollars one way or another. Business is thriving, our new house is zooming in value, we're buying two more houses for investment, and living better than ever! It was a terrific move for us. Wouldn't you say so, Roger?"

"Yes, dear."

On the other hand, sometimes people deliberately look for quieter places, with lower living costs and a more placid environment. Your aim in this case might be more for savings and security than for "getting rich quick." If you are retired, for example, you probably will be more concerned about expenses than about income possibilities. Or you may prefer a location, such as some areas in New England, where tradition and old-fashioned ways are still valued so much more than the bustling transitions of thriving economic growth.

We have friends who came back to rural upstate New York after trying several booming areas around the nation. They recently purchased a beautiful 150-year-old home with two acres and a lovely brook for $25,000. It is located only three scenic miles from a pretty village with good shopping, and only 20 minutes from Saratoga Springs, a famous resort area

They heat with firewood, which costs nearly nothing if you don't count bruises and burns. They burn only three cords of wood per year, at $60 per cord if they buy it and free if they cut their own. And they say that wood heat warms the body twice . . . once when you cut it and once when you burn it.

Property taxes are only $300 per year. Both are professionals who earn a little less than they would in much of the nation, but most of what they earn can be saved or spent as they will. They and most of their neighbors are extremely happy that the nation is tending to move south and west, for they love their Grandma Moses scenery and peaceful uncrowded living. The calendar for them seems to have stopped somewhere around 1951, or perhaps 1927.

Some Crucial Questions

As you consider the best places to live, you will raise some very important questions regarding income and costs. You might well ask, "But if I move there, how much will it cost to live? Will I be able to afford housing and food? Should I plan to rent a small garret and perhaps eat only occasionally?"

Economic questions are important. It is essential to give some careful consideration to the expenses to be found during and at the end of any move. And if you get a raise of $3000 but discover that renting a house costs more than the raise itself, have you made any gain by moving?

43

The following sections outline the economic facts you will need before making your best decisions. Let's recognize, however, that the relationship between various costs and expected changes in income are best understood by giving them your own personal application.

For example, we will provide, among many others, a chart outlining the differences among the costs of houses across the nation. Now before you react to some of the high prices with, "Oh oh, I can't afford a house *there*!" consider the fact that the higher-cost house in the new area may *earn* you much more money in appreciation in value than you might make by working all year. If you like investments, then you will have a different view of the cost of housing chart than will someone who prefers to rent.

Where to Make the Most Money

In some parts of our nation, where time has lingered and the old ways persist, it is said that an entire town can be sustained with just one ten dollar bill. And the only difference between good times and hard times is that during good times the ten dollar bill moves around town a little faster.

If you are looking for yesteryear, with old fashioned speech, values, and lifestyles, you can find it in many back-waters of America.

But, friends, they are not the best places to go if you are interested in making a lot of money. Where should you relocate to earn the most money? Your chances are best if you go where money is being made, and spent, in heaping quantities.

You could become wealthy in any of the 50 states or any of our 82 areas, and it is possible to achieve an excellent and glamorous lifestyle in just about every corner of the map. But your chances of doing so are much better where the money action is.

Where are your best places for making the most money? We have provided several charts to show you where the chances are greatest. Chart 1 shows the "spendable income" earned in each of the 82 areas.

Income You Can Spend

After you pay your taxes to the federal and state governments, you have left what is frequently referred to as "disposable income" or "spendable income." The very excellent Standard Rate and Data publication terms it "consumer spendable income." Whatever you call it, it provides an excellent clue to prospering possibilities for each area.

The income-after-taxes figures shown in Chart 1 are for 1982, courtesy of Standard Rate and Data Service. The incomes represent incomes per household, ranked from highest to lowest.

Also shown in Chart 1 are the portions of the populations which earn from $8000 to $9999, $10,000 to $14,999, and so forth. By reviewing the numbers for the different places, you will be able to make your best judgments regarding income amounts and income distribution.

As you can see from Chart 1, the range of incomes is tremendous. In fact, the economic distance from Hartford, at the top of the list, to Tampa at the bottom, is almost as great as the geographical distance.

INCOME YOU CAN SPEND
(After-tax income ranked highest to lowest)

Rank	Area*	Consumer Spendable Income Per Household	$8000-9999	$10,000-14,999	$15,000-24,999	$25,000 & over	Reactions
1	Hartford	$39,180	5.8%	14.4%	32.2%	45.1%	
2	Anchorage	36,181	4.0	7.9	25.6	61.0	
3	Washington, D.C.	33,352	5.1	10.8	28.3	53.4	
4	Nassau-Suffolk	33,089	4.7	12.9	30.7	49.5	
5	Newark	31,515	6.1	13.7	29.9	47.1	
6	Boston	31,390	8.1	16.7	31.6	39.5	
7	San Francisco	29,324	5.9	12.6	29.6	49.0	
8	Houston	28,983	6.8	13.2	28.4	49.1	
9	Detroit	28,883	6.2	14.7	32.6	43.5	
10	Seattle	27,809	6.3	14.4	32.0	44.5	
11	Wilmington	27,720	8.2	16.4	30.4	41.3	
12	Casper	27,700	6.9	13.9	30.6	46.2	
13	Chicago	27,644	6.2	14.4	31.7	44.6	
14	Portland, Me.	27,314	10.8	18.3	30.6	35.5	
15	Minneapolis	27,199	6.7	15.5	32.3	42.8	
16	Dallas	27,180	7.8	14.6	29.0	45.1	
17	Rochester	26,966	6.7	16.0	33.8	40.1	

Rank	Area*	Consumer Spendable Income Per Household	$8000-9999	$10,000-14,999	$15,000-24,999	$25,000 & over	Reactions
18	Cleveland	$29,964	7.4%	16.9%	31.3%	39.4%	
19	Philadelphia	26,552	8.3	16.8	31.3	39.4	
20	Honolulu	26,512	6.0	11.4	29.4	50.5	
21	Milwaukee	26,407	7.3	17.3	32.7	39.4	
22	Denver	26,400	6.8	13.7	29.8	47.1	
23	Baton Rouge	26,379	8.8	15.4	29.6	42.5	
24	Beaumont	26,182	10.7	18.1	30.4	36.3	
25	Los Angeles	25,964	7.5	14.5	29.5	44.7	
26	New Orleans	25,916	9.8	15.7	27.9	42.2	
27	Kansas City	25,810	8.6	17.0	31.1	39.2	
28	Las Vegas	25,777	6.2	12.5	29.7	49.3	
29	New York	25,726	8.3	14.8	27.9	44.0	
30	Manchester	25,203	8.6	17.1	32.4	38.3	
31	Richmond	25,064	9.1	16.4	29.9	40.2	
32	Akron	25,017	8.6	19.3	33.6	34.2	
33	Cincinnati	25,014	9.6	18.0	31.2	36.4	
34	St. Louis	24,888	9.2	18.5	31.6	35.9	
35	Raleigh	24,886	9.3	15.4	28.4	43.1	
36	Wichita	24,561	11.0	18.1	29.9	35.8	
37	Grand Rapids	24,540	9.0	18.7	32.2	35.8	
38	Indianapolis	24,505	8.5	17.7	32.2	37.4	
39	Sacramento	24,475	8.1	15.4	31.0	41.8	
40	Atlanta	24,456	8.1	14.9	30.1	43.2	
41	Louisville	24,366	10.3	18.3	30.2	36.4	
42	Albany	24,334	9.3	18.2	31.6	36.1	

Rank	Area*	Consumer Spendable Income Per Household	$8000-9999	$10,000-14,999	$15,000-24,999	$25,000 & over	Reactions
43	Columbus	$24,224	9.2%	17.4%	31.2%	37.9%	
44	Pittsburgh	24,211	11.3	19.8	30.2	32.8	
45	San Antonio	24,127	11.7	16.9	27.7	38.5	
46	Miami	24,038	9.0	14.4	26.0	46.3	
47	Providence	23,969	10.9	19.5	30.4	33.5	
48	Oklahoma City	23,931	10.3	16.9	29.1	39.1	
49	Portland, Or.	23,903	8.0	16.1	30.7	41.5	
50	Buffalo	23,889	9.9	19.8	31.0	34.1	
51	Des Moines	23,781	8.9	17.3	32.4	37.7	
52	Austin	23,579	8.7	14.3	27.4	46.3	
53	El Paso	23,531	12.2	17.4	28.0	36.7	
54	Corpus Christi	23,445	12.4	18.0	28.9	34.7	
55	Columbia	23,443	9.9	16.5	29.6	38.9	
56	Omaha	23,320	9.3	17.3	31.2	37.9	
57	Phoenix	23,169	7.7	14.1	28.8	46.3	
58	Norfolk	23,033	11.7	17.8	29.5	35.4	
59	Charleston, W.V.	22,998	12.6	19.3	30.1	32.1	
60	San Diego	22,870	7.8	14.2	29.4	45.1	
61	Orlando	22,562	9.6	15.5	28.4	42.4	
62	Nashville	22,433	11.2	17.8	28.8	36.9	
63	Shreveport	22,238	12.8	18.8	29.1	33.0	
64	Boise	22,063	9.0	15.9	29.5	42.0	
65	Tulsa	21,970	10.9	17.8	29.0	37.3	
66	Baltimore	21,920	8.7	16.9	31.2	38.8	
67	Great Falls	21,835	12.5	19.6	29.9	31.5	

Rank	Area*	Consumer Spendable Income Per Household	$8000-9999	$10,000-14,999	$15,000-24,999	$25,000 & over	Reactions
68	Memphis	-$21,812	11.5%	17.8%	28.6%	36.2%	
69	Fargo	21,809	10.2	17.3	30.1	38.3	
70	Salt Lake City	21,798	9.3	17.2	30.7	38.7	
71	Burlington	21,785	8.2	16.0	31.8	40.3	
72	Tucson	21,774	9.2	15.3	28.5	43.4	
73	Fresno	21,627	11.3	17.4	29.3	36.1	
74	Little Rock	21,610	12.1	18.0	29.1	35.3	
75	Sioux Falls	20,943	11.3	19.3	31.7	33.1	
76	Bakersfield	20,904	11.6	18.4	30.8	32.9	
77	Mobile	20,784	13.2	19.0	28.1	33.2	
78	Charleston, S.C.	20,620	12.9	18.7	29.7	33.0	
79	Albuquerque	20,612	9.8	15.5	29.3	41.0	
80	Birmingham	20,287	14.1	19.6	27.2	32.1	
81	Biloxi	19,416	15.8	20.3	28.8	28.1	
82	Tampa	19,383	12.6	17.7	27.1	37.1	

*Standard Metropolitan Statistical Area

Sources for all charts and maps may be found on pages 385–88.

Per Capita Incomes

Chart 2 shows a different kind of comparison of incomes, because we have compared incomes against the national average. As you can see, the average income earned in Grand Rapids is right at the national average. Incomes in Anchorage are 50% higher than the average, and Casper, San Francisco, and Washington, D.C., also are much higher than the average.

Please keep in mind that it is possible to prosper financially even in places considerably below the national average. This is especially true if living costs are concomitantly lower. As you make your decisions about the best places to thrive, be sure to compare *income* with the *cost of living* figures which are provided later in this chapter. As you will notice, many of the places with high incomes also have elevated living costs. The trick is to find those places which have a lost cost of living but high incomes. The variety of charts and discussions included in this chapter can help you find those best places for you to thrive financially.

PER CAPITA PERSONAL INCOMES
(Figures show percentages above or below national average—ranked from high to low)

Rank	Area*	Percentage	Reactions
1	Anchorage	+ 50.0	
2	Casper	+ 48.0	
3	San Francisco	+ 36.7	
4	Washington D.C.	+ 35.3	
5	Nassau-Suffolk	+ 28.9	
6	Seattle	+ 24.9	
7	Houston	+ 24.7	
8	Newark	+ 22.9	
9	Chicago	+ 19.8	
10	Hartford	+ 19.8	
11	Los Angeles	+ 19.3	
12	Minneapolis	+ 19.1	
13	Denver	+ 18.8	
14	Cleveland	+ 18.1	
15	Detroit	+ 17.8	
16	New York	+ 16.6	
17	Dallas	+ 16.1	
18	Des Moines	+ 15.8	
19	Wichita	+ 15.6	

Rank	Area*	Percentage	Reactions
20	Milwaukee	+14.7	
21	Boston	+13.6	
22	Portland, Or	+12.0	
23	Richmond	+11.7	
24	Kansas City	+10.9	
25	Wilmington	+10.6	
26	Honolulu	+10.3	
27	Oklahoma City	+9.3	
28	Tulsa	+8.9	
29	Las Vegas	+8.5	
30	St. Louis	+8.3	
31	Rochester	+7.9	
32	Pittsburgh	+7.8	
33	Sacramento	+7.1	
34	Philadelphia	+6.6	
35	Indianapolis	+6.0	
36	Omaha	+5.7	
37	Beaumont	+5.4	
38	Baltimore	+5.3	
39	Atlanta	+5.1	
40	San Diego	+4.7	
41	Cincinnati	+3.8	
42	New Orleans	+2.9	
43	Manchester	+2.5	
43	Sioux Falls	+2.5	
44	Charleston, W.V.	+2.2	
46	Boise	+1.9	
47	Fresno	+1.4	

Rank	Area*	Percentage	Reactions
48	Phoenix	+1.3	
49	Miami	+.9	
50	Columbus	+.3	
51	Grand Rapids	+.2	
52	Great Falls	−0.5	
53	Buffalo	−0.6	
53	Providence	−0.6	
55	Baton Rouge	−0.8	
56	Raleigh	−1.3	
57	Albany	−1.8	
58	Akron	−2.1	
59	Louisville	−2.5	
60	Portland, Me.	−2.7	
61	Fargo	−3.3	
62	Little Rock	−3.4	
63	Austin	−3.8	
64	Bakersfield	−4.2	
65	Birmingham	−6.3	
66	Nashville	−7.3	
67	Shreveport	−7.5	
68	Orlando	−7.7	
69	Corpus Christi	−8.0	
70	Tampa	−8.2	
71	Memphis	−8.6	
72	Burlington	−8.7	
73	Tucson	−8.9	
74	Norfolk	−9.2	
75	Albuquerque	−9.3	

Rank	Area*	Percentage	Reactions
76	San Antonio	−11.2	
77	Salt Lake City	−12.2	
78	Columbia	−13.1	
79	Mobile	−19.5	
80	Charleston, S.C.	−22.8	
81	Biloxi	−27.4	
82	El Paso	−29.8	

*Standard Metropolitan Statistical Area

Where Incomes Are Going to Rise

Inflation is likely to cause incomes to appear to go up everywhere. In some areas, however, incomes are going to *jump* up. In other places, your financial progress may be low and slow . . . as dangerous to your bank balance as it is in flying. Chart 3 shows the projected increases in income through 1990.

You need to know where the money is going to be made and whether it is worth your while to be there.

Where? The south shall rise again! And so shall its incomes. Granted that the earnings in the south and southwest have lagged behind the rest of the nation in the past. But they probably will soon catch up with the traditionally higher paid northeast and north central, and likely will surpass them in the not distant future.

Why? What has caused this oh-so-dramatic shift of economic power from the north to the south? Did the Confederates secretly win the Civil War? And what has caused the financial shift of tide, or even tidal wave, from the east to the west?

Several factors have been in force. First, federal support, primarily in the form of defense spending, has been moving from the north and east to the south and west. Elected officials who have been in office for a long time build up enormous power. Southern Congressmen, and westerners to a

WHERE INCOMES ARE PREDICTED TO RISE DURING THE 80's
(Ranked by predicted percentage growth in real personal income)

Rank	Area*	Percentage Growth	Reactions
1	Tampa	43.20	
2	Orlando	42.89	
3	Houston	41.69	
4	Bakersfield	41.45	
5	Dallas	40.89	
6	Tulsa	40.44	
7	Denver	39.88	
8	Corpus Christi	39.17	
9	Phoenix	38.42	
10	Miami	38.14	
11	San Diego	38.13	
12	Fresno	37.91	
13	El Paso	37.66	
14	Tucson	37.33	
15	Austin	36.85	
16	Las Vegas	36.16	
17	Charleston, S.C.	35.50	
18	Salt Lake City	33.47	

Rank	Area*	Percentage Growth	Reactions
19	San Antonio	33.23	
20	Beaumont	33.11	
21	Oklahoma City	32.20	
22	New Orleans	31.64	
23	Mobile	31.14	
24	Columbia	29.89	
25	Baton Rouge	29.30	
26	Shreveport	29.24	
27	Portland, Or.	28.85	
28	San Francisco	28.11	
29	Nashville	27.52	
30	Albuquerque	27.04	
31	Seattle	27.02	
32	Norfolk	26.02	
33	Richmond	25.58	
34	Raleigh	25.46	
35	Sacramento	24.98	
36	Atlanta	24.87	
37	Honolulu	23.98	
38	Minneapolis	23.74	
39	Wichita	23.45	
40	Memphis	23.22	
41	Little Rock	23.19	
42	Birmingham	22.68	
43	Los Angeles	22.60	
44	Boston	20.84	
45	Milwaukee	20.40	

Rank	Area*	Percentage Growth	Reactions
46	Louisville	19.75	
47	Columbus	19.10	
48	Grand Rapids	18.72	
49	Baltimore	18.66	
50	Cincinnati	18.08	
51	Omaha	17.41	
52	Kansas City	17.17	
53	Rochester	17.10	
54	Washington, D.C.	16.92	
55	Philadelphia	16.24	
56	New York	16.11	
57	Hartford	15.30	
58	Pittsburgh	15.08	
59	Indianapolis	14.67	
60	Chicago	14.21	
61	Akron	14.11	
62	Providence	13.75	
63	Wilmington	13.09	
64	Newark	12.94	
65	Cleveland	12.68	
66	St. Louis	11.94	
67	Albany	11.87	
68	Buffalo	11.59	
69	Detroit	6.50	

*Standard Metropolitan Statistical Area

lesser extent, are well known for their longevity in office and their efforts to win military and research allocations for their home areas. As a result, more than three-quarters of the Defense Department's payroll is spent in the south and west. In fact just California and Georgia together have more defense employees than the entire northeast and midwest combined!

Second, those areas which have benefited from increased defense spending also gain advantages from the technological advances and reseach findings which usually accompany today's sophisticated defense requirements. Scientific breakthroughs for the military quickly become adapted to civilian products. As a result, "silicone valleys" and "electronic communities" spring up with remarkable financial vigor and excellent income opportunities.

Third, once growth begins in an area, it is very likely to quickly become faster and self-fulfilling. Much of the growth is psychological . . . the area becomes "the place to be." As they say in sports, "They've got the momentum." Increased earning power brings more spending power and even greater vigor and enthusiasm to booming regions. In short order, boomlets can produce new centers of financial and political strength.

Fourth, energy costs have contributed to the shift of population and income opportunity. In the same way that turkey and chicken production has moved from the north to the south to save heating costs, so have new companies and industries sprung up in the warmer climates. Established companies in the frostbelt have not been replaced when they have been discontinued. It is not so much that companies have actually moved to the sunbelt from elsewhere, as one often hears, but attrition has decreased northern enterprises and new companies now are less frequently formed in the north.

What about the losers? Unfortunately, the old established regions, mostly in the northeast and north central, will continue to lose their vitality and their populations at the expense of the newly emerging powerhouses in the west and south. Some areas, such as New York and Chicago, will have a long way to slip before they lose enough of their strength to be considered less than powerful and influential, but like the old stags and stallions, in time they will have to give way to the younger and more vital.

Other regions with fewer assets and smaller populations will fade more quickly from earlier positions of dominance and quietly give way to the south and west.

The question is, do you want to hitch your future to a region which is vigorously growing, or to one which is relatively stable, or to a place which is generally in decline?

Not everyone will choose a booming area. Some will prefer to live in more settled places, with zoning and neighborhoods established, usually better cultural opportunities, and even an excellent chance to live in a splendid home at relatively low cost with fine public services available.

Income Predictions by State

To help you further in making your location decisions, Chart 4 provides personal income predictions for each of the 50 states.

The estimates parallel those for the regions in Chart 3, with south and west getting stronger and north and east losing earning power. We have included the growth rate for the past decade also, to give you a better historical perspective.

You will notice that the predicted income growth is much more conservative than the actual growth over the last ten years. That is because guesses for the future can never be as accurate as what we know from the past. Likely there will be even greater income growth than we predict, but the element of surprise is one of the things that makes life so exciting.

There are some big changes predicted. Alaska is expected to drop a long way in its income growth, primarily because the oil pipelines will have been built. However, if more gold is discovered, or another oil deposit located, or if a decision is made to develop federally owned lands, or some other economic booster comes along to surprise everyone, then incomes will zoom upward again.

In a similar manner, if ecological laws are relaxed and the nation's coal deposits are used more extensively, those states with coal reserves will likely benefit even more than they are now. Recent business problems experienced by the Boeing Aircraft Company in the state of Washington make the state's predicted growth rate probably too optimistic. If foreign companies continue to have such great interest in investing in the United States, they are likely to increase their development of factories and markets in the northeast (if European companies) and the far west (if Japanese).

INCOME PREDICTIONS BY STATE, 1979-89
(Ranked by predicted percentage growth during decade)

Rank	State	80's Growth Rate	70's Growth Rate	Reactions
1	Wyoming	49.20%	77.40%	
2	Florida	44.10	58.80	
3	Texas	40.20	58.40	
4	Colorado	39.20	56.60	
5	South Carolina	38.00	44.90	
6	Idaho	37.40	54.60	
7	Arizona	37.10	64.50	
8	New Hampshire	36.60	45.10	
9	Utah	35.80	52.50	
10	Arkansas	35.40	46.20	
11	North Dakota	35.20	42.20	
12	Vermont	35.10	30.00	
13	Mississippi	34.50	40.70	
14	New Mexico	34.40	54.90	
15	Nevada	34.30	66.80	
16	California	33.70	40.60	
17	North Carolina	33.60	37.90	
18	Louisiana	33.50	49.80	
19	Tennessee	33.30	41.80	

Rank	State	80's Growth Rate	70's Growth Rate	Reactions
20	South Dakota	33.20%	24.70%	
21	Kentucky	32.70	38.50	
22	Oklahoma	32.40	50.70	
23	Oregon	32.10	50.90	
24	Montana	31.30	37.20	
25	Virginia	29.60	42.10	
26	Alaska	29.50	61.30	
27	Nebraska	28.60	28.30	
27	Kansas	28.60	37.50	
29	Alabama	28.30	41.10	
30	Washington	27.80	48.70	
31	Georgia	27.50	38.20	
32	Minnesota	26.10	32.00	
33	Wisconsin	25.40	31.50	
34	Maine	25.20	33.00	
35	Iowa	25.00	29.40	
36	Maryland	24.10	28.90	
37	Missouri	23.40	27.20	
38	Connecticut	22.50	21.30	
39	Rhode Island	21.90	20.40	
40	Indiana	21.80	27.40	
40	Washington, D.C.	21.80	10.50	
42	Hawaii	21.50	32.50	
43	Delaware	21.40	24.30	
43	New York	21.40	8.50	
45	Ohio	20.80	21.60	
46	West Virginia	20.50	39.30	

Rank	State	80's Growth Rate	70's Growth Rate	Reactions
47	Michigan	19.20%	26.90%	
48	Pennsylvania	18.90	21.50	
49	New Jersey	18.50	19.30	
50	Illinois	15.80	23.50	
51	Massachusetts	15.70	19.20	

Jobs, and Where to Find Them

The most important reason for moving, for most people who do move, is economic. They are looking for better jobs. Other factors, such as quality of life, weather, crime, pollution, or various potential disasters, also have an important influence on decisions to relocate. They may be extremely important to you. But the fact remains, most people move to find better jobs.

Where will the best job market be in the coming decade: Orlando heads the list, as Chart 5 shows. The growth in the job market is predicted to be nothing short of phenomenal in the south and west.

As people flock in to fill developing job opportunities, they themselves create new employment for others. When areas are burgeoning, and as people pour in, they create new jobs in housing, schools, shopping facilities, transportation, and all of the diverse services needed.

It is apparent that much of the job market in the west and south is related to construction (both of buildings and interstate highways), services (education, medicine, etc.), and trade (wholesale and retail). These are outgrowths of large and growing populations . . . highways and buildings to hold the people, services to care for them, and trade to feed and clothe them. But the job opportunities stemming from population growth may dwindle rapidly when the growth process slows or stops.

You should be informed that the job market is not good in manufacturing. In fact, it appears that manufacturing is on the

JOBS, AND WHERE TO FIND THEM DURING THE 80's
[Ranked by predicted percentage growth (high to low) in total nonagricultural employment]

Rank	Area*	Percentage Growth	Reactions
1	Orlando	42.32	
2	Tucson	41.69	
3	Las Vegas	40.22	
4	Tampa	39.20	
5	Houston	39.07	
6	Tulsa	37.44	
7	Dallas	37.05	
8	Phoenix	36.15	
9	San Diego	34.20	
10	Austin	34.11	
11	El Paso	33.88	
12	Bakersfield	32.82	
13	Salt Lake City	32.14	
14	Corpus Christi	32.13	
15	Miami	31.76	
16	Charleston, S.C.	31.75	
17	Denver	31.57	

Rank	Area*	Percentage Growth	Reactions
18	San Antonio	31.43	
19	Fresno	30.54	
20	Baton Rouge	30.17	
21	Albuquerque	29.88	
22	Oklahoma City	29.67	
23	Shreveport	28.29	
24	Mobile	27.42	
25	Columbia	27.20	
26	Nashville	25.72	
27	Raleigh	25.56	
28	New Orleans	25.23	
29	Portland, Or.	24.21	
30	Beaumont	23.46	
31	Seattle	21.84	
32	San Francisco	21.23	
33	Wichita	21.08	
34	Atlanta	20.69	
35	Little Rock	20.67	
36	Norfolk	19.46	
37	Minneapolis	18.50	
38	Grand Rapids	17.72	
39	Omaha	17.33	
40	Honolulu	16.95	
41	Richmond	16.60	
42	Milwaukee	16.10	
43	Los Angeles	15.61	
44	Memphis	15.53	

Rank	Area*	Percentage Growth	Reactions
45	Hartford	15.12	
46	Sacramento	15.08	
47	Boston	14.93	
48	Cincinnati	13.70	
49	Birmingham	13.42	
50	Columbus	13.38	
51	Wilmington	11.42	
52	Washington, D.C.	10.97	
53	Rochester	10.73	
54	New York	10.67	
55	Louisville	10.44	
56	Indianapolis	9.78	
57	Kansas City	9.43	
58	Chicago	8.96	
59	Providence	7.07	
60	Baltimore	7.05	
61	Pittsburgh	6.94	
62	Philadelphia	6.08	
63	Akron	5.69	
64	Newark	5.51	
65	Cleveland	4.53	
66	Albany	3.89	
67	St. Louis	3.41	
68	Detroit	1.71	
69	Buffalo	.55	

*Standard Metropolitan Statistical Area

decline throughout the United States. Some plants are opening in the south and west, but closings outnumber openings across the nation. One begins to suspect that we Americans have decided that manufacturing is beneath our dignity, or perhaps we are too wound up in governmental red tape to make it worthwhile. At any rate, we now increasingly import the goods which once we produced here.

Recent Unemployment Rates

As you are no doubt aware, unemployment rates change from month to month, but their change is slow enough to provide important clues to the economic health of an area. Chart 6 shows the extent of unemployment in April, 1982, ranked from lowest to highest rates. You will notice that unemployment in some areas is almost four times greater than in others.

CHART

6

RECENT UNEMPLOYMENT RATES
(Ranked least to most, for April, 1982.)

Rank	Area*	Percentage Unem- ployed	Reactions
1	Raleigh	4.1	
2	Oklahoma City	4.5	
3	Sioux Falls	4.6	
4	Houston	5.0	
5	Casper †	5.1	
6	Nassau-Suffolk	5.2	
6	Tulsa	5.2	
8	Dallas	5.3	
8	Fargo	5.3	
10	Honolulu	5.5	
11	Denver	5.6	
11	Minneapolis	5.6	
11	Richmond	5.6	
14	Atlanta	5.8	
15	Washington, D.C.	5.9	
16	Albany	6.0	
17	Rochester	6.1	
18	Hartford	6.2	
19	Omaha	6.4	

Rank	Area*	Percentage Unemployed	Reactions
19	Portland, Me.	6.4	
21	Columbia	6.5	
22	Boston	6.7	
22	Phoenix	6.7	
24	San Antonio	6.9	
25	Orlando	7.0	
26	Albuquerque	7.1	
27	San Francisco	7.2	
27	Utah †	7.2	
29	Boise	7.4	
29	Norfolk	7.4	
29	Wichita	7.4	
32	Tampa	7.5	
32	Tucson	7.5	
34	Des Moines	7.7	
35	Little Rock	7.8	
36	Miami	7.9	
36	Wilmington	7.9	
38	Kansas City	8.0	
39	Great Falls	8.1	
39	Memphis	8.1	
39	Nashville	8.1	
42	Charleston, W.V.	8.2	
43	Charleston, S.C.	8.3	
43	Manchester	8.3	
43	Newark	8.3	

Rank	Area*	Percentage Unemployed	Reactions
43	New York	8.3	
47	Baton Rouge	8.5	
47	Los Angeles	8.5	
47	Philadelphia	8.5	
50	Shreveport	8.6	
51	St. Louis	8.7	
52	Milwaukee	9.0	
52	Burlington †	9.0	
54	Columbus	9.1	
55	Indianapolis	9.2	
56	New Orleans	9.3	
57	Las Vegas	9.4	
58	Chicago	9.5	
59	Biloxi †	9.6	
60	Baltimore	9.8	
60	Cleveland	9.8	
62	Portland, Or.	10.1	
63	Cincinnati	10.2	
63	Providence	10.2	
65	Seattle	10.5	
66	Pittsburgh	10.6	
67	Anchorage †	10.7	
68	Akron	11.4	
69	Buffalo	11.6	
70	Birmingham	11.7	
70	Sacramento	11.7	

Rank	Area*	Percentage Unemployed	Reactions
72	Louisville	11.8	
73	Grand Rapids	12.0	
74	Mobile	12.4	
75	Bakersfield	12.7	
76	Fresno	15.1	
77	Detroit	15.3	

*Standard Metropolitan Statistical Area
†Statewide figure

Predicted Job Markets by State

The state with the highest predicted employment growth rate for this decade is Florida, with Wyoming and Nevada close behind. Remember, however, that Wyoming and Nevada have relatively small populations, so their growth rates and employment opportunities look better by percentages than they would with actual numbers of jobs. The same is true for New Mexico and Arizona, both high on Chart 7. Texas, which is ninth on the list, is certainly large enough to absorb many more employees moving to the "Lone Star State."

One surprise among all the western and southern states is New Hampshire, in eighth place. The reason is that the business climate there is considered quite favorable. They provide tax incentives for new companies, a stable, experienced labor force, and many new firms (especially electronics) are setting up shop there. In contrast, the neighboring state of Vermont seems more concerned with preserving a rural lifestyle. Interestingly, many of those at the forefront of keeping Vermont rural are ex-residents of New York City who moved to the country.

71

CHART

7

PREDICTED JOB MARKETS
BY STATE DURING THE 80's
(Ranked from high to low by predicted percentage growth.)

Rank	State	80's Growth Rate	70's Growth Rate	Reactions
1	Florida	41.30%	52.00%	
2	Wyoming	40.50	66.20	
3	Nevada	40.10	70.00	
4	New Mexico	39.30	46.80	
5	Arizona	36.70	62.50	
6	Utah	36.10	44.40	
7	Idaho	33.70	47.30	
8	New Hampshire	30.60	40.70	
9	Texas	30.50	50.50	
10	Colorado	29.40	52.50	
11	Louisiana	28.80	42.80	
12	California	28.50	35.40	
13	South Carolina	28.10	35.00	
13	North Dakota	28.10	41.60	
15	Montana	27.60	35.00	
16	Oregon	27.20	39.00	
16	Oklahoma	27.20	40.70	
18	Vermont	27.10	30.40	

Rank	State	80's Growth Rate	70's Growth Rate	Reactions
19	Georgia	25.10%	32.60%	
20	Nebraska	24.00	26.70	
21	Arkansas	23.90	33.40	
22	Alaska	23.00	61.80	
23	North Carolina	22.80	29.60	
24	Mississippi	22.70	35.90	
25	Tennessee	22.30	27.10	
26	Kansas	22.10	34.10	
27	Kentucky	21.70	23.90	
28	Wisconsin	21.20	24.30	
29	Washington	20.60	40.60	
30	South Dakota	20.10	30.70	
31	Alabama	19.70	30.00	
32	Virginia	18.20	34.00	
33	Maryland	17.80	23.10	
34	Hawaii	16.20	32.40	
35	Iowa	15.80	23.10	
36	Connecticut	15.70	17.50	
36	Minnesota	15.70	30.20	
38	Delaware	13.50	17.70	
39	Maine	13.30	23.60	
40	Missouri	13.00	16.80	
41	Ohio	12.50	12.60	
42	New Jersey	11.80	16.00	
43	West Virginia	11.60	22.60	
44	Indiana	11.50	14.60	
45	New York	10.90	.70	

Rank	State	80's Growth Rate	70's Growth Rate	Reactions
46	Rhode Island	9.80%	14.80%	
47	Pennsylvania	9.30	8.90	
48	Michigan	9.20	14.10	
49	Illinois	8.50	11.80	
50	Massachusetts	7.70	15.90	
51	Washington, D.C.	5.20	8.20	

How Much Per Hour?

Another excellent measure of an area's value to you is represented by the average hourly wages paid, the total income earned, and the directions in which salaries are going. Chart 8 shows all of these for factory workers.

Even if you decide against moving, with this information you might want to demand a raise!

As a supplement to Chart 8, we have provided eight more charts at the end of Chapter Three. They show the incomes earned for selected occupations in different parts of the nation.

AVERAGE SALARIES OF FACTORY WORKERS
(Ranked from high to low by hourly average pay, 1982)

Rank	Area*	Avg. Hourly Earning	Income of Avg. factory Worker	Factory Worker's Salary Compared with a year ago (%)	Reaction
1	Anchorage†	$13.25	$NA	NA	
2	Detroit	11.81	25,197	+14.4	
3	Baton Rouge	11.34	NA	NA	
4	Seattle	11.23	23,308	+11.4	
5	Las Vegas	10.68	22,119	+12.8	
6	Buffalo	10.44	21,507	+ 5.0	
7	Charleston, W.V.	10.43	22,512	+10.0	
7	Des Moines	10.43	21,499	+16.7	
9	Pittsburgh	10.40	21,740	+ 5.2	
10	Milwaukee	10.33	21,296	+10.2	
11	Rochester	10.16	21,709	+ 4.8	
12	Houston	10.12	22,764	+ 8.3	
13	Wilmington	10.08	19,714	+ 5.5	
14	Cleveland	9.95	20,760	+ 4.5	
15	Akron	9.89	NA	NA	
16	Portland, Or.	9.85	19,130	+ 8.9	
17	Indianapolis	9.84	19,917	+ 4.9	

Rank	Area*	Avg. Hourly Earning	Income of Avg. factory Worker	Factory Worker's Salary Compared with a year ago (%)	Reaction
18	Louisville	$9.62	$20,155	+10.5	
19	Great Falls†	9.55	NA	NA	
20	St. Louis	9.46	18,944	+ 9.3	
21	Kansas City	9.42	19,535	+13.6	
22	Cincinnati	9.38	19,271	+ 5.4	
23	Grand Rapids	9.37	18,867	+11.1	
24	Minneapolis	9.35	19,105	+ 7.4	
25	Wichita	9.32	20,128	+11.8	
26	Mobile	9.25	19,269	+ 8.1	
26	Tulsa	9.25	19,085	+ 8.9	
28	New Orleans	9.23	18,453	+ 6.3	
29	Richmond	9.14	19,238	+ 7.6	
30	Columbus	9.13	18,671	+ 7.9	
31	Bakersfield†	9.07	NA	NA	
31	Fresno†	9.07	15,888	+ 5.0	
31	Los Angeles†	9.07	17,932	+ 9.9	
31	Sacramento†	9.07	18,720	+ 7.2	
31	San Diego†	9.07	18,302	+14.1	
31	San Francisco†	9.07	21,893	+ 7.7	
31	Washington, D.C.	9.07	17,915	+ 1.0	
38	Baltimore	8.97	18,952	+ 7.0	
39	Newark	8.73	18,674	+ 8.3	
40	Philadelphia	8.69	17,753	+ 5.5	
41	Hartford	8.64	17,837	+ 1.8	
42	Chicago	8.61	17,386	+ 8.3	

Rank	Area*	Avg. Hourly Earning	Income of Avg. factory Worker	Factory Worker's Salary Compared with a year ago (%)	Reaction
43	Phoenix	$8.59	$16,916	+ 4.3	
43	Tucson	8.59	16,830	+11.4	
45	Oklahoma City	8.58	17,674	+ 4.0	
46	Omaha	8.51	17,227	+ 5.1	
47	Albany	8.46	NA	NA	
48	Denver	8.42	17,223	+ 4.2	
49	Casper	8.31	16,913	+11.3	
50	Boise	8.22	16,333	+17.6	
50	Shreveport	8.22	NA	NA	
52	Sioux Falls	8.18	21,746	− 3.9	
53	Birmingham	8.11	16,996	+ 2.5	
54	Dallas	8.04	16,999	+10.7	
55	Nassau-Suffolk	7.97	NA	NA	
56	Honolulu	7.94	15,542	+ 5.7	
57	Nashville	7.93	NA	NA	
58	Atlanta	7.91	16,536	+10.3	
58	Salt Lake City	7.91	16,208	+ 9.6	
60	Burlington	7.83	16,869	+ 9.6	
61	Little Rock	7.58	15,197	+ 7.8	
62	Fargo	7.47	15,913	+13.2	
63	Orlando	7.41	NA	NA	
64	Memphis	7.40	16,446	+ 6.6	
65	New York	7.39	14,199	+ 6.8	
66	Albuquerque	7.35	14,797	+13.0	
66	Norfolk	7.35	15,623	+10.1	

Rank	Area*	Avg. Hourly Earning	Income of Avg. factory Worker	Factory Worker's Salary Compared with a year ago (%)	Reaction
68	Raleigh	$7.28	$NA	NA	
69	Charleston, S.C.†	7.19	14,462	+ 1.3	
70	Portland, Me.	6.87	14,380	+12.1	
71	Tampa	6.82	14,161	+ 3.8	
72	Providence	6.42	12,907	+ 5.2	
73	Manchester	6.39	13,040	+ 6.8	
74	Columbia	6.33	NA	NA	
75	San Antonio	6.26	12,866	+ 7.7	
76	Miami	5.88	11,864	+ 4.6	
77	Boston	NA	15,927	+ 8.7	

*Standard Metropolitan Statistical Area
†Statewide figure

Where Shoppers Will Do Their Thing

The predictions shown for growth in department store sales indicate the relative strengths of the economies throughout the nation. Chart 9 is headed by Tampa, with an anticipated growth rate of over 43 percent during the next decade!

Other sunbelt areas also are prominent in the top part of the chart. Some northeast and north central regions are expected to lose sales over the next ten years. Perhaps if they gave more redeemable stamps. . . .

WHERE SHOPPERS ARE PREDICTED TO BUY, 1980–89
(Ranked high to low by predicted percentage growth in department store sales)

Rank	Area*	Predicted Growth Rate During the 80's	Reaction
1	Tampa	43.13%	
2	Orlando	39.81	
3	Dallas	37.34	
4	Corpus Christi	37.27	
5	Tulsa	35.72	
6	Houston	35.34	
7	Bakersfield	35.27	
8	Tucson	35.08	
9	Shreveport	34.42	
10	San Diego	35.82	
11	El Paso	32.58	
12	Denver	29.55	
13	Miami	28.85	
13	Baton Rouge	28.85	
15	Oklahoma City	28.28	
16	Phoenix	28.08	

Rank	Area*	Predicted Growth Rate During the 80's	Reaction
17	San Antonio	27.81%	
18	Charleston, S.C.	27.07	
19	Columbia	26.37	
20	Fresno	26.14	
21	New Orleans	25.18	
22	Little Rock	24.06	
23	Albuquerque	21.70	
24	Raleigh	21.01	
25	Mobile	20.76	
26	Atlanta	18.30	
27	Sacramento	17.78	
28	San Francisco	16.68	
29	Portland, Or.	16.28	
30	Seattle	16.20	
31	Richmond	15.39	
32	Minneapolis	15.28	
33	Los Angeles	14.57	
34	Norfolk	12.04	
35	Washington, D.C.	11.28	
36	Louisville	10.53	
37	Grand Rapids	10.25	
38	Memphis	9.39	
39	Kansas City	8.80	
40	Columbus	8.79	
41	Honolulu	8.50	
42	Pittsburgh	7.25	

Rank	Area*	Predicted Growth Rate During the 80's	Reaction
43	Hartford	6.82%	
44	St. Louis	5.42	
45	Birmingham	5.27	
46	Baltimore	4.79	
47	Cincinnati	4.73	
48	Boston	4.71	
49	Rochester	3.76	
50	Philadelphia	3.31	
51	Indianapolis	3.09	
52	Omaha	3.06	
53	Albany	1.85	
54	New York	1.45	
55	Buffalo	.01	
56	Providence	−0.66	
57	Chicago	−2.43	
58	Milwaukee	−3.19	
59	Newark	−3.87	
60	Cleveland	−5.90	
61	Detroit	−6.11	

*Standard Metropolitan Statistical Area

Where the Houses Will Be Built

If you sell doorknobs, or happen to be a plumber or bank mortgage officer, you will find Chart 10 very useful. For the rest of us, it has value also, because it shows where the houses are going to be built in the next decade, which gives a big hint about best areas for our own economic gains.

You will be especially interested to know that lots of houses are going to be built during this decade. The interest rates will have a major influence on timing, but the famous baby boom of WWII has turned into a young adult boom. And after all, these young adults will have to raise their own little boomlets somewhere!

No, the houses will not be built around New York. No, not very many around Buffalo, Boston, or Pittsburgh either. By this time you will not be surprised to learn that they are going to be constructed in the sunbelt, for the most part. In fact, *fifteen times* as many houses per thousand people will be built in some areas as in others.

Several implications are apparent from Chart 10. If you are a construction-related professional, you already know about the migratory nature of your job. Construction workers are used to living much of their lives on wheels. For the rest of us, it is important to know that where houses will be built, land values are most likely to rise and an excellent chance for real estate speculation will emerge. It also indicates all sorts of opportunities for new jobs, new businesses, and new lifestyles. Where there is growth there is change, and some of you will thrive on it.

WHERE THE HOUSES WILL BE BUILT DURING THE 80's
(Predicted housing starts, per one thousand people—ranked high to low)

Rank	Area*	Units/1000	Reactions
1	Las Vegas	23.07	
2	Houston	21.12	
3	Phoenix	20.99	
4	Tucson	19.21	
5	Orlando	17.41	
5	Tampa	17.41	
7	Austin	15.70	
8	Dallas	14.29	
9	Seattle	13.99	
10	Charleston, S.C.	13.52	
11	Albuquerque	13.25	
12	Denver	13.20	
13	Sacramento	13.14	
14	Atlanta	12.68	
15	Salt Lake City	12.20	
16	Miami	12.10	
17	Richmond	11.17	
18	Oklahoma City	11.00	
19	Fresno	10.98	

Rank	Area*	Units/1000	Reactions
20	San Diego	9.95	
21	Portland, Or.	9.57	
22	Bakersfield	9.40	
23	Tulsa	9.06	
24	Norfolk	9.01	
25	Baton Rouge	8.95	
26	El Paso	8.65	
27	New Orleans	8.54	
28	Washington, D.C.	8.40	
29	Nashville	7.96	
30	San Antonio	7.90	
31	Minneapolis	7.34	
32	Kansas City	6.93	
33	Honolulu	6.90	
34	Omaha	6.80	
35	Baltimore	6.45	
36	Columbus	6.21	
37	San Francisco	6.11	
37	Cincinnati	6.11	
39	Indianapolis	6.02	
40	Birmingham	5.62	
41	St. Louis	5.27	
42	Grand Rapids	5.16	
43	Little Rock	4.98	
44	Los Angeles	4.59	
45	Milwaukee	4.58	
46	Chicago	4.25	
47	Akron	4.20	

Rank	Area*	Units/1000	Reactions
48	Providence	4.13	
49	Wilmington	3.98	
50	Cleveland	3.38	
51	Albany	3.30	
52	Philadelphia	3.22	
53	Newark	2.44	
54	Rochester	2.33	
55	Detroit	2.25	
56	Pittsburgh	2.21	
57	Boston	2.04	
58	Buffalo	1.85	
59	New York	1.67	

*Standard Metropolitan Statistical Area.

Cost of Houses

What a range of prices! From an average of $54,573 for a new home in Columbia, S.C., to $146,244 in New Orleans. Keep in mind that the type of construction, size, and land sites are not identical throughout the nation, but these are the cost comparisons for average new dwellings in each region.

Notice on Chart 11 that Orlando and Tampa are among the leaders, just as they were on our previous charts dealing with income growth, job markets, and housing starts. With their relatively low housing costs, they continue to offer the classic combination for real estate speculation. Florida real estate deals have continued for so many years that one has to wonder if they will ever diminish. Even swamps and marshes change hands with gusto and profits, but as the old joke goes, "Why, that land isn't for building on. It's just for trading!"

Denver also is an excellent candidate for consideration, with a relatively good future predicted and low cost housing available. As you study the charts, you undoubtedly will discover other places just right for you to prosper.

Real estate markets shift and change with a speed that can be dazzling, and the only way to keep abreast is to stay close to a telephone or local newspapers. When one of the authors lived in Seattle in the early 70's, houses could be bought for a song, or even a hum. The economy was depressed and houses could be had just for taking over the mortgages. Oh, couldn't we just kick ourselves for not grabbing them up! Now they have leaped in value, and are likely to continue to escalate. They still are excellent investment opportunities. But the trick is to find those areas in the process of or about to burgeon with still relatively low housing costs.

An excellent example of real estate investment savvy are the parents of college students in Houston who purchase condominiums in which the students reside. Upon graduation from college the condominiums are sold and the profits from the sales usually more than offset the entire costs of the college education!

Keep in mind that housing costs are largely tax deductible, and if you can afford a high investment in a thriving area, you are more likely to make a substantial profit than if you purchased a lower cost home in a declining region.

COST OF HOUSES, 1980
(Ranked low to high by average purchase price of new single family houses)

Rank	Area*	New Houses	Existing Houses	Reactions
1	Columbia	$54,573	$53,533	
2	Norfolk	60,391	68,593	
3	Wichita	66,976	78,184	
4	Nashville	67,286	57,110	
5	Orlando	69,164	49,728	
6	Denver	69,273	85,366	
7	Rochester	69,438	51,379	
8	Tucson	69,569	64,122	
9	Richmond	70,168	53,112	
10	Wilmington	70,518	60,441	
11	Buffalo	75,041	46,617	
12	Tampa	76,235	59,350	
13	Salt Lake City	77,783	104,927	
14	Baltimore	78,012	76,261	
15	St. Louis	78,425	64,378	
16	Philadelphia	78,685	54,452	
17	Boston	78,894	70,649	
18	Raleigh	79,385	43,301	
19	San Antonio	79,598	76,936	

Rank	Area*	New Houses	Existing Houses	Reactions
20	Houston	$81,505	$95,341	
21	Cincinnati	84,011	51,835	
22	Sacramento	86,085	91,556	
23	Indianapolis	86,548	68,472	
24	Oklahoma City	84,578	62,736	
25	Austin	86,669	73,841	
26	Seattle	88,034	81,108	
27	Kansas City	88,066	64,493	
28	Chicago	88,424	74,898	
29	Miami	88,833	84,288	
30	Atlanta	89,181	67,021	
31	Louisville	89,281	51,648	
32	Hartford	90,327	66,069	
33	Portland, Or.	90,728	67,883	
34	Tulsa	90,916	72,636	
35	Minneapolis	93,731	74,210	
36	Fresno	97,962	55,987	
37	Dallas	102,208	96,243	
38	Cleveland	106,728	64,794	
39	Phoenix	107,564	84,226	
40	New York	108,784	84,490	
41	Washington, D.C.	109,118	101,932	
42	Detroit	110,509	60,083	
43	Pittsburgh	112,938	57,003	
44	Los Angeles	113,105	105,094	
45	Honolulu	113,753	111,410	
46	Newark	114,246	94,240	

Rank	Area*	New Houses	Existing Houses	Reactions
47	Nassau-Suffolk	$120,023	$75,820	
48	Columbus	123,046	59,826	
49	San Francisco	135,802	108,897	
50	New Orleans	146,244	103,375	
51	Albany	NA	44,732	
51	Bakersfield	NA	116,042	

*Standard Metropolitan Statistical Area

Where Taxes Bite Deepest

Psst. Hey Bud. Over here. Heard about the latest way to lower your taxes? Interested? Of course you are. It's one of the reasons that the so-called underground economy has flourished, with flea markets and ''off-the-books'' income making up an astounding portion of the national economy. And it's certainly another reason that people all over the United States are thinking about moving to places which don't take out such a large chunk at tax bite time.

Make no misteak! Ooops. Make no mistake! There are dramatic differences among the various parts of the country in terms of state and local taxes. Chart 12 is based on 1980 census data, and shows that the national average for state and local taxes is 12% of the worker's personal income. (This does not include federal income tax, by the way.) Another way of saying this is that the average income earner paid $934 in state and local taxes. Still another way of saying it is, OUCH!

As you can see from Chart 12, state and local tax rates in some states are *more than twice as high* as in others. And you can expect to pay *more than four times as much* in actual dollars in some states.

Alaska residents paid the highest rate, at $234 per each $1000 earned, with New York and Wyoming not too far behind.

At the other end of the scale we find Indiana and Ohio, with a relatively low 9.8 percent, and Arkansas and Missouri at only 9.9 percent. Perhaps we should not say "only," because it is still a fairly large bite.

Although you might be tempted to choose your best location based on lower expenses, including taxes, you should bear in mind that higher taxes generally translate to greater public services. You're not sure they are worth it? No one really is, but nevertheless, the services do depend upon the taxes.

An excellent example of a dubious service is provided each autumn on Long Island, where the authors live. The two counties on Long Island, not counting parts of New York City, have the highest tax rates in the United States.

While most of the nation rakes leaves and dumps them behind their homes in compost piles, Long Islanders pile their leaves in long windrows along the street or in mounds on the curbs. In a few weeks, along comes a crew of workers, complete with huge dumptrucks and a medium-size frontloader. They carefully scoop and sweep up all of Long Island's huge crop of leaves, from some of the most prolific trees in the nation, and truck them miles away to town dumps. To newcomers, it seems amazing that the highest taxes in the nation have paid for the harvesting and hauling of leaves!

Another example of such services was the experience of one of the authors shortly after moving to Long Island from the west coast. He was out one morning collecting debris on the side of the road near his home when a young boy approached him saying, "Doctor, what are you doing? The town will do that for you."

CHART
12

WHERE STATE TAXES HIT HARDEST
(Ranked high to low by percent of personal income expanded for state taxes)

Rank	State	% of Personal Income	Tax Collections Per Person	Reactions
1	Alaska	23.4%	$2,546	
2	New York	16.6	1,370	
3	Wyoming	15.9	1,291	
4	Massachusetts	14.8	1,176	
5	Hawaii	14.6	1,194	
6	Arizona	14.2	1,004	
7	Minnesota	14.0	1,096	
7	Vermont	14.0	905	
9	Wisconsin	13.7	1,021	
10	Montana	13.4	900	
11	Washington, D.C.	13.1	1,336	
12	Rhode Island	13.0	975	
13	New Mexico	12.9	830	
14	Maine	12.8	798	
14	Utah	12.8	805	
16	Nevada	12.7	1,126	
17	Maryland	12.6	1,054	

Rank	State	% of Personal Income	Tax Collections Per Person	Reactions
18	Colorado	12.5%	$972	
19	Michigan	12.4	1,050	
20	Louisiana	12.2	807	
20	New Jersey	12.2	1,067	
20	Oregon	12.2	956	
23	California	12.1	1,058	
23	Delaware	12.1	1,036	
23	Washington	12.1	992	
	National Avg.	12.0	934	
26	Nebraska	11.9	896	
26	Pennsylvania	11.9	921	
28	West Virginia	11.8	773	
29	Mississippi	11.6	636	
30	Connecticut	11.4	1,013	
31	Georgia	11.3	751	
31	Idaho	11.3	767	
31	Kentucky	11.3	738	
34	Illinois	11.2	998	
34	Iowa	11.2	894	
34	Kansas	11.2	878	
37	North Carolina	10.9	711	
37	South Carolina	10.9	679	
39	South Dakota	10.8	740	
40	Virginia	10.7	815	
41	North Dakota	10.6	757	
41	Oklahoma	10.6	753	

Rank	State	% of Personal Income	Tax Collections Per Person	Reactions
43	Florida	10.5%	$771	
44	Tennessee	10.2	663	
45	Alabama	10.0	623	
45	New Hampshire	10.0	722	
45	Texas	10.0	749	
48	Arkansas	9.9	594	
48	Missouri	9.9	726	
50	Indiana	9.8	749	
50	Ohio	9.8	768	

Property Taxes

Three of the top four states on the property tax chart (Chart 13) also were in the top five for state and local taxes (Chart 12). Shall we therefore declare Alaska, Massachusetts, and Wyoming to be the NATION'S TOP TAXERS and give New York a runner-up award?

Again, remember that higher taxes generally mean better services. In this case, property taxes largely are the source of revenue for the schools. Can we then say that the states with highest property taxes have the best schools? This has not been demonstrated all that clearly, but it is evident that good educational programs require adequate financial support.

As you make your decisions regarding moving, you will need to think about whether you value services and can bear the tax expense for them, or whether you might prefer lower tax costs and fewer services provided. As you can see from Chart 13, you certainly have a wide range of choices.

CHART
13

PROPERTY TAX COLLECTIONS BY STATE
(Ranked high to low by amount collected per $1,000 of personal income)

Rank	State	Amounts per $1,000	Reactions
1	Alaska	$76	
2	Massachusetts	72	
3	Montana	66	
4	Wyoming	64	
4	California	64	
6	New York	62	
6	New Hampshire	62	
8	Vermont	61	
9	New Jersey	60	
10	South Dakota	54	
10	Connecticut	54	
10	Arizona	54	
13	Rhode Island	53	
13	Oregon	53	
15	Nebraska	52	
16	Maine	51	
17	Wisconsin	48	

Rank	State	Amounts per $1,000	Reactions
18	Kansas	$47	
19	Michigan	46	
20	Colorado	45	
21	Iowa	44	
22	Minnesota	43	
23	Illinois	42	
24	Nevada	41	
25	Washington	39	
25	North Dakota	39	
27	Texas	38	
28	Maryland	37	
28	Idaho	37	
30	Utah	36	
30	Indiana	36	
32	Ohio	35	
32	Florida	35	
34	Georgia	32	
34	Washington, D.C.	32	
36	Virginia	31	
37	Missouri	30	
38	Tennessee	26	
38	Mississippi	26	
38	North Carolina	26	
41	South Carolina	25	
42	Hawaii	23	
43	Arkansas	22	
43	Pennsylvania	22	

Rank	State	Amounts per $1,000	Reactions
43	Oklahoma	$22	
46	New Mexico	21	
46	Kentucky	21	
48	West Virginia	20	
49	Delaware	19	
50	Louisiana	17	
51	Alabama	12	

Cost of Living, Here and There

The pioneers were looking for lots of things . . . a place to earn a better living, religious freedom, more open spaces. And not to be overlooked, a place where living costs were lower.

Can't you just imagine old Jeb Longrifle crabbing at his wife and half-deaf mother-in-law that,

"The price of tobaccy went up to a penny, dagnabbit! And flour is durn near three cents a bag. And now they're startin' talk of taxes! That does it. We're moving to where we can grow our own and live off the fat of the land. It just costs too dadburned much to live here!"

Well, Mr. Longrifle's concern is probably not too different from that of most of us. Ding bust it, we also see taxes leaping upward, energy costs scaring us half to death, and the price of a single family house beginning to approximate the national budget of a small developing nation.

Little wonder that we too think about moving to a land of milk and honey, where wild blueberries ripen in the sun, cashews and apples just wait to be picked, and (Please, God!) taxes and home heating oil are not so costly.

The good news is that some places are much less expensive than others!

We have determined that the main cost of living differences among the many regions we have described in this book are due to:

1. Energy (gas, oil, electricity, etc.)
2. Housing
3. Transportation
4. State and local taxes

Other differences in such factors as food, medical costs, home furnishing and management, clothing, social security, federal taxes, and so forth are significant but not as great across the nation. In other words, they are high most places.

To help you make informed judgments regarding the cost of living, Charts 14, 15, and 16 provide a comparison of expenses for different areas around the United States. The information is adapted from hypothetical budgets constructed at regular intervals for imaginary families of four by the U.S. Department of Labor. Because inflation has made the actual costs for today ever higher, we have shown the area comparisons by percentages above or below the national average.

Chart 14 shows comparisons based on a relatively high income. Chart 15 is for an intermediate budget, and Chart 16 shows comparisons for a relatively low budget.

Some of the differences among the areas are very interesting. For example, rent in Chicago is low, but medical expenses are relatively high. Boston has relatively low medical costs, so it might pay to take the bus from Chicago to Boston if you feel like you are getting the mumps. And just don't plan to get sick in Anchorage.

ANNUAL COSTS FOR HIGHER FAMILY BUDGET

(Ranked from lowest to highest for a 4 person family, expressed as percent above or below U.S. average for metropolitan areas.)

Rank	Area*	Budget	Food	Rent	Home-owner	Medical	Trans-portation	Reactions
1	Dallas	−13.7	−5.0	+15.4	−16.9	+9.5	−1.1	
2	Atlanta	−11.5	−4.9	−30.7	−26.8	−12.6	−7.0	
3	Houston	−11.2	−0.3	−25.5	−17.1	−5.0	+13.9	
4	St. Louis	−8.1	+3.4	−31.4	−20.5	−11.5	+2.1	
5	Cincinnati	−6.4	−0.3	−39.1	−8.0	−6.3	−11.6	
6	Pittsburgh	−6.1	+0.7	−34.2	−11.8	−10.9	+1.1	
7	Denver	−5.5	−5.3	−2.1	−12.6	−5.0	+10.4	
8	Kansas City	−5.4	−0.6	−25.2	−13.8	−4.3	−0.9	
9	Chicago	−4.5	−2.1	−4.5	−5.1	+5.1	+10.8	

Rank	Area*	Budget	Food	Rent	Home-owner	Medical	Trans-portation	Reactions
10	Seattle	-4.4	-0.7	+18.5	+0.4	-5.4	-9.7	
11	Cleveland	-4.2	-0.7	-30.3	-0.4	-2.5	-6.5	
12	Detroit	-3.6	-0.5	-7.1	+4.1	-0.8	-9.1	
12	San Diego	-3.6	-4.9	+11.5	+4.1	-7.8	+18.8	
14	Baltimore	-2.6	-4.5	-13.7	-11.8	-7.5	-9.9	
15	Los Angeles	-1.5	-0.5	+27.7	-4.8	+3.5	+27.1	
16	Minneapolis	-1.1	-3.2	-11.1	-11.6	-15.6	-8.7	
17	Buffalo	-0.5	-3.4	-2.4	-7.9	-21.6	-4.2	
18	Philadelphia	+1.1	+8.8	+12.2	-3.4	+7.0	+3.6	
19	Milwaukee	+1.5	-2.6	-21.6	+0.8	-6.3	-6.1	
20	San Francisco	+4.6	+1.5	+24.4	-2.9	+4.7	+13.6	
21	Washington, D.C.	+5.2	+0.2	-0.6	-0.8	-1.5	-1.2	
22	Boston	+14.6	-1.9	+9.4	+36.2	-10.9	+25.3	
23	Anchorage	+15.3	+7.5	+40.8	+18.4	+11.5	+54.7	
24	New York	+21.0	+11.0	+34.9	+26.2	-2.1	+3.3	
25	Honolulu	+28.6	+29.2	+26.0	+20.6	+3.0	+7.3	

*Standard Metropolitan Statistical Area

ANNUAL COSTS FOR INTERMEDIATE FAMILY BUDGET
(Ranked from lowest to highest for a 4 person family, expressed as percent above or below U.S. average for metropolitan areas.)

Rank	Area*	Budget	Food	Rent	Home-owner	Medical	Trans-portation	Reactions
1	Dallas	-12.4	-5.9	-4.7	-20.7	+10.1	+2.4	
2	Atlanta	-10.1	-5.1	-21.4	-26.7	-12.6	-3.1	
3	Houston	-8.9	-1.7	-17.7	-18.7	+13.3	-1.3	
4	St. Louis	-5.4	+2.8	-17.4	-15.0	-11.3	-3.2	
5	Kansas City	-5.3	-3.2	-15.3	-16.2	-3.7	+3.9	
6	Pittsburgh	-4.5	+2.1	-20.3	-15.1	-10.9	+5.1	
7	San Diego	-4.3	-5.8	+1.1	-2.8	+18.5	+0.5	
8	Denver	-4.1	-7.4	-13.3	-9.3	-10.1	+1.9	
9	Los Angeles	-3.4	-3.6	+20.6	-9.1	+26.7	+3.5	
10	Baltimore	-3.0	-6.6	+7.6	-13.7	-9.9	-3.7	

Rank	Area*	Budget	Food	Rent	Home-owner	Medical	Trans-portation	Reactions
11	Detroit	−2.6	−4.9	−10.4	+3.2	−1.4	−4.8	
12	Chicago	−2.1	−2.3	+0.8	+0.2	+5.7	+5.0	
13	Cincinnati	−1.6	+0.4	−21.7	−1.5	−6.3	−2.9	
14	Cleveland	−1.1	−0.9	−19.1	+3.6	−2.6	−0.9	
15	Minneapolis	−0.4	−5.2	−0.8	−0.8	−15.7	−1.3	
16	Seattle	−0.1	−0.6	+34.5	−0.8	+10.3	+2.7	
17	Buffalo	+2.2	−0.4	−10.2	−2.9	−21.7	+5.6	
18	Philadelphia	+2.6	+10.2	−17.2	+3.4	+3.3	−1.9	
19	Milwaukee	+3.8	−4.3	−5.2	+7.5	−5.8	+1.8	
20	San Francisco	+4.6	−0.2	+47.3	−2.3	+13.0	+6.9	
21	Washington, D.C.	+5.6	+0.9	+12.1	+0.2	−0.9	−0.9	
22	Boston	+12.8	+0.1	+14.7	+33.3	+11.1	+16.9	
23	New York	+14.1	+11.2	+5.6	+26.9	−2.4	−9.2	
24	Honolulu	+23.2	+28.9	+40.4	+8.7	+7.4	+1.7	
24	Anchorage	+23.2	+11.3	+82.1	+18.4	+55.8	+23.9	

*Standard Metropolitan Statistical Area

CHART
16

ANNUAL COSTS FOR LOWER FAMILY BUDGET

(Ranked from lowest to highest for a 4 person family, expressed as percent above or below U.S. average for metropolitan areas.)

Rank	Area*	Budget	Food	Rent	Medical	Trans-portation	Reactions
1	Dallas	−7.0	−6.1	−8.0	+10.0	−1.8	
2	Atlanta	−6.9	−5.7	−17.4	−13.0	+0.8	
3	Buffalo	−5.0	−1.8	−17.8	−21.8	−3.6	
4	Houston	−4.3	−2.6	−14.2	+14.0	−7.3	
5	Kansas City	−3.6	−1.1	−16.7	−3.9	+0.2	
6	Denver	−2.5	−4.5	−11.4	−10.7	+2.6	
7	Cincinnati	−2.4	+3.0	−18.5	−6.7	−8.3	
7	Detroit	−2.4	+0.9	−16.3	−1.6	−1.1	
7	Pittsburgh	−2.4	+0.4	−9.8	−11.1	+7.2	

Rank	Area*	Budget	Food	Rent	Medical	Trans-portation	Reactions
7	St. Louis	− 2.4	+ 5.0	− 12.3	− 11.5	+ 3.1	
11	Minneapolis	− 2.3	− 0.3	+ 0.2	− 15.9	− 1.6	
12	Cleveland	− 2.0	+ 0.5	− 13.3	− 3.0	+ 2.2	
13	Baltimore	− 1.1	− 0.2	+ 4.5	− 9.9	− 1.2	
14	Milwaukee	+ 0.2	− 5.6	− 1.4	− 0.6	+ 0.1	
15	Chicago	0.7	+ 0.2	− 1.3	+ 6.1	+ 9.3	
15	Philadelphia	+ 0.7	+ 4.6	− 14.4	+ 3.4	− 1.8	
17	New York	+ 1.4	+ 7.8	− 3.2	− 2.2	− 12.9	
17	San Diego	+ 1.4	− 2.4	+ 11.5	+ 17.9	+ 7.3	
19	Boston	5.9	− 3.4	+ 21.7	− 11.2	+ 18.4	
20	Los Angeles	+ 7.3	− 1.2	+ 29.9	+ 27.1	+ 12.3	
21	Washington, D.C.	+ 7.9	− 0.7	+ 22.5	− 0.6	− 0.3	
22	San Francisco	+ 10.3	+ 1.9	+ 31.7	+ 13.0	+ 9.1	
23	Seattle	+ 10.6	+ 0.9	+ 38.9	+ 10.1	+ 6.6	
24	Honolulu	+ 31.3	+ 32.9	+ 45.8	+ 7.3	+ 3.1	
25	Anchorage	+ 48.2	+ 17.0	+ 95.8	+ 56.2	+ 76.1	

*Standard Metropolitan Statistical Area

103

Costs For a Retired Couple

Comparisons for costs of living for retired couples for various parts of the country are shown in Charts 17, 18, and 19. The three charts reflect high, intermediate, and low budgets. Again, there are some interesting differences among the regions for food, rent, home ownership, transportation, and medical expenses.

ANNUAL COSTS FOR LOWER BUDGET FOR RETIRED COUPLE

(Ranked from lowest to highest for retired couple, expressed as a percent above or below U.S. average for metropolitan areas.)

Rank	Area*	Budget	Food	Rent	Home-owner	Trans-portation	Medical	Reaction
1	Atlanta	−10.5	−6.7	−25.4	−48.5	−2.2	+35.7	
2	Dallas	−7.4	−8.7	−13.6	−30.1	+2.1	+35.1	

Rank	Area*	Budget	Food	Rent	Home-owner	Trans-portation	Medical	Reaction
3	Chicago	-7.1	+2.2	+1.9	-14.3	+1.5	-77.2	
4	Houston	-4.3	-4.7	-24.8	-21.7	+5.8	+27.1	
5	Philadelphia	-4.0	+7.9	-11.3	+10.3	-1.1	-74.2	
6	San Diego	-3.5	-4.1	+8.4	-29.5	+4.1	+41.1	
7	Baltimore	-3.4	-6.4	-6.2	-19.3	-3.6	+30.3	
7	Cincinnati	-3.4	+3.7	-23.6	-17.9	-0.6	+20.0	
9	Denver	-3.3	-4.9	-22.7	-19.9	-3.1	+35.7	
10	Kansas City	-2.3	+0.4	-21.0	-21.1	+3.2	+32.1	
11	St. Louis	-1.7	+6.5	-15.5	-22.4	-3.9	+33.4	
12	Los Angeles	-0.8	-2.4	+24.8	-37.1	+8.4	+54.1	
13	Detroit	-0.4	+0.4	-0.3	-4.4	-1.5	+31.5	
14	Minneapolis	-0.2	-0.2	+12.9	-15.1	-6.3	+23.7	
15	Pittsburgh	-0.1	+1.2	-14.6	-6.9	-1.8	+40.0	
16	Milwaukee	+0.6	-4.1	+2.9	+0.1	-1.1	+30.8	
17	Cleveland	+2.2	+0.3	-6.8	+7.2	-4.6	+27.6	
18	Buffalo	+3.3	+0.8	-13.6	+13.7	-7.0	+41.6	

Rank	Area*	Budget	Food	Rent	Home-owner	Trans-portation	Medical	Reaction
19	San Francisco	+6.3	+2.2	+25.8	−21.4	+7.5	+56.1	
20	New York	+6.4	+8.0	+3.2	53.6	−0.5	−77.4	
21	Boston	+6.5	+1.6	+12.8	+55.9	−3.9	−73.3	
22	Washington, D.C.	+7.7	+3.0	+24.2	+3.0	+3.0	+32.4	
23	Seattle	+9.6	+0.4	+37.4	−0.3	+2.8	+43.4	
24	Honolulu	+15.0	+30.3	+36.7	−32.7	+0.8	+59.7	
25	Anchorage	+36.1	+25.6	+77.5	+22.9	+22.2	+102.1	

*Standard Metropolitan Statistical Area

ANNUAL COSTS FOR INTERMEDIATE BUDGET
FOR RETIRED COUPLE

*(Ranked from lowest to highest for retired couple,
expressed as a percent above or below
U.S. average for metropolitan areas.)*

Rank	Area*	Budget	Food	Rent	Home-owner	Trans-portation	Medical	Reaction
1	Atlanta	-10.1	-5.7	-27.9	-44.7	-2.4	+12.0	
2	Dallas	-7.7	-1.7	-10.7	-28.5	+2.6	+10.4	
3	San Diego	-6.6	-5.7	+4.9	-30.0	+4.7	+10.1	
4	Chicago	-5.7	-0.9	-3.5	-15.6	+1.4	-9.7	
5	Cincinnati	-5.2	+0.6	-24.0	-15.7	-0.8	-1.5	
5	Denver	-5.2	-7.6	-22.4	-25.1	-2.8	+8.1	

Rank	Area*	Budget	Food	Rent	Home-owner	Trans-portation	Medical	Reaction
7	Houston	−5.2	−3.1	−24.7	−17.5	+5.8	+2.9	
8	Kansas City	−4.4	−2.5	−25.6	−20.0	+2.8	+7.1	
9	Baltimore	−4.1	−4.7	−8.7	−26.3	−3.4	+6.2	
10	Los Angeles	−3.7	−4.5	+18.6	−34.7	+8.5	+17.5	
11	St. Louis	−3.4	+3.2	−19.7	−20.1	−3.3	+11.6	
12	Minneapolis	−2.9	−2.9	+7.3	−19.3	−6.3	+4.6	
13	Detroit	−2.0	−2.7	−1.0	−0.3	−1.5	+5.6	
14	Pittsburgh	−1.0	+2.6	−18.7	−3.0	−1.3	+12.5	
15	Milwaukee	−0.5	−4.5	−2.4	+4.2	−0.7	+8.6	
16	Cleveland	+0.9	−0.7	−1.7	+6.2	−4.5	+5.5	
16	Philadelphia	+0.9	+10.1	−4.9	+10.5	−0.5	+12.5	
18	Buffalo	+2.5	+2.1	−6.5	+8.0	−6.9	+13.5	
19	San Francisco	+3.7	−0.5	+23.6	−23.2	+7.3	+22.1	
20	Washington, D.C.	+5.4	+4.5	+5.9	+0.9	+3.1	+8.7	
21	Seattle	+5.8	−0.9	+35.2	−6.2	+2.8	+9.0	
22	New York	+9.8	+10.4	+12.4	+53.8	−0.8	−29.6	

Rank	Area*	Budget	Food	Rent	Home-owner	Trans-portation	Medical	Reaction
23	Honolulu	+12.6	+26.6	+42.7	-28.3	+1.2	+21.3	
24	Boston	+13.4	+4.2	+19.5	+60.7	-3.7	+3.1	
25	Anchorage	+25.9	+18.7	+66.1	+23.9	+21.8	+25.3	

*Standard Metropolitan Statistical Area

C H A R T
19

ANNUAL COSTS FOR HIGHER BUDGET FOR RETIRED COUPLE

(Ranked from lowest to highest for retired couple, expressed as a percent above or below U.S. average for metropolitan areas.)

Rank	Area*	Budget	Food	Rent	Home-owner	Trans-portation	Medical	Reaction
1	Atlanta	-11.2	-4.8	-34.1	-42.3	-2.2	+0.8	
2	Cincinnati	-7.7	+0.2	-39.3	-20.0	-0.5	-6.6	

Rank	Area*	Budget	Food	Rent	Home-owner	Trans-portation	Medical	Reaction
3	San Diego	-6.4	-3.7	+12.3	-26.4	+5.5	-0.5	
4	Dallas	-5.0	-4.6	+9.9	-27.1	+2.5	+6.2	
4	St. Louis	-5.0	+4.5	-37.7	-27.0	-3.7	+10.1	
6	Baltimore	-4.6	-2.2	-23.4	-25.5	-3.3	+0.5	
7	Minneapolis	-4.4	+0.4	-10.4	-21.1	-6.0	-3.3	
8	Denver	-4.2	-4.0	-18.5	-25.5	-2.8	+1.9	
9	Chicago	-4.0	+0.1	+0.4	-14.1	+1.0	-8.1	
10	Kansas City	-2.8	+1.7	-26.4	-17.7	+2.8	+4.1	
11	Houston	-2.7	-0.9	+1.9	-17.3	+5.9	+0.9	
12	Pittsburgh	-1.6	+1.7	-26.8	-1.6	-1.5	+5.7	
13	Milwaukee	-1.5	-2.2	-14.8	+6.4	-1.2	-1.4	
14	Los Angeles	-0.9	-0.2	+54.4	-33.0	+8.2	+11.6	
15	Cleveland	-0.6	-1.1	-15.5	+5.4	-3.8	-1.6	
16	Philadelphia	+0.4	+9.7	+6.1	+1.8	-0.2	-8.6	
17	Buffalo	+0.9	-0.6	+5.7	+1.8	-7.0	+4.6	
18	Detroit	+1.0	-2.1	+10.6	+16.4	-1.2	-3.9	

Rank	Area*	Budget	Food	Rent	Home-owner	Trans-portation	Medical	Reaction
19	Seattle	+2.0	−1.1	+17.6	−11.4	+3.0	+0.1	
20	San Francisco	+2.6	+1.0	+7.3	−23.8	+7.6	+16.0	
21	Washington, D.C.	+4.3	+3.4	−5.8	+8.9	+3.1	+3.9	
22	Honolulu	+9.7	+28.5	+25.2	−17.3	+1.5	+0.8	
23	New York	+10.5	+8.1	+15.1	+50.9	−0.7	−6.8	
24	Boston	+18.3	+2.4	+23.1	+88.1	−3.5	+7.2	
25	Anchorage	+20.7	+19.2	+32.0	+22.0	+21.5	+14.8	

*Standard Metropolitan Statistical Area

Electric Bills

What an amazing range of costs for electricity across the nation. As you can see from Chart 20, the lowest rates (combining winter and summer) are found in Seattle and the highest are in New York. Seattle's rates are low because hydroelectric power is not subject to OPEC's machinations . . . unless OPEC buys the Columbia River.

TYPICAL ELECTRIC BILLS FOR RESIDENCES DURING WINTER AND SUMMER
(Ranked from least to most by winter rates)

Rank	Area*	Cost for 2500 KWh[1] in Winter	Cost for 2500 KWh in Summer	Reaction
1	Sacramento	$46.25	$68.50	
2	Seattle	50.59	40.84	
3	Boise	71.09	NA	
4	Indianapolis	73.22	NA	
5	Great Falls	76.39	NA	
6	Omaha	76.82	98.77	
7	Dallas	76.83	111.96	
8	St. Louis	77.96	129.35	
9	Shreveport	79.08	90.58	
10	Casper	82.73	75.18	
11	Sioux Falls	85.59	112.25	
12	Oklahoma City	87.52	109.28	
13	Austin	88.23	138.73	
14	Portland, Or.	88.38	80.52	
15	Louisville	88.82	122.45	
16	Little Rock	89.16	126.27	
17	Wichita	89.52	129.08	

Rank	Area*	Cost for 2500 KWh[1] in Winter	Cost for 2500 KWh in Summer	Reaction
18	Burlington	$90.84	$NA	
19	New Orleans	91.44	98.59	
20	Nashville	94.36	NA	
21	Tulsa	95.28	120.16	
22	Memphis	96.86	NA	
23	Minneapolis	97.47	135.94	
24	San Antonio	97.95	113.17	
25	Atlanta	98.79	135.41	
26	Fargo	99.91	NA	
27	Cincinnati	102.48	NA	
28	Las Vegas	102.93	NA	
29	Des Moines	103.14	136.55	
30	Chicago	104.31	183.89	
31	Charleston, W.V.	104.43	NA	
32	Baton Rouge	104.97	112.57	
33	Anchorage	106.16	NA	
34	Kansas City	107.55	137.24	
35	Baltimore	109.37	143.55	
36	Albany	109.70	NA	
36	Buffalo	109.70	NA	
38	Houston	111.12	140.95	
39	Columbus	112.55	159.21	
40	Corpus Christi	113.84	NA	
41	Denver	115.26	NA	
42	Milwaukee	116.25	148.25	
43	Beaumont	117.20	133.20	

Rank	Area*	Cost for 2500 KWh[1] in Winter	Cost for 2500 KWh in Summer	Reaction
44	Tucson	$117.53	$151.23	
45	Raleigh	117.79	130.20	
46	Salt Lake City	117.95	NA	
47	Washington, D.C.	118.55	149.51	
48	Phoenix	119.81	146.60	
49	Bakersfield	120.63	172.38	
49	Fresno	120.63	172.38	
49	San Francisco	120.63	172.38	
52	Norfolk	120.72	158.50	
52	Richmond	120.72	158.50	
54	Birmingham	121.42	NA	
54	Mobile	121.42	NA	
56	Biloxi	121.76	135.01	
57	Pittsburgh	123.54	155.07	
58	Charleston, S.C.	125.99	NA	
58	Columbia	125.99	NA	
60	Cleveland	127.91	162.92	
61	Orlando	129.59	NA	
62	Grand Rapids	131.50	NA	
63	Detroit	132.58	NA	
64	Miami	133.06	NA	
65	Wilmington	134.08	201.48	
66	Akron	134.32	NA	
67	Tampa	142.53	NA	
68	Rochester	142.64	NA	
69	Philadelphia	143.92	198.18	

Rank	Area*	Cost for 2500 KWh[1] in Winter	Cost for 2500 KWh in Summer	Reaction
70	Portland	$148.59	$NA	
71	Hartford	166.75	NA	
72	Albuquerque	167.38	171.08	
73	Los Angeles	170.15	NA	
74	Newark	180.42	207.62	
75	El Paso	184.94	NA	
76	Manchester	190.00	NA	
77	Boston	192.70	221.21	
78	Nassau-Suffolk	202.94	260.50	
79	Providence	211.05	214.90	
80	Honolulu	220.20	NA	
81	San Diego	245.66	270.91	
82	New York	269.59	309.38	

[1]Data based on rates effective during utility-specified winter or summer period for one month.
*Standard Metropolitan Statistical Area

Supplemental Charts

Charts 21 through 28 are provided as supplements to Chart 8. They show the incomes earned for selected occupations in various parts of the United States.

CHART
21

AVERAGE ANNUAL SALARY OF CLASSROOM TEACHERS
(Ranked from high to low)

Rank	Area†	Annual Salary	Reaction
1	Anchorage	$29,926	
2	Washington, D.C.	22,190	
3	Philadelphia	21,427	
4	Los Angeles	20,692	
5	Denver	20,209	
6	San Diego	20,197	
7	Sacramento	20,154	
8	Seattle	20,034	
9	New York	19,832	
10	Detroit	19,683	
11	Boston	18,091	
12	Casper	17,980	
13	Milwaukee	17,760	
14	St. Louis	17,725	
15	Wilmington	17,705	
16	Pittsburgh	17,549	
17	Miami	17,481	
18	Phoenix	17,327	
19	Fargo	17,200	

Rank	Area†	Annual Salary	Reaction
20	San Francisco	$17,125	
21	Las Vegas	16,753	
22	Nashville	16,508	
23	Tulsa	16,357	
24	Atlanta	16,033	
25	Newark	16,017	
26	Austin	16,000	
27	Louisville	15,938	
28	Baltimore	15,910	
29	Salt Lake City	15,723	
30	Dallas	15,623	
31	Baton Rouge	15,500	
31	Indianapolis	15,500	
33	New Orleans	15,450	
34	Houston	15,289	
35	Tucson	15,061	
36	Shreveport	15,047	
37	Wichita	15,045	
38	Sioux Falls	15,013	
39	Charleston, W.V.	14,966	
40	San Antonio	14,900	
41	Albuquerque	14,639	
42	Little Rock	14,605	
43	Norfolk	14,547	
44	Orlando	14,518	
45	Columbia	14,049	
46	Raleigh	13,990	

Rank	Area†	Annual Salary	Reaction
47	Memphis	$13,693	
47	Mobile	13,652	
49	Tampa	13,452	
50	Birmingham	13,446	
51	Corpus Christi	13,000	
52	El Paso	12,905	
53	Oklahoma City	12,903	
54	Kansas City	11,838	
55	Richmond	11,835	

†Incorporated City

22

AVERAGE WEEKLY SALARY OF SECRETARIES
(Ranked from high to low)

Rank	Area*	Weekly Salary	Reaction
1	Detroit	$374.50	
2	Seattle	318.00	
3	Houston	314.50	
4	Albany	298.00	
5	Wichita	297.50	

Rank	Area*	Weekly Salary	Reaction
6	San Francisco	$296.00	
7	Chicago	294.50	
8	Portland, Or.	294.00	
9	Los Angeles	293.50	
10	Cleveland	292.50	
11	New York	289.00	
12	Pittsburgh	288.00	
13	Washington, D.C.	287.00	
14	Atlanta	286.50	
14	Newark	286.50	
16	Boston	282.00	
17	Milwaukee	281.00	
18	Baltimore	280.50	
18	Cincinnati	280.50	
18	Fresno	280.50	
21	Denver	274.50	
22	Nassau-Suffolk	274.00	
23	Indianapolis	270.50	
23	Louisville	270.50	
23	Oklahoma City	270.50	
23	St. Louis	270.50	
27	San Diego	265.50	
28	Dallas	263.00	
30	Buffalo	261.00	
31	Minneapolis	259.00	
32	Sacramento	257.00	
33	New Orleans	254.00	

Rank	Area*	Weekly Salary	Reaction
34	Kansas City	$252.50	
35	Richmond	251.00	
36	Miami	250.00	
37	Corpus Christi	248.50	
38	Salt Lake City	248.00	
39	Hartford	247.50	
40	Columbus	243.00	
41	Omaha	239.50	
42	Memphis	237.50	
43	Providence	235.00	
44	Norfolk	234.50	
45	San Antonio	232.50	
46	Portland, Me.	231.00	

*Standard Metropolitan Statistical Area

CHART
23

AVERAGE WEEKLY SALARY OF COMPUTER PROGRAMMERS
(Ranked from high to low)

Rank	Area*	Weekly Salary	Reactions
1	Detroit	$437.50	
2	Houston	425.00	
3	Cleveland	410.00	
4	New York	404.50	
5	Miami	401.50	
6	Nassau-Suffolk	400.50	
7	Los Angeles	399.50	
8	Chicago	395.50	
9	San Diego	392.00	
10	Denver	388.50	
11	Seattle	386.50	
12	Sacramento	383.50	
13	Washington, D.C.	381.50	
14	San Francisco	380.50	
15	Albany	379.00	
16	Milwaukee	375.50	
17	Baltimore	374.50	
18	Omaha	373.50	
19	Boston	373.00	

Rank	Area*	Weekly Salary	Reactions
19	Minneapolis	$373.00	
21	Oklahoma City	371.50	
22	Newark	371.00	
23	Corpus Christi	369.50	
24	St. Louis	367.50	
24	Wichita	367.50	
26	Salt Lake City	364.50	
27	Cincinnati	361.00	
27	Pittsburgh	361.00	
29	Hartford	360.00	
30	Atlanta	359.00	
31	Portland, Or.	353.00	
32	Philadelphia	352.50	
33	Kansas City	347.50	
34	Dallas	344.50	
35	Buffalo	342.00	
36	Richmond	341.50	
37	Columbus	338.50	
38	New Orleans	334.50	
39	Indianapolis	333.50	
40	Memphis	328.00	
41	Norfolk	327.50	
42	San Antonio	322.50	
43	Louisville	312.50	
44	Providence	312.00	

*Standard Metropolitan Statistical Area

CHART
24

AVERAGE WEEKLY SALARY OF
REGISTERED NURSES
(Ranked from high to low)

Rank	Area*	Weekly Salary	Reactions
1	Detroit	$455.50	
2	Seattle	411.50	
3	Baltimore	395.50	
4	Indianapolis	392.00	
5	Cleveland	389.00	
6	Houston	388.50	
7	Atlanta	388.00	
8	San Francisco	385.00	
9	Los Angeles	381.00	
10	St. Louis	374.00	
11	Milwaukee	369.50	
12	Pittsburgh	369.00	
13	Chicago	368.00	
14	Dallas	366.50	
14	San Diego	366.50	
16	Cincinnati	366.00	
17	Buffalo	362.00	
18	Albany	360.00	
19	Wichita	357.00	

Rank	Area*	Weekly Salary	Reactions
20	Boston	$255.50	
21	New York	355.00	
22	Minneapolis	354.50	
23	Denver	353.00	
24	Louisville	348.50	
25	Nassau-Suffolk	341.50	
25	Philadelphia	341.50	
27	Kansas City	340.00	
28	Richmond	335.50	
29	Newark	334.50	
30	Hartford	328.00	
31	Omaha	321.00	
32	Columbus	309.00	
32	Memphis	309.00	
34	Providence	308.00	

*Standard Metropolitan Statistical Area

AVERAGE HOURLY WAGE OF MAINTENANCE CARPENTERS
(Ranked from high to low)

Rank	Area*	Hourly Wage	Reactions
1	Detroit	$12.01	
2	Corpus Christi	11.98	
3	Cleveland	11.79	
4	Houston	11.69	
5	San Francisco	11.39	
6	Portland, Or.	11.19	
7	Milwaukee	10.99	
8	Chicago	10.88	
9	Minneapolis	10.81	
10	Pittsburgh	10.68	
11	Cincinnati	10.58	
12	Richmond	10.48	
13	Denver	10.46	
14	Indianapolis	10.45	
15	Baltimore	10.30	
16	Buffalo	10.29	
17	Louisville	10.25	
18	Washington, D.C.	10.08	
19	Sacramento	9.96	

Rank	Area*	Hourly Wage	Reactions
20	Philadelphia	$9.83	
21	Los Angeles	9.81	
22	Newark	9.64	
23	Salt Lake City	9.56	
24	St. Louis	9.51	
25	San Diego	9.46	
26	Atlanta	9.41	
27	Kansas City	9.37	
28	Nassau-Suffolk	9.32	
28	Wichita	9.32	
30	Hartford	9.17	
31	Boston	9.10	
32	Dallas	9.00	
33	New York	8.83	
34	Memphis	8.82	
35	Oklahoma City	8.79	
36	Albany	8.46	
37	New Orleans	8.03	
38	Miami	7.80	
39	Omaha	7.41	
40	Providence	7.17	
41	Portland, Me.	6.29	

*Standard Metropolital Statistical Area

AVERAGE HOURLY WAGE OF ELECTRICIANS
(Ranked from high to low)

Rank	Area*	Hourly Wage	Reactions
1	Detroit	$12.50	
2	Portland, Or.	12.15	
3	San Francisco	11.95	
4	Milwaukee	11.93	
5	Cleveland	11.90	
6	Baltimore	11.78	
7	Houston	11.65	
8	Oklahoma City	11.64	
9	Richmond	11.61	
10	Corpus Christi	11.56	
11	Chicago	11.41	
12	Minneapolis	11.25	
13	Buffalo	11.02	
14	St. Louis	10.98	
15	Pittsburgh	10.94	
16	Indianapolis	10.93	
17	Washington, D.C.	10.85	
18	Atlanta	10.83	
19	Louisville	10.74	

Rank	Area*	Hourly Wage	Reactions
20	Sacramento	$10.73	
21	Cincinnati	10.69	
21	Los Angeles	10.69	
23	Kansas City	10.54	
24	San Diego	10.46	
25	Memphis	10.33	
26	New York	10.23	
26	Norfolk	10.23	
28	Dallas	10.13	
29	Newark	10.10	
30	Salt Lake City	9.99	
31	Boston	9.95	
32	New Orleans	9.87	
33	Philadelphia	9.81	
34	Albany	9.80	
35	Fresno	9.74	
36	Wichita	9.72	
37	Denver	9.62	
38	Hartford	9.51	
39	Nassau-Suffolk	9.48	
40	Columbus	9.43	
41	Omaha	9.18	
42	San Antonio	8.81	
43	Miami	8.51	
44	Providence	8.34	
45	Portland, Me.	7.79	

*Standard Metropolitan Statistical Area

AVERAGE HOURLY WAGE OF
MECHANICS
(Ranked from high to low)

Rank	Area*	Hourly Wage	Reactions
1	Richmond	$12.25	
2	Detroit	12.07	
3	Cleveland	12.03	
4	Baltimore	11.76	
5	Portland, Or.	11.63	
6	Corpus Christi	11.53	
7	Seattle	11.49	
8	Buffalo	11.42	
9	San Francisco	11.31	
10	Sacramento	11.06	
11	Houston	10.74	
12	Pittsburgh	10.71	
13	Indianapolis	10.64	
14	Chicago	10.59	
15	Louisville	10.47	
16	Milwaukee	10.23	
17	Minneapolis	9.88	
18	San Diego	9.65	
19	St. Louis	9.61	

Rank	Area*	Hourly Wage	Reactions
20	Los Angeles	$9.58	
21	Cincinnati	9.55	
22	Kansas City	9.47	
22	New York	9.47	
24	Memphis	9.45	
25	Newark	9.42	
26	New Orleans	9.40	
27	Dallas	9.27	
28	Denver	9.24	
29	Philadelphia	9.21	
30	Salt Lake City	9.17	
31	Wichita	9.13	
32	Columbus	9.12	
33	Oklahoma City	9.07	
34	Boston	9.01	
35	Fresno	8.99	
36	Omaha	8.93	
37	Atlanta	8.92	
38	Hartford	8.71	
39	Nassau-Suffolk	8.58	
40	Albany	8.07	
41	Norfolk	7.74	
42	Miami	7.72	
43	San Antonio	7.65	
44	Providence	7.36	
45	Portland, Me.	6.39	

*Standard Metropolitan Statistical Area

CHART
28

AVERAGE HOURLY WAGE OF TRUCK DRIVERS
(Ranked from high to low)

Rank	Area*	Hourly Wage	Reactions
1	Chicago	$12.17	
2	Seattle	11.60	
3	San Francisco	11.56	
4	Minneapolis	11.15	
5	Portland, Or.	11.12	
6	Detroit	10.38	
7	Cleveland	10.36	
8	St. Louis	10.30	
9	Milwaukee	10.20	
10	Nassau-Suffolk	10.16	
10	Philadelphia	10.16	
12	Newark	10.09	
13	Cincinnati	9.98	
14	Albany	9.97	
15	Pittsburgh	9.91	
16	Baltimore	9.85	
17	Boston	9.80	
18	Fresno	9.76	
19	Sacramento	9.69	
20	Providence	9.68	

Rank	Area*	Hourly Wage	Reactions
21	New York	$9.67	
22	Buffalo	9.63	
23	Columbus	9.59	
24	Kansas City	9.42	
25	Indianapolis	9.33	
26	Los Angeles	9.30	
27	Omaha	9.20	
28	San Diego	9.10	
29	Salt Lake City	8.77	
30	Denver	8.65	
31	Hartford	8.59	
32	Louisville	8.56	
33	Atlanta	8.48	
34	Wichita	8.33	
35	Houston	8.26	
36	Oklahoma City	8.19	
37	Portland, Or.	8.03	
38	Richmond	7.98	
39	Washington, D.C.	7.89	
40	Corpus Christi	7.88	
41	Memphis	7.63	
42	Dallas	7.49	
43	New Orleans	7.32	
44	San Antonio	6.83	
45	Miami	6.81	
46	Norfolk	5.80	

*Standard Metropolitan Statistical Area

Directions: Rate only those cities below which are on your Tentative Interest List. Give a 5 to those cities with predominance of (+) ratings on the various charts in this chapter. Give a 3 if a city has only enough (+) marks to remain of interest. Give a 1 to those with few (+) marks. Eliminate from your Tentative Interest list those cities for which you've lost all interest; add additional cities as interest develops and rate them as above.

SUMMARY GRID

		Rating (5, 3, or 1)	Comments
1	Akron, Ohio		
2	Albany, New York		
3	Albuquerque, New Mexico		
4	Anchorage, Alaska		
5	Atlanta, Georgia		
6	Austin, Texas		
7	Bakersfield, California		
8	Baltimore, Maryland		
9	Baton Rouge, Louisiana		
10	Beaumont, Texas		
11	Biloxi, Mississippi		
12	Birmingham, Alabama		
13	Boise, Idaho		
14	Boston, Massachusetts		
15	Buffalo, New York		
16	Burlington, Vermont		
17	Casper, Wyoming		

		Rating (5, 3, or 1)	Comments
18	Charleston, South Carolina		
19	Charleston, West Virginia		
20	Chicago, Illinois		
21	Cincinnati, Ohio		
22	Cleveland, Ohio		
23	Columbia, South Carolina		
24	Columbus, Ohio		
25	Corpus Christi, Texas		
26	Dallas, Texas		
27	Denver, Colorado		
28	Des Moines, Iowa		
29	Detroit, Michigan		
30	El Paso, Texas		
31	Fargo, North Dakota		
32	Fresno, California		
33	Grand Rapids, Michigan		
34	Great Falls, Montana		
35	Hartford, Connecticut		
36	Honolulu, Hawaii		
37	Houston, Texas		
38	Indianapolis, Indiana		
39	Kansas City, Missouri		
40	Las Vegas, Nevada		
41	Little Rock, Arkansas		
42	Los Angeles, California		
43	Louisville, Kentucky		
44	Manchester, New Hampshire		

		Rating (5, 3, or 1)	Comments
45	Memphis, Tennessee		
46	Miami, Florida		
47	Milwaukee, Wisconsin		
48	Minneapolis, Minnesota		
49	Mobile, Alabama		
50	Nashville, Tennessee		
51	Nassau-Suffolk, New York		
52	Newark, New Jersey		
53	New Orleans, Louisiana		
54	New York, New York		
55	Norfolk, Virginia		
56	Oklahoma City, Oklahoma		
57	Omaha, Nebraska		
58	Orlando, Florida		
59	Philadelphia, Pennsylvania		
60	Phoenix, Arizona		
61	Pittsburgh, Pennsylvania		
62	Portland, Maine		
63	Portland, Oregon		
64	Providence, Rhode Island		
65	Raleigh, North Carolina		
66	Richmond, Virginia		
67	Rochester, New York		
68	Sacramento, California		
69	Salt Lake City, Utah		
70	San Antonio, Texas		
71	San Diego, California		

		Rating (5, 3, or 1)	Comments
72	San Francisco, California		
73	Seattle, Washington		
74	Shrovoport, Louisiana		
75	Sioux Falls, South Dakota		
76	St. Louis, Missouri		
77	Tampa, Florida		
78	Tucson, Arizona		
79	Tulsa, Oklahoma		
80	Washington, D.C.		
81	Wichita, Kansas		
82	Wilmington, Delaware		

4

Whither For The Weather?

Songwriters are amazing. They describe things so well, and set it to music too! And later on the scientists make the discoveries that the songwriters have been providing for years. Take the relationship between personality and weather, for example.

How long have you been singing about crossing over to the sunny side of the street, or getting the blues when it rains, or having stormy weather in a relationship, or zipadeedooda-ing it with wonderful sunshiny days?

And we even talk about the weather itself as reflecting personality. We say, "What a gloomy day," or "Those clouds look grim." And we frequently describe people with weather related adjectives, such as having a "sunny outlook" or a "stormy temperament."

Well, the researchers have just recently been discovering what we have been singing and talking about for a long time . . . the influence of weather on personality can be dramatic indeed!

These discoveries reflect what psychotherapists have known

138

for some time. When the weather turns sour, clients begin to pour through the door. In our own programs we have found that patients often refer to two weeks of rainy weather or a hot and humid spell as "... the last straw, Doctor. This weather, along with everything else, is really getting to me."

Not everyone is so reactive to weather extremes, however. Some people seem to thrive on the dynamic surges of the seasons, nature's splendiferous vicissitudes, and being close to the excitement of change. Not everyone will be happy with one balmy day after another in San Diego or Honolulu. We recently had an ice storm on Long Island which showed how dramatically different are people's reactions to nature:

> The scene was incredible ... it looked like a crystal dream. Thick ice sparkled on every tree, and the lawn tinkled like a glass chandelier when even the smallest child walked across it. The ice storm was breathtaking.
>
> But then the wind began to moan and the chiming of the ice-encrusted limbs was punctuated with the sudden explosions of huge trees beginning to snap and shatter in the wind. Electric power and telephone lines were swept down as tree tops suddenly plunged to the earth. Soon the area looked like a huge battlefield, with uprooted trees and limbs covering the streets and lawns. Houses grew cold in the dark, water pipes froze and burst.

How did Long Islanders respond to the storm? Some panicked, sure that the ice age had precipitously descended and the azaleas would never bloom again. Many felt their only chance for survival was a quick retreat to Miami and airline switchboards were jammed with calls. Others, less reactive to weather, appeared to enjoy the adventure and the break from normal routine. They stoked up dusty campstoves, scrounged up firewood for fireplaces, and accepted the downed limbs as part of nature's awesome power.

As a result of that one storm, which was not all that devastating in retrospect, a surprising number of people came to us for counseling. They were agitated, depressed, anxious, and even frightened, triggered in part by their reaction to the weather. In fairness to Long Island, it should be said that the weather is considered quite moderate most of the time. But for some, particularly those who are most weather-reactive, it was not the right place to live that winter.

How much does your happiness and success depend upon Mother Nature? Probably much more than you think. Some of us are extremely influenced by the weather and have very strong likes and dislikes. Even those who are not as concerned about the climatological characteristics (say that three times fast) of where they live are still going to be influenced to some degree by the weather. The number of times that doctors advise their patients to "Take a vacation in the sun!" is not just a coincidence. In fact, they generally justify their own frequent flights to sunny getaways in this manner.

How wonderful it is that in the United States virtually everyone's weather preferences can be accommodated. If you like the weather mild with few temperature extremes, a number of areas have excellent weather for you. If you prefer maximum sun, minimum rain, and warm temperatures, there are the areas which will suit you just fine, thank you. If you like the four seasons in all their intensity, try those regions with warm summers, long gorgeous falls, deep winters, and lush verdant springs.

And we should point out that if you somehow thrill to monsoons and violent thunderstorms, heat waves searing enough to bake your brains, or humidity sufficient to render one gasping and helpless, you might find a few such places hidden in the charts too.

In this chapter, you will find a careful analysis of the climate in our major areas. We have tried to include information which will be most useful to you in considering where to live in America.

The Sunshiny Places

Americans love the sun, no doubt about it. And our love affair with Old Sol has helped make the sunbelt regions boom. It's not just a coincidence that the sunniest areas are also at the top of the list for population growth, with Las

Vegas heading the charts and sunny Phoenix and Tucson also packing the people in.

We have arranged Chart 1 from the sunniest areas to the cloudiest. It reflects the percentage of days that the sun can be expected to shine during the year.[1]

If you are a weather-reactive person, who thrives on sunshine and shrivels in the shade, give some careful consideration to both ends of this list. Perhaps the sunshine factor will be a deciding variable when you make your decisions. At least it will help you decide whether to pack a swimming suit or an umbrella.

---

[1]Well, of course, the sun does shine all the time, even at night. We mean days on which the sun shines on the ground more than 50% of the daylight hours.

THE SUN SHINES BRIGHT...
(Percent of annual sunshine ranked from most to least)

Rank	Area†	% of possible sunshine	Reaction
1	Phoenix	86	
1	Tucson	86	
3	Las Vegas	85	
4	El Paso	83	
5	Fresno	82	
6	Sacramento	79	
7	Albuquerque	77	
7	Bakersfield	77	
9	Los Angeles	73	
10	Denver	70	
10	Salt Lake City	70	
12	Honolulu	68	
13	Boise	67	
13	Kansas City	67	
13	Miami	67	
13	Oklahoma City	67	
13	San Diego	67	
13	San Francisco	67	
19	Orlando	66	

Rank	Area†	% of possible sunshine	Reaction
19	Tampa	66	
21	Charleston, S.C.	65	
21	Memphis	65	
21	Wichita	65	
24	Columbia	64	
24	Corpus Christi	64	
24	Dallas	64	
24	Shreveport	64	
28	Great Falls	63	
28	Little Rock	63	
28	Norfolk	63	
31	Omaha	62	
31	Tulsa	62	
33	Atlanta	61	
33	Austin	61	
33	Richmond	61	
33	San Antonio	61	
37	Baton Rouge	60	
37	Boston	60	
37	Casper	60	
37	Des Moines	60	
37	Mobile	60	
37	Raleigh	60	
43	Nassau-Suffolk	59	
43	New Orleans	59	
43	New York	59	

Rank	Area†	% of possible sunshine	Reaction
43	St. Louis	59	
47	Beaumont	58	
47	Birmingham	58	
47	Fargo	58	
47	Hartford	58	
47	Indianapolis	58	
47	Minneapolis	58	
47	Nashville	58	
47	Newark	58	
47	Philadelphia	58	
47	Portland, Me.	58	
47	Sioux Falls	58	
47	Washington, D.C.	58	
59	Baltimore	57	
59	Chicago	57	
59	Cincinnati	57	
59	Houston	57	
59	Louisville	57	
59	Providence	57	
65	Milwaukee	56	
66	Wilmington	55	
67	Detroit	54	
67	Rochester	54	
69	Albany	53	
70	Buffalo	52	
70	Cleveland	52	

Rank	Area†	% of possible sunshine	Reaction
70	Columbus	52	
73	Burlington	51	
74	Grand Rapids	50	
75	Charleston, W.V.	48	
75	Portland, Or.	48	
77	Akron	47	
78	Anchorage	46	
79	Seattle	45	
80	Pittsburgh	42	

†Incorporated City

How Often It Rains...And How Much

Unless you are a farmer or own your own hydroelectric dam or have some other special interest, you will be more concerned about number of "rainy days" than total rainfall. For this reason we have ranked our areas by *number of days* in which 1/100th or more inches of rain falls during the year. In the second column we have provided total rainfall.

The rainy day champions? Buffalo, Seattle, and Cleveland, where they have learned to live, love and be successful despite the drizzles and downpours. And it is not true that they have to shave their moss and wring out their hair twice a day. The driest places? Las Vegas, Phoenix, Los Angeles and Bakersfield, all of which are proof positive that you can make deserts bloom.

Which are best for you? It depends upon whether you enjoy growing cacti or water lilies, baking on the beach or singing in the rain, enjoy your clouds wet and scudding or white and seldom. As you can see from the Rainy Day Chart, the range across the United States is surprisingly broad, with lots of choices available for you.

CHART
2

HOW OFTEN IT RAINS...
AND HOW MUCH
(Ranked from fewest to most days with rain)

Rank	Area†	# days of rain .01″ or more per year	Annual Average total inches	Reaction
1	Las Vegas	27	3.76	
2	Bakersfield	35	5.72	
2	Los Angeles	35	14.05	
4	Phoenix	36	7.05	
5	San Diego	42	9.75	
6	Fresno	44	10.24	
7	El Paso	47	7.77	
8	Tucson	50	11.05	
9	Sacramento	57	17.22	
10	Albuquerque	59	7.77	
11	San Francisco	66	20.66	
12	Dallas	77	32.30	
13	Corpus Christi	78	28.53	
14	San Antonio	80	27.54	
15	Austin	82	32.49	
15	Oklahoma City	82	31.37	
17	Wichita	85	30.58	

Rank	Area†	# days of rain .01″ or more per year	Annual Average total inches	Reaction
18	Denver	86	15.51	
19	Boise	89	11.50	
19	Salt Lake City	89	15.17	
21	Tulsa	90	36.90	
22	Casper	93	11.22	
23	Sioux Falls	94	24.72	
24	Omaha	98	30.18	
24	Shreveport	98	44.72	
26	Kansas City	99	37.00	
27	Fargo	100	19.62	
27	Great Falls	100	14.99	
29	Honolulu	101	22.90	
30	Little Rock	103	48.52	
31	Beaumont	104	55.07	
32	Des Moines	105	30.85	
32	Memphis	105	49.10	
34	Baton Rouge	108	54.05	
34	Houston	108	48.19	
34	Tampa	108	49.38	
37	St. Louis	110	35.89	
38	Columbia	111	46.36	
38	Raleigh	111	42.54	
38	Washington, D.C.	111	38.89	
41	Baltimore	112	40.46	
41	New Orleans	112	56.77	

Rank	Area†	# days of rain .01" or more per year	Annual Average total inches	Reaction
43	Atlanta	113	48.34	
43	Minneapolis	113	25.94	
43	Richmond	113	39.03	
46	Charleston, S.C.	114	52.12	
46	Philadelphia	114	39.93	
48	Anchorage	115	14.74	
48	Norfolk	115	44.68	
50	Wilmington	116	40.25	
51	Nassau-Suffolk	117	41.53	
51	Orlando	117	51.21	
53	Birmingham	118	53.23	
54	Nashville	120	46.00	
54	New York	120	40.19	
56	Newark	121	41.45	
57	Chicago	124	34.44	
57	Indianapolis	124	38.74	
57	Louisville	124	43.11	
57	Providence	124	42.75	
61	Milwaukee	125	29.07	
61	Mobile	125	66.98	
63	Portland, Me.	126	40.80	
64	Boston	128	42.52	
65	Hartford	129	43.37	
66	Cincinnati	130	40.03	
67	Miami	131	59.80	
68	Detroit	133	31.69	

Rank	Area†	# days of rain .01" or more per year	Annual Average total inches	Reaction
69	Columbus	136	37.01	
70	Albany	137	33.36	
71	Grand Rapids	145	32.39	
72	Pittsburgh	146	36.22	
73	Charleston, W.V.	150	40.75	
74	Burlington	152	32.54	
75	Akron	153	35.13	
75	Seattle	153	35.65	
77	Portland, Or.	154	37.61	
78	Cleveland	156	34.99	
79	Rochester	157	34.99	
80	Buffalo	169	36.11	
80	Biloxi	NA	57.99	
80	Manchester	NA	43.20	

†Incorporated City

The Sweat Factor

Whenever we had summer visitors from the West Coast to our homes in New York, we were always surprised to hear them complain about the humidity. Frankly, it can get sticky on Long Island, but as you can tell from the chart below, there are many places with much higher humidity. But if you look at the ratings for most of the West Coast, you'll discover what we learned too. West Coasters are not used to perspiring. In fact, they consider it to be in very poor taste. No wonder West Coasters look with awe and some amazement at

East Coasters happily wiping away torrents of perspiration from their faces and proclaiming, "Isn't this weather great!"

Your own degree of comfort with humidity is different from others' reactions to sticky weather. Some people say they can't stand to feel sweaty, and others don't seem to mind much at all. The Temperature-Humidity Index we have for you is based on average temperatures and humidity figures for the various areas across the United States. Findings from the formula have been shown with symbols, so you can tell at a glance where you can expect to sweat most in America and where perspiring has become almost a lost art.

In order to translate the findings into useful information, we have relied generally on accepted ratings of expert meterologists and climatologists. Essentially what they have done is to ask people whether or not they felt comfortable under various degrees of humidity. A high rating of from 84 to 91 means that almost everyone feels extremely uncomfortable and it is very difficult to work. At the other end of the scale, a rating of 69 or below means that almost no one feels uncomfortable.

Please don't take these ratings literally. People can and do survive in Austin, Birmingham, Corpus Christi, Dallas and other places with high ratings. In fact, these are, generally speaking, the areas where people are flocking. But if you are uncomfortable with high heat and humidity, you will want to consider carefully whether those high-rated places will be desirable for you. Or whether you are willing to pay the high air conditioning costs associated with keeping cool and dry. Yes, we have provided a chart for this too, a little later in this chapter.

CHART

3

THE SWEAT FACTOR: TEMPERATURE HUMIDITY INDEX
(Ranked from most comfortable to least comfortable)

What the symbols indicate:

☆	=	69 or below	Everyone feels comfortable
☐	=	70–74	Almost everyone feels comfortable
○	=	75–78	Half of the people are comfortable
⊗	=	79–83	Almost no one is comfortable
●	=	84–91	Everyone suffers and no one is comfortable

Rank	Area†	May	June	July	Aug.	Sept.	Oct.	Reactions
1	Anchorage	☆	☆	☆	☆	☆	☆	
2	Great Falls	☆	☆	☐	☐	☆	☆	
2	San Francisco	☆	☆	☆	☐	☐	☆	
2	Seattle	☆	☆	☐	☐	☆	☆	
5	Portland, Me.	☆	☐	☐	☐	☆	☆	
5	Portland, Or.	☆	☆	☐	☐	☐	☆	
5	San Diego	☆	☆	☐	☆	☐	☐	
8	Boston	☆	☐	○	☐	☆	☆	
8	Buffalo	☆	☐	○	☐	☆	☆	
8	Burlington	☆	☐	○	☐	☆	☆	
8	Casper	☆	☐	○	☐	☆	☆	
8	Detroit	☆	☐	○	☐	☆	☆	

Rank	Area†	May	June	July	Aug.	Sept.	Oct.	Reactions
13	Los Angeles	☆	☆	☐	☐	☐	☐	
14	Fargo	☆	☐	○	○	☆	☆	
14	Milwaukee	☆	☐	○	○	☆	☆	
14	Minneapolis	☆	☐	○	○	☆	☆	
17	Akron	☆	☐	○	○	☐	☆	
17	Albany	☆	☐	○	○	☐	☆	
17	Boise	☆	☐	○	○	☐	☆	
17	Chicago	☆	☐	○	○	☐	☆	
17	Cleveland	☆	☐	○	○	☐	☆	
17	Denver	☆	☐	○	○	☐	☆	
17	Grand Rapids	☆	☐	○	○	☐	☆	
17	Hartford	☆	☐	○	○	☐	☆	
17	Pittsburgh	☆	☐	○	○	▨	☆	
17	Providence	☆	☐	○	○	☐	☆	
17	Rochester	☆	☐	○	○	☐	☆	
17	Salt Lake City	☆	☐	○	○	☐	☆	
17	Sioux Falls	☆	☐	○	○	☐	☆	
30	Newark	☆	○	○	○	☐	☆	
31	Albuquerque	☐	○	○	○	☐	☆	
32	Memphis	☆	☐	⊗	○	☐	☆	
33	New York	☆	○	⊗	○	☐	☆	
33	Nassau-Suffolk	☆	○	⊗	○	☐	☆	
33	Wilmington	☆	○	⊗	○	☐	☆	
36	Charleston, W.V.	☐	○	⊗	○	☐	☆	
36	Columbus	☐	○	⊗	○	☐	☆	
38	Indianapolis	☐	○	⊗	○	○	☆	
38	Norfolk	☐	○	⊗	○	○	☆	
40	Fresno	☐	○	⊗	○	○	☐	

Rank	Area†	May	June	July	Aug.	Sept.	Oct.	Reactions
40	Sacramento	□	⊙	⊗	○	○	□	
42	Baltimore	□	○	⊗	⊗	□	☆	
42	Cincinnati	□	○	⊗	⊗	□	☆	
42	Des Moines	□	⊙	⊗	⊗	□	☆	
42	Philadelphia	□	○	⊗	⊗	□	☆	
42	Washington, D.C.	□	○	⊗	⊗	□	☆	
47	Kansas City	□	○	⊗	⊗	○	☆	
47	Louisville	□	○	⊗	⊗	○	☆	
47	Richmond	□	○	⊗	⊗	○	☆	
50	Bakersfield	□	○	⊗	⊗	○	□	
50	El Paso	□	○	⊗	⊗	○	□	
50	Las Vegas	□	○	⊗	⊗	○	□	
53	Atlanta	□	⊗	⊗	⊗	○	☆	
53	Raleigh	□	⊗	⊗	⊗	○	☆	
53	St. Louis	□	⊗	⊗	⊗	○	☆	
53	Wichita	□	⊗	⊗	⊗	○	☆	
57	Nashville	○	⊗	⊗	⊗	○	□	
57	Omaha	□	○	⊗	⊗	⊗	○	
59	Oklahoma City	□	⊗	⊗	⊗	⊗	□	
60	Charleston, S.C.	○	⊗	⊗	⊗	⊗	□	
60	Orlando	○	⊗	⊗	⊗	⊗	□	
62	Honolulu	○	⊗	⊗	⊗	⊗	○	
63	Baton Rouge	⊗	⊗	⊗	⊗	⊗	○	
64	Columbia	○	⊗	●	⊗	⊗	□	
65	Tucson	○	⊗	⊗	⊗	⊗	●	
66	Miami	⊗	⊗	⊗	●	⊗	⊗	
67	Tulsa	□	⊗	●	●	⊗	□	
68	Birmingham	○	⊗	●	●	⊗	□	

Rank	Area†	May	June	July	Aug.	Sept.	Oct.	Reactions
68	Dallas	○	⊗	●	●	⊗	□	
68	Little Rock	○	⊗	●	●	⊗	□	
68	Mobile	○	⊗	●	●	⊗	□	
68	Shreveport	○	⊗	●	●	⊗	□	
73	Phoenix	○	⊗	●	●	⊗	○	
74	Austin	⊗	●	●	●	⊗	○	
74	Beaumont	⊗	●	●	●	⊗	○	
74	Corpus Christi	⊗	●	●	●	⊗	○	
74	Houston	⊗	⊗	●	●	●	○	
74	New Orleans	⊗	●	●	●	⊗	○	
74	San Antonio	⊗	●	●	●	⊗	○	
74	Tampa	⊗	●	●	●	⊗	○	

†Incorporated City

Keeping Cool

Because energy costs have been screaming skyward and are likely to continue doing so, people are concerned about the cost of heating their homes and, if they head south to escape heating bills, they must be aware of the high cost of cooling their homes too.

We have presented Chart 4 in the form of cooling degree days. Now you should know that the experts do not really agree about the meaning of this term or what formula should be used. However, our purpose is not different from yours in this matter. We would like at least a good comparison of estimated costs for a year. The problems is that electricity rates are quite different around the nation. Moreover, each residence has its own characteristics, making it impossible for energy experts to provide per residence estimates for various places. We have had to compromise a little with this chart, therefore, but it can still be extremely useful to you.

We have provided comparisons, based on cooling degree days, for the various regions we have described in this book. Please bear in mind that you are not obligated to buy and use an air conditioner in any place on the chart. One of the authors lived for a while in the Micronesian Islands in the South Pacific, and upon returning to Hawaii discovered that it seemed comparatively cold. He looked a bit out of place wearing a sweater on Waikiki. But it goes to show that your body can become accustomed to warmer climates, especially if you are willing to melt a little in the process of adaptation.

CHART
4

KEEPING COOL:
THE AIR CONDITIONING FACTOR
*(Cooling degree days[1] ranked
from fewest to most)*

Rank	Area†	Cooling Degree Days	Reaction
1	Anchorage	0	
2	San Francisco	39	
3	Seattle	183	
4	Portland, Me.	252	
5	Portland, Or.	300	
6	Great Falls	339	
7	Burlington	396	
8	Buffalo	437	
9	Milwaukee	450	
10	Casper	458	
11	Fargo	473	
12	Rochester	531	
13	Providence	532	
14	Albany	574	
15	Grand Rapids	575	
16	Hartford	584	
17	Minneapolis	585	
18	Cleveland	613	

Rank	Area†	Cooling Degree Days	Reaction
19	Denver	625	
20	Akron	634	
21	Detroit	654	
22	Boston	661	
23	Boise	714	
24	Sioux Falls	719	
25	San Diego	722	
26	Columbus	809	
27	Nassau-Suffolk	861	
28	Chicago	925	
29	Salt Lake City	927	
30	Des Moines	928	
31	Pittsburgh	948	
32	Indianapolis	974	
33	Wilmington	992	
34	Newark	1024	
35	Charleston, W.V.	1055	
36	New York	1068	
37	Philadelphia	1104	
38	Baltimore	1108	
39	Sacramento	1159	
40	Omaha	1173	
41	Los Angeles	1185	
42	Cincinnati	1188	
43	Louisville	1268	
44	Albuquerque	1316	
45	Richmond	1353	

Rank	Area†	Cooling Degree Days	Reaction
46	Raleigh	1394	
47	Washington, D.C.	1415	
48	Norfolk	1441	
49	St. Louis	1475	
50	Atlanta	1589	
51	Kansas City	1609	
52	Fresno	1671	
53	Wichita	1673	
54	Nashville	1694	
55	Oklahoma City	1876	
56	Little Rock	1926	
57	Birmingham	1928	
58	Tulsa	1949	
59	Memphis	2029	
60	Charleston, S.C.	2078	
61	Columbia	2087	
62	El Paso	2098	
63	Bakersfield	2179	
64	Shreveport	2538	
65	Mobile	2577	
66	Baton Rouge	2585	
67	Dallas	2587	
68	New Orleans	2706	
69	Beaumont	2798	
70	Tucson	2814	
71	Houston	2889	
72	Austin	2908	

Rank	Area†	Cooling Degree Days	Reaction
73	Las Vegas	2946	
74	San Antonio	2994	
75	Orlando	3226	
76	Tampa	3300	
77	Corpus Christi	3474	
78	Phoenix	3508	
79	Miami	4038	
80	Honolulu	4221	

†Incorporated City

[1]Most people begin to feel uncomfortable when the temperatures reach 80° and higher and, if air conditioning is available, to use it at such times. Cooling Degree Days is defined as the sum of the minimum and maximum temperatures divided by 2, less 65° from that number. For example, with maximum temperature at 84° and minimum temperature at 62° there would be 8 cooling degree days: $84 - 62 = 146 \div 2 = 73 - 65 = 8$.

How Long Is the Winter, Mom?

The official winter and the cold season are two entirely different things. Official winter is from December . . . uh . . . December something to March something. It's on the calendar. But when does it get cold and how long does it last . . . that's what we are interested in when we choose a place to prosper. Some places don't even have a real winter of the sort we usually think of. And others have cold seasons which linger for the majority of the year.

Probably the best way to indicate the relative durations of the cold season in the different locations is to list the first and last days of frost on the average. This we have provided in Chart 5. For example, Albany has a very long cold season by this standard . . . more than six months! The authors have owned farms near Albany and learned quickly how risky corn cropping and alfalfa growing can be in that region. But the long autumns are breathtaking in their splendor! And the snowy winters are the lovely scenes of Currier and Ives and Grandma Moses.

Cold seasons are not for everyone. Heating costs are driving many out of the north. But if you enjoy snuggling on cold evenings, you'll find plenty of cold nights in Manchester, Minneapolis, Denver, Great Falls, and Buffalo, among others.

Quite a few areas have no frost at all in their average years. Whether they are of interest to you or not will depend on your preferences for distinct seasons, or whether you received a pair of skis for your birthday.

HOW LONG IS THE WINTER, MOM?
(Ranked by time between first and last frost)

Rank	Area†	First Frost in Fall	Last Frost in Spring	Months	Weeks	Reactions
1	Honolulu	*	*	—	—	
1	Los Angeles	*	*	—	—	
1	Miami	*	*	—	—	
1	San Diego	*	*	—	—	
1	San Francisco	*	*	—	—	
6	Tampa	12/26	1/10	0	2	
7	Orlando	12/17	1/31	1	2	
7	Phoenix	12/11	1/27	1	2	
7	Sacramento	12/11	1/24	1	2	
10	Corpus Christi	12/12	2/9	1	3	
11	Fresno	12/3	2/3	2	0	
11	Mobile	12/12	2/17	2	0	
11	New Orleans	12/12	2/13	2	0	
14	Biloxi	12/12	2/21	2	1	
14	Charleston, S.C.	12/10	2/19	2	1	
16	Bakersfield	11/28	2/14	2	2	
17	Portland, Or.	12/1	2/25	2	2½	
18	Beaumont	11/24	2/18	2	3	
18	Houston	12/11	2/5	2	3	
18	Seattle	12/1	2/23	2	3	

Rank	Area†	First Frost in Fall	Last Frost in Spring	Months	Weeks	Reactions
21	Austin	11/28	3/3	3	0	
21	Shreveport	11/27	3/1	3	0	
23	San Antonio	11/26	3/3	3	1	
24	Baton Rouge	11/15	3/1	3	2	
24	Tucson	11/23	3/6	3	2	
26	Columbia	11/21	3/14	3	3	
26	Norfolk	11/27	3/18	3	3	
28	Atlanta	11/19	3/20	4	0	
28	Dallas	11/22	3/18	4	0	
28	El Paso	11/12	3/14	4	0	
28	Las Vegas	11/13	3/13	4	0	
28	Little Rock	11/15	3/16	4	0	
33	Birmingham	11/14	3/19	4	1	
33	Memphis	11/12	3/20	4	1	
33	Raleigh	11/16	3/24	4	1	
36	Baltimore	11/17	3/28	4	1½	
37	Philadelphia	11/17	3/30	4	2	
38	Louisville	11/17	4/1	4	3	
38	Nashville	11/5	3/28	4	3	
38	Oklahoma City	11/7	3/28	4	3	
41	Richmond	11/8	4/2	4	3½	
41	St. Louis	11/8	4/2	4	3½	
43	Kansas City	10/31	4/5	5	0	
43	Sioux Falls	10/3	5/5	5	0	
43	Tulsa	11/2	3/31	5	0	
43	Wichita	11/1	4/5	5	0	
47	Newark	10/27	4/5	5	1	

Rank	Area†	First Frost in Fall	Last Frost in Spring	Months	Weeks	Reactions
48	Salt Lake City	11/1	4/12	5	1½	
49	Washington, D.C.	10/28	4/10	5	2	
50	Cincinnati	10/25	4/15	5	2¼	
50	Cleveland	11/2	4/21	5	2½	
50	Columbus	10/30	4/17	5	2½	
50	Providence	10/27	4/13	5	2½	
54	Albuquerque	10/29	4/16	5	3	
54	Boston	10/28	4/19	5	3	
54	Charleston, W.V.	10/28	4/18	5	3	
54	Chicago	10/28	4/19	5	3	
54	Indianapolis	10/27	4/17	5	3	
54	Wilmington	10/26	4/18	5	3	
60	Milwaukee	10/25	4/20	5	3½	
60	Nassau-Suffolk	10/20	4/13	5	3½	
60	New York	10/20	4/13	5	3½	
60	Omaha	10/20	4/14	5	3½	
64	Des Moines	10/19	4/20	6	0	
64	Detroit	10/23	4/25	6	0	
64	Hartford	10/19	4/22	6	0	
64	Pittsburgh	10/23	4/20	6	0	
68	Akron	10/20	4/29	6	1	
68	Buffalo	10/25	4/30	6	1	
68	Rochester	10/21	4/28	6	1	
71	Albany	10/13	4/27	6	2	
71	Boise	10/16	4/29	6	2	
71	Grand Rapids	10/13	4/25	6	2	
71	Manchester	10/13	4/29	6	2	

Rank	Area†	First Frost in Fall	Last Frost in Spring	Months	Weeks	Reactions
71	Minneapolis	10/15	4/29	6	2	
71	Portland, Me.	10/15	4/29	6	2	
77	Denver	10/14	5/2	6	2½	
78	Burlington	10/3	5/18	7	2	
78	Fargo	9/27	5/13	7	2	
80	Great Falls	9/26	5/14	7	2½	
81	Casper	9/25	5/18	7	3	
82	Anchorage	9/13	5/18	8	1	

†Incorporated City
*Most years no freezing weather.

Where Snowmen Live

Enjoy snowball fights, walking through hushed snowbound forests and beside frosty streams, building igloos, blasting over a snowy meadow on your Mach 2 Snowmobile, or sweeping down a silver glade on skis or sled? You won't find these in the sunbelt. Of course you also won't experience icy roads, shoveling sidewalks, or combing sleet from your hair. Snow is not everyone's pleasure, but for many of us it is one of the greatest gifts of nature. Where can you find it (or avoid it)?

We have arranged Chart 6 by snowy days rather than total accumulation on the assumption that most of you care more about traffic disruptions or the pristine wonderment of newly fallen snow than how much will fall during the year. However, usually one will find a high correlation between these two factors and accumulation is provided in the second column.

CHART
6

WHERE THE SNOW FLIES
(Ranked from fewest days to most days with snowfall)

Rank	Area†	# Days of snow 1 inch or more	Average Total Amt. of snow (in inches)	Reaction
1	Honolulu	0	0	
1	Los Angeles	0	T	
1	Miami	0	0	
1	Orlando	0	T	
1	Phoenix	0	T	
1	Sacramento	0	.1	
1	San Diego	0	T	
1	San Francisco	0	T	
1	Tampa	0	T	
10	Austin	*	1	
10	Bakersfield	*	T	
10	Baton Rouge	*	.2	
10	Beaumont	*	.5	
10	Birmingham	*	1.1	
10	Charleston, S.C.	*	.6	
10	Corpus Christi	*	.1	
10	Fresno	*	.1	
10	Mobile	*	.5	

Rank	Area†	# Days of snow 1 inch or more	Average Total Amt. of snow (in inches)	Reaction
10	New Orleans	*	.2	
10	San Antonio	*	.5	
10	Shreveport	*	1.7	
22	Atlanta	1	1.5	
22	Columbia	1	1.7	
22	Dallas	1	3.5	
22	Houston	1	.4	
22	Las Vegas	1	1.4	
22	Tucson	1	1.4	
28	El Paso	2	4.6	
28	Little Rock	2	5.4	
28	Memphis	2	5.5	
28	Norfolk	2	2.2	
28	Portland, Or.	2	7.3	
28	Raleigh	2	7.1	
34	Oklahoma City	3	9.2	
35	Albuquerque	4	10.6	
35	Nashville	4	11.2	
35	Richmond	4	13.9	
35	Tulsa	4	9.3	
35	Louisville	5	18.3	
35	Seattle	5	8.2	
35	Washington, D.C.	5	16.6	
35	Wichita	5	15.6	
43	Cincinnati	6	18.9	
43	Kansas City	6	19.8	

Rank	Area†	# Days of snow 1 inch or more	Average Total Amt. of snow (in inches)	Reaction
43	Philadelphia	6	21.1	
43	St. Louis	6	17.8	
43	Wilmington	6	20.8	
48	Indianapolis	7	22.0	
48	Newark	7	28.4	
50	Baltimore	8	21.7	
50	Boise	8	21.3	
50	Columbus	8	28.4	
50	New York	8	29.3	
50	Nassau-Suffolk	8	29.3	
55	Charleston, W.V.	9	30.9	
55	Pittsburgh	9	30.0	
57	Omaha	10	32.0	
57	Providence	10	39.2	
59	Boston	11	43.1	
59	Detroit	11	31.7	
59	Fargo	11	35.4	
59	Sioux Falls	11	39.0	
63	Chicago	12	42.6	
63	Des Moines	12	33.4	
65	Milwaukee	13	46.6	
66	Hartford	14	54.1	
66	Minneapolis	14	46.3	
68	Akron	15	48.2	
69	Albany	16	66.4	
70	Cleveland	18	52.5	

Rank	Area†	# Days of snow 1 inch or more	Average Total Amt. of snow (in inches)	Reaction
70	Denver	18	59.0	
70	Portland, Me.	18	74.5	
70	Salt Lake City	18	58.5	
74	Great Falls	20	58.0	
75	Anchorage	21	70.4	
76	Burlington	22	79.5	
77	Casper	23	75.3	
78	Grand Rapids	25	77.3	
79	Buffalo	26	92.9	
80	Rochester	27	88.4	

†Incorporated City

"T" in this column refers to a trace of snow.

*The asterisk stands for a small amount of snow but less than 1 inch.

Feeding the Furnace

America is rediscovering the woodstove, kerosene heaters, the modern miracle of coal, and if we continue to stay lucky, we might soon be collecting dried buffalo dung to feed our fires. Ah, progress! Well, with fuel oil at well over $1.30 a gallon and gas and electricity concomitantly high, we'll trundle off to bed in our longjohns and nightcaps.

The cost of heating a medium-sized home in the various regions in America is shown in Chart 7. We have estimated the costs for heating with oil. Of course, the cost of energy may be somewhat different around the United States. In addition, the costs seem to change radically (always upward) even between bills.

To help you obtain a pretty fair idea of the relative costs, based on heating degree days, in each of the regions, we have based the expenses on standard oil prices on Long Island, New York. We know we don't have to tell you that prices have continued to change and our figures were destined to be outmoded immediately. They do, however, provide *relative* expenses. The engineers who work with these kinds of estimates typically base their figures on a house of 1400 to 1600 square feet.

FEEDING THE FURNACE
[The cost (ouch) of heating is expressed in heating degree days,[1] ranked from lowest to highest]

Rank	Area†	Average Annual Heating Degree Days	Oil Costs	Reaction
1	Honolulu	0	$ 0	
2	Miami	206	53.56	
3	Tampa	718	186.68	
4	Orlando	733	190.58	
5	Corpus Christi	930	241.80	
6	Los Angeles	1245	323.70	
7	Houston	1434	372.84	
8	New Orleans	1465	380.90	
9	San Diego	1507	391.82	
10	Beaumont	1518	394.68	
11	Phoenix	1552	403.52	
12	San Antonio	1570	408.20	
13	Baton Rouge	1670	434.20	
14	Mobile	1684	437.84	
15	Austin	1737	451.62	
16	Tucson	1752	455.52	
17	Charleston, S.C.	2146	557.96	

Rank	Area†	Average Annual Heating Degree Days	Oil Costs	Reaction
18	Shreveport	2167	$563.42	
19	Bakersfield	2185	568.10	
20	Dallas	2382	619.32	
21	Columbia	2598	675.48	
22	Las Vegas	2601	676.26	
23	Fresno	2650	689.00	
24	El Paso	2678	696.28	
25	Sacramento	2843	739.18	
26	Birmingham	2844	739.44	
27	San Francisco	3080	860.80	
28	Atlanta	3095	804.70	
29	Memphis	3227	839.02	
30	Little Rock	3354	872.04	
31	Norfolk	3488	906.88	
32	Raleigh	3514	913.64	
33	Tulsa	3680	956.80	
34	Nashville	3696	960.96	
35	Oklahoma City	3695	960.70	
36	Richmond	3939	1024.14	
37	Washington, D.C.	4211	1094.86	
38	Albuquerque	4292	1115.92	
39	Charleston, W.V.	4590	1193.40	
40	Louisville	4640	1206.40	
41	Wichita	4687	1218.62	
42	Kansas City	4711	1224.85	
43	Seattle	4727	1229.02	

Rank	Area†	Average Annual Heating Degree Days	Oil Costs	Reaction
44	Baltimore	4729	$1229.54	
45	St. Louis	4750	1235.00	
46	Portland, Or.	4792	1245.92	
47	Cincinnati	4844	1259.44	
48	New York	4848	1260.48	
49	Philadelphia	4865	1264.90	
50	Wilmington	4940	1284.40	
51	Newark	5034	1308.84	
52	Nassau-Suffolk	5184	1347.84	
53	Pittsburgh	5278	1372.28	
54	Indianapolis	5577	1450.02	
55	Boston	5621	1461.46	
56	Columbus	5702	1482.52	
57	Boise	5833	1516.58	
58	Providence	5972	1552.72	
59	Salt Lake City	5983	1555.58	
60	Denver	6016	1564.16	
61	Omaha	6049	1572.74	
62	Chicago	6127	1593.02	
63	Cleveland	6154	1600.04	
64	Akron	6224	1618.24	
65	Detroit	6228	1619.28	
66	Hartford	6350	1651.00	
67	Des Moines	6710	1744.60	
68	Rochester	6719	1746.94	
69	Grand Rapids	6801	1768.26	

Rank	Area†	Average Annual Heating Degree Days	Oil Costs	Reaction
70	Albany	6888	$1790.88	
71	Buffalo	6927	1801.02	
72	Milwaukee	7444	1935.44	
73	Portland, Me.	7498	1949.48	
74	Casper	7555	1964.30	
75	Great Falls	7652	1989.52	
76	Sioux Falls	7838	2037.88	
77	Burlington	7876	2047.76	
78	Minneapolis	8159	2121.34	
79	Fargo	9271	2410.46	
80	Anchorage	10,911	2836.86	

†Incorporated City

[1]Heating Degree Days: Each degree of mean temperature below 65° is counted as one heating degree day. So, if the maximum temperature for the day is 70° and the minimum temperature is 52°, four heating degree days are produced. The formula for a heating degree day is the maximum temperature plus the minimum temperature divided by two. Hence, $70° + 52° = 122° \div 2 = 61°$, and $65° - 61° = 4$ heating degree days.

Should We Wear Our Woolies or Bikinis?

"The weather report is brought to you today by Fuzz and Lint, makers of fine sweaters since 1612. It's 53 degrees, and its going to be cold tonight, with temperatures in the low . . . ."

Judging by the amount of air time given over to temperature reports, we Americans certainly do care about how warm or cold the weather is. And when people think about moving to another location, one of the first things they talk about is something like, "But it gets too hot there, Harvey." Or, "I couldn't live there! I'd freeze my socks off!"

To help you make the best decisions regarding your location, we have included two charts here dealing with the average temperatures you can expect for each area.

Chart 8 holds some real surprises. It shows the temperatures (average) you will find during the year in each region. With this chart you can make convenient comparisons and decide whether your possible choices might actually be too hot or too cold for you and your family. For example, did you know that Phoenix and Las Vegas, to which people are flocking, reach a daily average of 91 and 90 degrees respectively during the month of July? And some places we often think of as hot spots really are not. For example, Los Angeles and San Diego only average 73 and 70 degrees in July. Rather temperate, wouldn't you say?

Like it cold? Prefer moderate winters? Some of the highs and lows during January are dramatic. The coldest place is not Anchorage or Minneapolis/St. Paul (they average 12 degrees), but is Fargo, with an average of 6 (count 'em) degrees in January. And Sioux Falls, with an average of 14 degrees, is not exactly toasty. None of the other regions even come close to these temperatures.

Warmest place in January? Honolulu, of course (72 degrees), and Miami (67 degrees). Orlando and Tampa (60 degrees) and Corpus Christi (56 degrees) also merit attention as very moderate during the winter.

As you look over Chart 8 you will notice the first column is for temperature range. These are the number of degrees difference between the warmest months and coldest months.

As you can see, most of the regions experience a wide range of temperatures, on the order of 40 to 50 degrees between January and July. These are the places with definite seasons, where change is often in the air, and where you can readily tell when spring arrives or summer disappears. Greatest range? It's found in Fargo (65 degrees) where summers are warm and lovely, perhaps to make up for the amazingly frigid winters. Minneapolis/St. Paul and Sioux Falls also experience an unusually wide range of temperatures during the year.

The narrowest range of temperatures is found in Honolulu and San Francisco (only eight degrees each during the year). Miami and San Diego (15 degrees) and Los Angeles (16 degrees) are remarkably consistent and Tampa (22 degrees), and Orlando (21 degrees) also have little range during the year. Other big changers are Omaha (54 degrees), Burlington (53 degrees), Kansas City and Milwaukee (51 degrees).

CHART
8

SHOULD WE WEAR OUR WOOLIES OR BIKINIS?
(Normal daily mean temperature, ranked by range—least to most)

Rank	Area†	Range	Jan.	March	May	July	Sept.	Nov.	Reactions
1	Honolulu	8	72	73	77	80	80	77	
1	San Francisco	8	51	54	57	59	62	57	
3	Miami	15	67	71	78	82	82	72	
3	San Diego	15	55	58	63	70	70	61	
5	Los Angeles	16	57	59	65	73	73	63	

Rank	Area†	Range	Jan.	March	May	July	Sept.	Nov.	Reactions
6	Orlando	21	60	66	76	81	80	67	
7	Tampa	22	60	66	77	82	81	67	
8	Seattle	26	40	46	56	66	61	46	
9	Biloxi	28	54	61	75	82	78	60	
10	Corpus Christi	29	56	65	78	85	81	65	
10	New Orleans	29	53	61	75	82	78	60	
10	Portland, Or.	29	38	46	57	67	62	45	
13	Sacramento	30	45	53	64	75	72	53	
14	Baton Rouge	31	51	60	75	82	78	59	
14	Beaumont	31	52	60	75	83	79	60	
14	Charleston, S.C.	31	49	57	72	80	75	56	
14	Houston	31	52	61	76	83	79	61	
14	Mobile	31	51	59	75	82	76	59	
19	San Antonio	34	51	61	76	85	79	60	
20	Austin	35	50	60	75	85	79	59	
20	Birmingham	35	46	55	72	81	76	54	
20	Tucson	35	51	58	74	86	80	59	
23	Atlanta	36	42	51	69	78	72	51	
23	Bakersfield	36	48	57	70	84	77	56	
23	Columbia	36	45	54	72	81	75	54	
23	Fresno	36	45	54	67	81	74	54	
23	Shreveport	36	47	57	73	83	77	56	
28	Norfolk	37	41	48	67	78	72	52	
28	Raleigh	37	41	49	67	78	71	50	
30	El Paso	38	44	55	72	82	74	52	
31	Charleston, W.V.	40	35	45	65	75	68	45	
31	Dallas	40	45	55	73	85	78	56	
31	Phoenix	40	51	60	76	91	84	60	

Rank	Area†	Range	Jan.	March	May	July	Sept.	Nov.	Reactions
31	Richmond	40	38	47	67	78	70	49	
35	Little Rock	41	40	50	70	81	73	50	
35	Memphis	41	41	51	71	83	74	51	
37	Nashville	42	30	49	69	80	72	48	
38	Denver	43	30	37	57	73	63	39	
38	Washington, D.C.	43	32	42	63	75	67	48	
40	Albuquerque	44	35	46	65	79	70	45	
40	Baltimore	44	33	43	64	77	69	46	
40	Boston	44	29	38	59	73	65	45	
40	Cincinnati	44	32	43	64	76	68	45	
40	Cleveland	44	27	36	58	71	64	42	
40	Louisville	44	33	44	65	77	69	45	
40	Nassau-Suffolk	44	31	39	60	75	67	47	
40	Pittsburgh	44	31	40	62	75	67	44	
40	Providence	44	28	37	57	72	63	43	
40	Wilmington	44	32	42	62	76	68	46	
50	Newark	45	31	41	62	76	68	46	
50	New York	45	32	41	62	77	68	47	
50	Oklahoma City	45	37	48	68	82	73	49	
50	Philadelphia	45	32	42	63	77	68	46	
50	Tulsa	45	37	48	69	82	73	49	
55	Akron	46	26	36	59	72	64	41	
55	Anchorage	46	12	24	46	58	48	21	
55	Boise	46	29	41	57	75	63	40	
55	Buffalo	46	24	32	55	70	62	40	
55	Columbus	46	28	39	61	74	65	42	
55	Las Vegas	46	44	55	73	90	80	53	
55	Manchester	46	24	33	56	70	60	39	

Rank	Area†	Range	Jan.	March	May	July	Sept.	Nov.	Reactions
55	Portland, Me.	46	22	32	53	68	59	39	
63	Detroit	47	26	35	58	73	65	41	
63	Indianapolis	47	28	40	62	75	66	42	
63	Rochester	47	24	33	57	71	62	41	
66	Casper	48	23	31	53	71	59	34	
66	Great Falls	48	21	31	53	69	57	35	
66	Hartford	48	25	36	58	69	57	41	
66	St. Louis	48	31	43	66	73	63	45	
70	Chicago	49	23	36	58	72	64	39	
70	Grand Rapids	49	23	33	57	72	62	39	
70	Salt Lake City	49	28	40	58	77	65	39	
73	Albany	50	22	33	58	72	70	40	
73	Wichita	50	31	44	66	81	71	45	
75	Milwaukee	51	19	31	54	70	61	37	
75	Kansas City	51	27	41	64	78	68	42	
77	Burlington	53	17	29	55	70	59	37	
78	Omaha	54	23	37	63	77	66	40	
79	Des Moines	56	19	33	61	75	64	38	
80	Sioux Falls	59	14	30	58	73	61	33	
81	Minneapolis	60	12	28	57	72	60	32	
82	Fargo	65	6	24	55	71	58	29	

†Incorporated City

Daily Highs and Lows

As you are narrowing down your choices you should think about the changes in temperature you might expect during each day. How high and how low does it get on the average? If it is hot during the day, does it cool down at night? Boise certainly does, dropping from an average of 91 degrees during July days to an average of 59 degrees at night. So do such examples as Fresno, going from 98 to 63 degrees, Albuquerque, from 92 to 65 degrees, and Kansas City, from 87 to 67 degrees.

Hottest spots in the nation? Phoenix (average daily high of 105 degrees during July!) and Las Vegas (104 degrees!). Coldest days are found in Fargo (average daily low temperature of −4 degrees . . . brr) and Minneapolis/St. Paul (3 degrees) and Anchorage and Sioux Falls (4 degrees).

By reviewing the temperatures for the other months provided, you can learn a great deal about the springs and autumns of the regions under your consideration. Some regions have Septembers which are as warm as or warmer than their Julys, such as San Diego, Honolulu and Los Angeles. Others show remarkably little variation between night and day, as well as being quite consistent throughout the year (such as Honolulu, Seattle, San Diego and San Francisco).

AVERAGE DAILY HIGH—WARM SEASON TEMPERATURE
(Ranked from coolest maximum to warmest maximum temperature during July)

Rank	Area†	July Max.	Min.	September Max.	Min.	May Max.	Min.	Reaction
1	San Francisco	64	53	59	56	63	51	
2	Anchorage	66	50	56	40	55	37	
3	San Diego	75	64	77	63	69	57	
4	Seattle	76	56	71	50	66	47	
5	Portland, Me.	79	57	70	47	64	42	
5	Portland, Or.	79	55	74	51	67	46	
7	Buffalo	80	61	71	52	64	46	
7	Milwaukee	80	59	72	51	65	43	
9	Boston	81	65	72	57	67	50	
9	Burlington	81	59	70	49	66	44	
9	Providence	81	63	73	54	67	47	
12	Cleveland	82	61	78	54	68	48	
12	Minneapolis	82	61	71	49	68	46	
12	Rochester	82	60	48	33	67	46	
15	Akron	83	61	75	53	70	48	
15	Chicago	83	61	75	52	70	47	
15	Detroit	83	63	74	55	69	48	

Rank	Area†	July Max.	July Min.	September Max.	September Min.	May Max.	May Min.	Reaction
15	Fargo	83	59	70	46	67	42	
15	Grand Rapids	83	60	74	51	69	45	
15	Los Angeles	83	61	80	60	70	50	
15	Nassau-Suffolk	83	67	75	59	68	51	
22	Albany	84	60	74	50	70	46	
22	Great Falls	84	55	70	45	65	42	
22	Hartford	84	61	75	51	70	46	
22	Pittsburgh	84	65	77	56	72	52	
26	Columbus	85	62	78	53	73	49	
26	Des Moines	85	65	75	54	71	51	
26	Indianapolis	85	65	78	55	73	52	
26	New York	85	68	77	60	71	53	
26	Sioux Falls	85	62	73	49	70	46	
31	Charleston, W.V.	86	64	79	56	52	44	
31	Newark	86	67	77	59	73	52	
31	Washington, D.C.	86	64	79	55	75	51	
31	Wilmington	86	66	78	58	73	52	
35	Atlanta	87	69	81	63	79	59	
35	Baltimore	87	67	79	58	75	53	
35	Casper	87	55	74	43	66	39	
35	Cincinnati	87	66	80	57	75	54	
35	Denver	87	59	78	48	70	44	
35	Honolulu	87	73	87	73	84	70	
35	Louisville	87	66	81	58	76	54	
35	Norfolk	87	70	80	64	76	57	
35	Philadelphia	87	67	78	58	74	52	
35	Kansas City	87	67	79	57	74	54	

Rank	Area†	July Max.	July Min.	September Max.	September Min.	May Max.	May Min.	Reaction
45	Raleigh	88	67	82	60	79	55	
45	Richmond	88	68	81	59	78	55	
45	St. Louis	88	69	80	59	76	56	
48	Charleston, S.C.	89	71	85	66	83	61	
48	Miami	89	76	88	75	85	71	
48	Omaha	89	67	79	54	74	52	
51	Birmingham	90	70	85	63	83	58	
51	Nashville	90	69	84	61	80	57	
51	New Orleans	90	73	87	70	85	65	
51	Orlando	90	73	88	72	87	66	
51	Tampa	90	74	89	73	88	67	
56	Baton Rouge	91	73	87	68	85	64	
56	Boise	91	59	78	49	71	44	
56	Mobile	91	73	87	68	85	65	
59	Albuquerque	92	65	93	57	80	51	
59	Beaumont	92	74	89	69	84	66	
59	Columbia	92	70	85	64	85	60	
59	Memphis	92	72	84	63	81	61	
59	Wichita	92	70	82	59	77	55	
64	Little Rock	93	70	86	61	81	38	
64	Oklahoma City	93	70	85	61	79	58	
64	Sacramento	93	58	88	55	79	50	
64	Salt Lake City	93	61	80	49	72	44	
64	Tulsa	93	71	85	62	79	58	
69	Corpus Christi	94	75	90	72	87	69	
69	Houston	94	73	90	68	86	66	
69	Shreveport	94	73	88	67	84	63	

Rank	Area†	July Max.	July Min.	September Max.	September Min.	May Max.	May Min.	Reaction
72	Austin	95	74	89	68	85	65	
72	El Paso	95	70	87	61	87	57	
74	Dallas	96	74	89	67	83	62	
74	San Antonio	96	74	90	69	86	66	
76	Fresno	98	63	91	57	83	52	
76	Tucson	98	74	93	67	90	58	
78	Bakersfield	99	69	91	62	84	56	
79	Las Vegas	104	75	95	65	88	59	
80	Phoenix	105	78	98	69	93	60	

†Incorporated City

AVERAGE DAILY LOW—COLD SEASON TEMPERATURE
(Ranked from warmest minimum to coldest minimum temperature during January)

Rank	Area†	January Min.	January Max.	March Min.	March Max.	November Min.	November Max.	Reaction
1	Honolulu	65	79	66	80	70	83	
2	Miami	59	76	63	80	65	80	
3	Orlando	50	71	56	76	57	76	
3	Tampa	50	71	56	76	56	77	
5	Los Angeles	47	67	50	69	52	73	
6	Corpus Christi	46	67	54	76	55	75	
6	San Diego	46	65	50	66	52	70	
6	San Francisco	46	56	49	60	52	63	
9	New Orleans	44	62	51	70	50	70	
10	Beaumont	42	62	50	71	49	71	
11	Houston	42	63	50	72	49	73	
12	Baton Rouge	41	62	49	73	48	71	
12	Mobile	41	62	49	71	47	70	
14	San Antonio	40	62	49	73	48	71	
15	Austin	39	60	48	71	48	70	
16	Phoenix	38	65	45	75	45	75	
16	Shreveport	38	57	46	67	45	67	

Rank	Area†	January Min.	January Max.	March Min.	March Max.	November Min.	November Max.	Reaction
16	Tucson	38	65	44	72	45	72	
19	Bakersfield	37	58	45	69	44	68	
19	Charleston, S.C.	37	60	45	60	44	08	
19	Sacramento	37	53	42	64	42	64	
22	Fresno	36	55	41	67	41	66	
23	Seattle	35	45	38	53	40	51	
24	Birmingham	34	54	42	65	40	64	
24	Columbia	34	57	42	67	41	67	
24	Dallas	34	56	43	67	44	68	
27	Atlanta	33	51	41	61	41	62	
27	Las Vegas	33	56	42	68	41	66	
27	Portland, Or.	33	44	37	54	39	52	
30	Memphis	32	49	41	61	40	62	
30	Norfolk	32	49	39	57	43	61	
32	El Paso	30	57	40	69	37	66	
32	Raleigh	30	51	37	61	38	62	
34	Little Rock	29	50	39	62	38	62	
34	Nashville	29	48	38	59	38	59	
36	Richmond	28	47	36	58	37	61	
37	New York	26	39	34	48	41	54	
37	Oklahoma City	26	48	37	60	37	61	
37	Tulsa	26	47	37	60	38	61	
40	Baltimore	25	42	33	53	36	56	
40	Charleston, W.V.	25	44	34	55	35	56	
40	Louisville	25	42	34	54	35	55	
40	Nassau-Suffolk	25	38	32	47	39	54	
44	Albuquerque	24	47	32	59	32	57	

Rank	Area†	January Min.	January Max.	March Min.	March Max.	November Min.	November Max.	Reaction
44	Cincinnati	24	40	34	52	36	53	
44	Newark	24	39	32	49	38	54	
44	Pittsburgh	24	37	32	49	37	52	
44	Philadelphia	24	40	33	51	37	56	
44	Wilmington	24	46	32	51	36	55	
50	Boston	23	36	32	45	39	52	
50	St. Louis	23	40	34	53	36	54	
50	Washington	23	41	31	53	34	56	
53	Boise	21	37	31	52	31	49	
53	Providence	21	36	29	45	35	52	
53	Wichita	21	41	32	55	34	56	
56	Cleveland	20	33	28	44	34	49	
56	Columbus	20	36	29	49	32	51	
56	Indianapolis	20	36	30	49	33	51	
59	Akron	19	34	27	45	33	49	
59	Detroit	19	32	28	43	34	48	
59	Salt Lake City	19	37	28	51	28	50	
62	Buffalo	18	30	25	39	34	46	
62	Kansas City	18	36	31	51	33	51	
62	Rochester	17	31	25	41	33	48	
65	Denver	16	44	24	50	25	53	
65	Grand Rapids	16	30	24	42	31	46	
65	Hartford	16	33	27	45	32	51	
68	Chicago	15	31	27	45	30	48	
69	Albany	13	30	24	43	31	48	
69	Casper	13	34	19	43	23	45	
71	Great Falls	12	29	21	40	26	43	

Rank	Area†	January Min.	Max.	March Min.	Max.	November Min.	Max.	Reaction
71	Omaha	12	23	26	48	29	51	
71	Portland, Me.	12	31	23	41	30	48	
71	Des Moines	11	28	25	43	29	46	
74	Milwaukee	11	27	23	39	29	44	
76	Burlington	8	26	20	38	30	44	
77	Anchorage	4	20	15	33	14	28	
77	Sioux Falls	4	25	20	40	23	44	
77	Minneapolis	3	21	20	37	24	41	
80	Fargo	−4	15	15	34	20	37	

†Incorporated City

Whether weather is a most important factor for you or less significant than the other variables described in the other chapters, these weather-related charts can help you make your best decisions. They tell us much about the nature of the different regions and hold lots of surprises. And as you are certainly aware, it's better to be surprised before you move to a new place than after you have unpacked all the dishes.

Directions: Rate only those cities below which are on your Tentative Interest List. Give a 5 to those cities with predominance of (+) ratings on the various charts in this chapter. Give a 3 if a city has only enough (+) marks to remain of interest. Give a 1 to those with few (+) marks. Eliminate from your Tentative Interest List those cities for which you've lost all interest; add additional cities as interest develops and rate them as above.

SUMMARY GRID

		Rating (5, 3 or 1)	Comments
1	Akron, Ohio		
2	Albany, New York		
3	Albuquerque, New Mexico		
4	Anchorage, Alaska		
5	Atlanta, Georgia		
6	Austin, Texas		
7	Bakersfield, California		
8	Baltimore, Maryland		
9	Baton Rouge, Louisiana		
10	Beaumont, Texas		
11	Biloxi, Mississippi		
12	Birmingham, Alabama		
13	Boise, Idaho		
14	Boston, Massachusetts		
15	Buffalo, New York		
16	Burlington, Vermont		
17	Casper, Wyoming		

		Rating (5, 3 or 1)	Comments
18	Charleston, South Carolina		
19	Charleston, West Virginia		
20	Chicago, Illinois		
21	Cincinnati, Ohio		
22	Cleveland, Ohio		
23	Columbia, South Carolina		
24	Columbus, Ohio		
25	Corpus Christi, Texas		
26	Dallas, Texas		
27	Denver, Colorado		
28	Des Moines, Iowa		
29	Detroit, Michigan		
30	El Paso, Texas		
31	Fargo, North Dakota		
32	Fresno, California		
33	Grand Rapids, Michigan		
34	Great Falls, Montana		
35	Hartford, Connecticut		
36	Honolulu, Hawaii		
37	Houston, Texas		
38	Indianapolis, Indiana		
39	Kansas City, Missouri		
40	Las Vegas, Nevada		
41	Little Rock, Arkansas		
42	Los Angeles, California		
43	Louisville, Kentucky		
44	Manchester, New Hampshire		

		Rating (5, 3 or 1)	Comments
45	Memphis, Tennessee		
46	Miami, Florida		
47	Milwaukee, Wisconsin		
48	Minneapolis, Minnesota		
49	Mobile, Alabama		
50	Nashville, Tennessee		
51	Nassau-Suffolk, New York		
52	Newark, New Jersey		
53	New Orleans, Louisiana		
54	New York, New York		
55	Norfolk, Virginia		
56	Oklahoma City, Oklahoma		
57	Omaha, Nebraska		
58	Orlando, Florida		
59	Philadelphia, Pennsylvania		
60	Phoenix, Arizona		
61	Pittsburgh, Pennsylvania		
62	Portland, Maine		
63	Portland, Oregon		
64	Providence, Rhode Island		
65	Raleigh, North Carolina		
66	Richmond, Virginia		
67	Rochester, New York		
68	Sacramento, California		
69	Salt Lake City, Utah		
70	San Antonio, Texas		
71	San Diego, California		

		Rating (5, 3 or 1)	Comments
72	San Francisco, California		
73	Seattle, Washington		
74	Shreveport, Louisiana		
75	Sioux Falls, South Dakota		
76	St. Louis, Missouri		
77	Tampa, Florida		
78	Tucson, Arizona		
79	Tulsa, Oklahoma		
80	Washington, D.C.		
81	Wichita, Kansas		
82	Wilmington, Delaware		

5

Population Winners and Losers

No doubt about it. America is once again on the move.

We have a heritage of climbing aboard a creaking Conestoga wagon, or a lashed-together raft, or a wheezing truck overloaded with family and possessions, and moving to where opportunities beckon.

Our population shifts seem to have come in waves and cycles, and another one is now under way. Our wagon trains are shorter, usually no longer than the station wagon and a rented truck. And we are less likely to yell "Westward ho!" than we are to shout, "Did you remember to make reservations, Herman?" But the zest for moving is as strong as ever.

Where is everybody going? And what are the implications for you and your family?

People are asking themselves whether they should join the apparent exodus to elsewhere, but they are uncertain about where they should go, or even if they should. Companies in the process of being formed or relocating are unsure about the best location for them and their employees. Everyone wonders about what they might find in the new place under consideration and whether they might like it there.

Not everyone wants to live where populations are growing. Many people become uneasy as new arrivals pour into their home areas, and it is not uncommon to hear old-timers muttering about the ruination of traditional lifestyles. Like Daniel Boone and Kit Carson, they start to wonder whether they should be moving out to less crowded places.

Big winners and losers in population are being created every day as the moving vans load and unload across the nation. The population changes create wonderful opportunities for you to find the best places to prosper. Your task is to identify the places where the population is exploding, those which are staying about the same, and those which are losing large numbers of citizens. Then you can decide which of these offer the greatest payoffs for you.

Please do not make the mistake of assuming that you can be a winner only in burgeoning areas. Those regions with stable or even declining populations also can offer terrific opportunities. We will discuss the advantages and disadvantages of growing, static, or decreasing populations a little later in this chapter.

The answers to three population questions will help you make the best location decisions. The three questions are:

1. How many people live there now?
2. Is the place growing, remaining the same, or losing population?
3. What are the people like?

This chapter is intended to help you find these answers and consider their implications for you.

Where Is Everybody Now?

The range of populations for our 82 areas is amazing, from over nine million to eighty thousand. Which is the best for you? Let us consider some of the reasons that you might select a highly populated area, and then review the advantages offered by less populated places.

WHERE THE FOLKS ARE NOW
(Ranked from greatest to least population, 1980 census.)

Rank	Area*	Population	Reaction
1	New York	9,080,777	
2	Los Angeles	7,445,721	
3	Chicago	7,057,853	
4	Philadelphia	4,700,996	
5	Detroit	4,344,139	
6	San Francisco	3,226,867	
7	Washington, D.C.	3,045,399	
8	Dallas	2,964,342	
9	Houston	2,891,146	
10	Boston	2,759,800	
11	Nassau-Suffolk	2,605,813	
12	St. Louis	2,344,912	
13	Pittsburgh	2,260,919	
14	Baltimore	2,166,308	
15	Minneapolis	2,109,207	
16	Atlanta	2,010,368	
17	Newark	1,963,600	
18	Cleveland	1,895,997	
19	San Diego	1,859,623	
20	Denver	1,615,442	

Rank	Area*	Population	Reaction
21	Seattle	1,600,944	
22	Miami	1,573,817	
23	Tampa	1,550,035	
24	Phoenix	1,511,552	
25	Milwaukee	1,392,872	
26	Cincinnati	1,392,394	
27	Kansas City	1,322,156	
28	Buffalo	1,241,434	
29	Portland, Or.	1,236,294	
30	New Orleans	1,183,606	
31	Indianapolis	1,161,539	
32	Columbus	1,088,973	
33	San Antonio	1,070,245	
34	Sacramento	1,010,989	
35	Rochester	970,313	
36	Salt Lake City	935,280	
37	Providence	917,962	
38	Memphis	909,767	
39	Louisville	901,907	
40	Birmingham	834,067	
41	Oklahoma City	829,584	
42	Nashville	828,540	
43	Norfolk	799,853	
44	Albany	794,298	
45	Honolulu	762,020	
46	Hartford	726,036	
47	Orlando	694,645	
48	Tulsa	678,627	

Rank	Area*	Population	Reaction
49	Akron	660,233	
50	Richmond	630,965	
51	Grand Rapids	601,106	
52	Omaha	566,140	
53	Austin	532,811	
54	Tucson	531,895	
55	Raleigh	525,059	
56	Wilmington	523,386	
57	Fresno	507,005	
58	Baton Rouge	495,888	
59	El Paso	479,448	
60	Las Vegas	462,218	
61	Albuquerque	448,798	
62	Mobile	439,941	
63	Charleston, S.C.	416,012	
64	Wichita	410,121	
65	Bakersfield	401,540	
66	Columbia	395,775	
67	Little Rock	393,781	
68	Shreveport	376,704	
69	Beaumont	374,809	
70	Des Moines	338,048	
71	Corpus Christi	324,245	
72	Charleston, W.V.	260,037	
73	Biloxi	191,574	
74	Portland, Me.	183,457	
75	Anchorage	173,992	
76	Boise	172,843	

Rank	Area*	Population	Reaction
77	Manchester	160,443	
78	Fargo	137,493	
79	Sioux Falls	110,029	
80	Great Falls	00,039	

*Standard Metropolitan Statistical Area

Like Lots of Company?

A recent acquaintance, Claudia Ryan, explained her reasons for choosing life in a highly populated area:

"When I make a trip across this city, it's like visiting several different countries! We've got Little Italy, Chinatown, a garment section like New York's, a barrio of sorts, a kind of Harlem of our own but much smaller . . . really, I love the excitement and change which this city offers.

And there are cultural things going on here that make my old home town seem like Ma and Pa Kettle back on the farm. How could I live without the museums, opera, art galleries . . . even if I don't go very often it's great to know that they're there. And how could I give up the all-news radio stations, and all the choices of TV stations? Maybe that's what it boils down to . . . having lots of choices."

Indeed, choices are everywhere in highly populated places. Choices in careers, for example. One usually finds a delightful array of occupational and professional opportunities in populous cities, and if you have an interest in pursuing a specialty, it is more likely to be possible in Big Town. A cartoonist or electrical engineer, for example, has a much better chance of success in highly populated places.

Educational and professional training opportunities also are more available where the most people are. And children with special needs or talents are more likely to have programs available. Schools and institutes of all sorts can be found, from a variety of programs for gifted children to the best training in the performing arts.

There is another facet of living in more highly populated areas which may or may not be a benefit for you. It was a decided advantage for Kathy, a lovely professional colleague who recently moved from a small city to a major metropolis. In her words:

"To me, the biggest difference between living here and where I was raised is social expectancy. Frankly, I always disliked the small town practice of people just 'dropping in,' without phoning or any warning at all. It was sometimes embarrassing, but mostly it was such a waste of time! Here I can be alone, and people respect my not wanting to be friends or involved with everyone else. In a small town, just about everyone knows your business, and usually helps you mind it. I cherish my individuality, and find it is accepted and respected in a metropolitan region."

Choices, choices, and more choices. They are everywhere in highly populated places. How many newspapers do you like to read? If only one, do you at least want lots of choices? Shopping choices and convenience should be emphasized also. Big city regions are not only loaded with major shopping centers and stores, they are blessed with an incredible variety of specialty outlets. Like antiques? You'll find rows of shops. Need clothes to fit special sizes? Whatever your interests and needs, they are no problem in big city areas.

"Go get 'em, Tigers! Kill 'em, Vikings! Way to go, Islanders! Look at 'em . . . that's my team!" Whether your favorite sports team's name is derived from the animal kingdom (Lions, Penguins), people (Vikings, Pirates), engine parts (Pistons), or clothing (various colored socks . . . even knickerbockers!), the fact remains: the major sports teams are found in the major metropolitan areas.

Do you enjoy sampling a wide variety of restaurants and nightlife? Or are you content with pot roast and bean soup, or perhaps the Skookum Chuck Burger Special found just about everywhere in America? The degree of sophistication and variety found after dark largely depends on the size of the population.

Finally, medical and mental health facilities are both more specialized and more comprehensive in the more populated places. It is no secret that the major metropolitan regions house most of the most prestigious research and treatment centers, and medical care tends to be better. The chapter on quality of life treats this issue in more detail.

Not Quite So Crowded, Please

Of course, not all of us are convinced that the advantages of large populations outweigh the desirable qualities found in less populated areas. Let us consider the arguments outlined by Marisa M., who had lived in several big cities and chose to reside in a less crowded area:

"My major dissatisfaction concerned the lack of involvement in the places I lived. There were just so many people that their value, it seemed to me, became diminished. I mean, there are so many that they somehow seemed less important than when in a less populated area.

Take driving, for example. In a small town, people don't cut in, or honk, or drive so dangerously. I think the reason is that you might be cutting off the high school principal, or your neighbor's sister, and people take care of each other more. They are more sensitive and aware of the other person's worth."

Some of us prefer a less populated region because it offers what might be considered a more peaceful and orderly life. The pace tends to be slower, and roles are more defined. In a smaller community, one becomes more recognized as part of the social system.

One decided advantage in growing up in less populated

areas is the opportunity to be a "bigger fish in a smaller pond." Girls and boys have more chances to be class leaders, active participants in competitions, recognized as important in various clubs or activities . . . in short, more chances to be recognized as winners. This opportunity tends to increase confidence and achievement of potential. It is not just a coincidence that so many of America's leaders have come from places with smaller populations.

Traditions are generally more established and understandable, and one can readily put down "roots" in less populated areas. This is not to say, however, that very small towns always accept newcomers easily. In some old established areas with fairly small populations, "breaking into socially accepted circles" can be difficult. The thinking almost sounds like this: "Yes, we have been in this area for five generations now. I have the feeling that soon we are going to be accepted." We have heard farmers in New England complain that although they have worked the same land for more than thirty years, they still are considered newcomers.

There is so much that can be said for places with smaller populations, but for the most part they probably can be reduced to "the pleasures of small town living." It is the feeling of being home, knowing that if you knock on a door requesting to use a telephone that you are likely to be welcomed rather than threatened with the police. Once a region becomes a metropolis, the small town essence disappears. In our view, the transition population figure is around one million.

Predicted Changes in Population

More than 90 percent of America's growth in population in the last decades has been in the south and west. People have been moving from the industrial north and east at startling rates. Will the trend continue?

Chart 2 shows the predicted rates for the next decade for the majority of our 82 areas. We are indebted to Chase Econometrics for their consideration in providing these projections.

Please keep in mind that the projections are a splendid resource, providing invaluable clues for future population changes. But even an excellent economic consultation firm like Chase Econometrics is limited in its projections to best guesses. These are predictions, based on past trends and likely probabilities. They cannot be guaranteed, of course, because many unforeseen circumstances can influence predictions. For example, new solar heating breakthroughs might make the move to warmer climates less desirable. An earthquake or volcanic eruption could slow the influx of newcomers, or even cause a massive exodus of residents.

Also keep in mind that growth rates, based on percentages, can be misleading. Statistics themselves can fool us. For example, a fairly small town could double its population and not really change much. A metropolis could add or lose hundreds of thousands of people and the changes would not be reflected by much of a percentage change.

The Big Winners

Perhaps it is fitting that the home of all those casinos would be the big winner at the top of Chart 2. And the predictions for Austin, Houston, and Tucson are almost as high. But Las Vegas, Austin, and Tucson are all around the half million mark, while Houston has almost three million. Houston's predicted 25 percent growth rate with its huge population makes it, in our view, our best candidate for the title of "Big Population Winner!"

Other winners include the northwest twins, Seattle, Wash. and Portland, Oregon. Their populations are already large enough (about a million and a half) that their predicted growth rates mean a virtual flood of people will pour into those areas.

The other regions with predicted growth rates over twelve percent or so also should be considered excellent prospects for relocating, if you are looking for a place with ferment and change.

Will the Losers Really Lose?

At the other end of the list, the losses of people from Buffalo, Albany, Newark, New York, and Cleveland is nothing short of staggering.

Is the decline of the northeast and north central inevitable? A recent presidential panel suggested that this was the case. Its members even urged Congress to find fair ways to move huge parts of the northern populations to the sunbelt.

On the other hand, various coalitions, Congressional committees, and study groups of all kinds are dedicated to stemming the losses and revitalizing the old industrialized regions of our country. How successful they will be remains to be seen. One result of recent population shifts has been the additional loss of political power from the northern tier. Moreover, between 1975 and 1979 the 18 states comprising the northeastern and north central areas sent $165 billion *more* in taxes to the federal government than they received in federal support. Little wonder many in the frostbelt complain that the sunbelt is being developed with northern money!

Strengths of the frostbelt which might increase investments include a highly skilled and well educated work force, a concentration of universities, cultural depth and diversity, and sufficient water supplies to support a high rate of economic growth. Many European investors and new residents enjoy the north's similarity to their countries of origin.

Finally, some argue that the north will rise again because of a free market economy which favors the south and west at this time but will balance out in the near future. That is, production costs and living expenses are lower in the sunbelt at this time, but might be expected to catch up to northern levels soon.

PREDICTED CHANGES IN POPULATION DURING THE 80's
(Ranked from highest to lowest predicted population percentage growth during decade)

Rank	Area*	1980–89	Reaction
1	Las Vegas	32.15	
2	Austin	31.73	
3	Houston	25.49	
4	Tucson	25.24	
5	Phoenix	23.83	
6	San Diego	23.03	
7	El Paso	22.50	
8	Salt Lake City	22.34	
9	Tulsa	21.09	
10	Seattle	19.13	
11	Portland, Or.	18.84	
12	Dallas	18.78	
13	Orlando	18.16	
14	San Antonio	18.06	
15	Tampa	17.89	
16	Oklahoma City	17.48	
17	Denver	16.51	
18	Charleston, S.C.	15.81	

Rank	Area*	1980–89	Reaction
19	Bakersfield	15.06	
20	Corpus Christi	14.59	
21	Miami	13.59	
22	Nashville	13.38	
23	Mobile	13.02	
24	Columbia	12.72	
25	Fresno	12.29	
26	Shreveport	12.09	
27	Albuquerque	11.99	
28	Little Rock	11.64	
29	Beaumont	11.60	
30	Sacramento	11.10	
31	Baton Rouge	10.36	
32	New Orleans	9.55	
33	Raleigh	9.07	
34	Minneapolis	8.74	
35	Honolulu	8.61	
35	Norfolk	8.34	
37	Atlanta	8.02	
37	Richmond	7.70	
39	Memphis	7.34	
40	Wichita	6.44	
41	Birmingham	6.06	
42	San Francisco	5.58	
43	Omaha	5.57	
44	Los Angeles	5.23	
45	Milwaukee	5.10	
46	Grand Rapids	3.59	

Rank	Area*	1980-89	Reaction
46	Louisville	3.59	
48	Columbus	3.55	
49	Kansas City	2.89	
50	Chicago	1.98	
51	Wilmington	1.67	
52	Rochester	.54	
53	Baltimore	.15	
54	Indianapolis	.09	
55	Washington, D.C.	−0.50	
56	Cincinnati	−0.68	
57	Philadelphia	−0.97	
58	St. Louis	−1.20	
59	Detroit	−1.22	
60	Hartford	−1.40	
61	Pittsburgh	−3.05	
62	Boston	−3.12	
63	Providence	−4.00	
64	Akron	−5.92	
65	Cleveland	−6.88	
66	New York	−6.94	
67	Newark	−7.55	
68	Albany	−8.56	
69	Buffalo	−10.48	

*Standard Metropolitan Statistical Area

A Look At the Last Decade

Some amazing changes in population have taken place in the last decade. By reviewing Chart 3 you will gain a better understanding of what has happened to various areas and the implications for you.

The population changes in Chart 3 are arranged from highest growth to highest losses.

The growth rates of some areas over the past ten years have been absolutely phenomenal. The biggest winner from a percentage standpoint has been Las Vegas, with a host of other big gainers scattered across the south and west.

As we mentioned earlier, when an already large metropolis registers large growth percentages, the influx of people has to have been tremendous. For this reason, the gains of Houston have been extremely impressive.

Significantly, not a single northeastern or north central area made it into the top 25 population gainers. Only Manchester made it into the top 40.

The big losers? Led by New York's loss of 9.0 percent of its population northeastern areas hold most of the places at the bottom of the list. And it is apparent that, because they are such highly populated places, northeastern areas have been losing extraordinarily large numbers of people to reflect the high percentages shown.

Please do not assume that the growing areas are necessarily your best choices for locating. There are some good reasons for choosing regions which are losing population. For example, real estate costs are much lower in most of the northeast than they are in much of the burgeoning south and west.

When one of the authors lived in southern California 15 years ago, houses were selling very inexpensively. Many people chose to just move away from their homes and let them be foreclosed rather than go to the bother of trying to resell them. Huge tracts were being built and then abandoned and vandalized because buyers did not materialize in the numbers anticipated. Of course, real estate speculators with foresight or luck, or both, made fortunes when the boom began in earnest.

Another of the authors lived in Texas, and remembers well the cheap real estate around Dallas, Fort Worth, and Houston. What a change! And the number of new Texans has created a fantastic market in cowboy hats and language instructors who specialize in teaching an "authentic drawl guaranteed in six weeks or your old accent back free of charge!"

New York is ranked last in terms of growth over the last ten years, but it remains indisputably the cultural center of the United States. Its homes are relatively inexpensive, with excellent quality, variety, and availability. You can even find waterfront mansions, of various sizes, in excellent nearby areas, for less money than a mediocre tract-built house on a concrete slab in the red-hot growth areas of the west.

Another implication of recent population change can be quite a surprise. The frontiers and open land are now found as much in the east and north as in the west and south! Farm land often has been allowed to revert back to natural woods, and the moose have returned to Maine in force. No, no bison have been sighted yet.

Of course, the disadvantages are significant of living in an area where population is dwindling. Slow growth in housing values, shrinking job opportunities, loss of some services and federal spending, and general deterioration of old highways and utilities are part of living in places where population is being lost.

CHART
3

A LOOK AT THE LAST DECADE
(Population changes ranked by % change from greatest to least growth.)

Rank	Area	Growth Rate (% change)	Reaction
1	Las Vegas	69.1	
2	Phoenix	55.6	
3	Boise	54.0	
4	Orlando	53.3	
5	Tucson	51.2	
6	Austin	47.8	
7	Houston	44.6	
8	Tampa	42.4	
9	Anchorage	37.7	
10	San Diego	37.0	
11	Albuquerque	34.7	
12	El Paso	33.4	
13	Salt Lake City	32.6	
14	Baton Rouge	32.0	
15	Denver	30.3	
16	Atlanta	26.0	
17	Sacramento	25.3	

Rank	Area	Growth Rate (% change)	Reaction
18	Raleigh	25.2	
19	Dallas	24.7	
20	Miami	24.1	
21	Charleston, S.C.	23.8	
22	Tulsa	23.6	
23	Portland, Or.	22.8	
24	Fresno	22.7	
25	Columbia	22.6	
26	Little Rock	21.8	
27	Bakersfield	21.6	
28	Manchester	21.1	
29	Honolulu	20.9	
30	San Antonio	20.5	
31	Biloxi	19.7	
32	Oklahoma City	18.7	
33	Nashville	18.5	
34	Mobile	16.8	
35	Sioux Falls	15.6	
36	Richmond	15.2	
37	Fargo	14.3	
38	Corpus Christi	13.8	
39	New Orleans	13.1	
40	Seattle	12.4	
41	Shreveport	12.1	
42	Grand Rapids	11.5	
43	Norfolk	9.2	
44	Memphis	9.1	

Rank	Area	Growth Rate (% change)	Reaction
45	Birmingham	8.7	
46	Portland, Me.	7.9	
47	Beaumont	7.8	
48	Des Moines	7.8	
49	Minneapolis	7.3	
50	Columbus	7.0	
51	Los Angeles	5.7	
52	Wichita	5.3	
53	Wilmington	4.8	
54	Baltimore	4.6	
54	Washington, D.C.	4.6	
56	Indianapolis	4.5	
57	Omaha	4.3	
58	Louisville	4.0	
59	Kansas City	3.8	
59	San Francisco	3.8	
61	Albany	2.1	
62	Nassau-Suffolk	2.0	
63	Charleston, W.V.	1.4	
64	Chicago	1.2	
65	Providence	1.0	
66	Rochester	0.9	
67	Hartford	0.8	
68	Cincinnati	0.4	
69	Milwaukee	− 0.8	
70	Great Falls	− 1.4	
71	Detroit	− 2.0	

Rank	Area	Growth Rate (% change)	Reaction
72	Philadelphia	−2.6	
73	St. Louis	−2.7	
74	Akron	−2.8	
75	Newark	−4.6	
76	Boston	−4.8	
77	Pittsburgh	−5.8	
78	Buffalo	−8.0	
79	Cleveland	−8.1	
80	New York	−9.0	

*Standard Metropolitan Statistical Area

Comparing the Last 10 Years To the Next 10

As you gain insights into the areas you are considering, it will help to compare the differences between Chart 2 and Chart 3. For example, you will see that Beaumont has not been growing rapidly until very recently. The 11.6 percent predicted gain will be due to the general strength of the Texas economy, energy issues (spelled OIL), and its location so close to Houston.

Seattle also will show a major increase in growth rate, from 12.4 percent to 19.1 percent. This 6.7 percent increase reflects a projected healthy economy, thanks in part to an increasing awareness of the area's cultural and natural bounty.

Corpus Christi will move from 13.8 percent to 14.6 percent. Like Beaumont, its growth is due to a combination of sunbelt attraction, revitalization of the southwestern oil industry, and the apparent intention of Texans to make their state the economic center of America . . . if not the universe. They have made great strides already.

Other already growing regions which will continue their high growth rates include:

1. Portland, Oregon
2. Tulsa
3. Oklahoma City

Portland's gains have been uneven, with economic highs and lows. Spillover from California, however, has put population pressure on Oregon, as Californians discover the relatively open spaces and lower costs of their neighbors to the north. Oregonians have been known to put signs along the highway welcoming the visitors but urging them not to stay . . . but their western hospitality, the scenic beauty, and the mild climate are not easy to disguise. In addition, the state has a long tradition of maintaining an ecologically balanced environment, with a wonderful array of public beaches and parks.

Tulsa and Oklahoma City are, of course, in a state whose economic growth has been dramatic. Energy development has provided much of the impetus for the population upsurge, but they are not just "oil towns" by any means. They are becoming lovely cosmopolitan centers.

It has been popular to conjecture that metropolitan areas, like animate organisms, have a life and death cycle. Therefore, as the theory goes, such places as New York, Buffalo, Akron, St. Louis, Pittsburgh, Providence, Cincinnati, and Newark have had their heyday and are now in a dying phase.

On the other hand, the wonderful examples of Paris, Cairo, Rome, and other classic cities of the world can be cited as arguments against the relatively short lifespan assigned to our comparatively young metropolitan areas. One of our dear friends, a recent immigrant from Egypt, was polite but hardly thrilled when shown a building in Boston built in the 1700's. "Really?" replied Dr. Saad. "A.D. or B.C.?"

State Population Changes

The 1980 census figures show an American population of 226 million, an increase of 11 percent over 1970. But the increases are not spread evenly throughout the states . . . and two states (New York and Rhode Island) experienced a decrease. Chart 4 shows in graph form how the states have fared.

POPULATION CHANGES BY STATE, 1970–80
(Ranked by percentage from greatest to least growth during decade)

Rank	State	Change	Reaction
1	Nevada	63.8%	
2	Arizona	52.9	
3	Wyoming	41.1	
4	Florida	41.1	
5	Utah	37.3	
6	Alaska	32.3	
6	Idaho	32.3	
8	Colorado	30.2	
9	New Mexico	26.9	
10	Texas	26.4	
11	Hawaii	25.3	
12	Oregon	25.1	
13	New Hampshire	24.6	
14	Washington	20.4	
15	Arkansas	18.6	
16	South Carolina	18.4	
17	California	17.7	
18	Georgia	17.6	

Rank	State	Change	Reaction
19	Oklahoma	17.2%	
20	Tennessee	15.6	
21	Louisiana	15.1	
22	North Carolina	15.0	
22	Vermont	15.0	
24	Virginia	14.4	
25	Maine	13.1	
25	Kentucky	13.1	
27	Montana	12.9	
27	Mississippi	12.9	
29	Alabama	12.2	
30	West Virginia	10.6	
31	Delaware	8.5	
32	Maryland	6.9	
32	Minnesota	6.9	
34	Wisconsin	6.1	
35	North Dakota	5.6	
36	Nebraska	5.3	
37	Indiana	5.0	
38	Missouri	4.8	
39	Kansas	4.7	
40	Michigan	4.0	
41	South Dakota	3.2	
42	Iowa	3.0	
43	New Jersey	2.3	
44	Connecticut	2.1	
45	Illinois	1.9	
46	Ohio	0.9	

Rank	State	Change	Reaction
47	Massachusetts	0.7%	
48	Pennsylvania	0.2	
49	New York	−0.3	
50	Rhode Island	−0.4	

Population Density, By State

No, density does not refer to impaired intellectual capacity. Rather, Chart 5 indicates the number of persons per square mile. Please keep in mind that some large but highly populated states have some areas where few people live, which makes their density figures appear lower than you will experience if you live there. California is an excellent case in point.

Alaska, with less than one person per square mile, has the lowest density, and even its cities are sprawled across miles of relatively undeveloped land. Two of the authors have lived in different places in Alaska, but in comparing notes found that even with the boom times in Anchorage and Fairbanks, living there is certainly uncrowded.

POPULATION DENSITY BY STATE
(Ranked from highest to lowest density)

Rank	State	Persons per square mile	Reaction
1	New Jersey	986.1	
2	Rhode Island	897.6	
3	Massachusetts	733.3	
4	Connecticut	637.9	
5	Maryland	428.6	
6	New York	370.6	
7	Delaware	308.0	
8	Pennsylvania	264.4	
9	Ohio	263.3	
10	Illinois	205.2	
11	Florida	179.9	
12	Michigan	162.8	
13	Indiana	152.8	
14	California	151.4	
15	Hawaii	150.2	
16	Virginia	134.6	
17	North Carolina	120.3	
18	Tennessee	111.6	
19	South Carolina	103.3	

Rank	State	Persons per square mile	Reaction
20	New Hampshire	102.4	
21	Louisiana	94.4	
22	Georgia	94.1	
23	Kentucky	92.3	
24	Wisconsin	86.4	
25	West Virginia	80.8	
26	Alabama	76.6	
27	Missouri	71.3	
28	Washington	62.1	
29	Vermont	55.1	
30	Texas	54.3	
31	Mississippi	53.4	
32	Iowa	52.1	
33	Minnesota	51.3	
34	Oklahoma	44.1	
35	Arkansas	43.9	
36	Maine	36.3	
37	Kansas	28.9	
38	Colorado	27.9	
39	Oregon	27.4	
40	Arizona	23.9	
41	Nebraska	20.5	
42	Utah	17.8	
43	Idaho	11.5	
44	New Mexico	10.7	
45	North Dakota	9.4	
46	South Dakota	9.1	

Rank	State	Persons per square mile	Reaction
47	Nevada	7.3	
48	Montana	5.4	
49	Wyoming	4.0	
50	Alaska	.7	

Pardon Me. Do You Speak English?

Contrary to popular opinion, languages other than English are the mother tongues of a large number of our citizens. In New Mexico, for example, only 55 percent of the people have been raised with English as their mother tongue. The rest are predominantly Spanish speaking. Over 40 percent of the Hawaiians learn their own language before English, and Rhode Islanders speak more French and Italian than most of us would realize.

LANGUAGE SPOKEN AS MOTHER TONGUE
(Ranked by percentage from high to low of those speaking English as first language)

Rank	State	% of Population for which Mother Tongue is					Reaction
		English	Spanish	German	French	Italian	
1	Alabama	94.3	.2	.4	.2	.1	
2	North Carolina	94.0	.2	.3	.2	.1	
3	Mississippi	93.9	.2	.2	.3	.1	
4	South Carolina	93.5	.2	.3	.2	.1	
5	Georgia	93.4	.3	.4	.2	.1	
5	Arkansas	93.4	.3	.6	.2	.1	
7	Tennessee	93.3	.2	.3	.1	.1	
8	Kentucky	93.2	.2	.9	.1	.1	
9	West Virginia	93.1	.1	.4	.1	.7	
10	Virginia	92.3	.5	.8	.4	.3	
11	Oklahoma	91.3	.8	1.3	.2	.1	
12	Indiana	90.0	.8	2.7	.2	.3	
13	Idaho	89.4	1.6	2.2	.3	.2	
14	Utah	88.9	2.7	1.2	.2	.4	
15	Missouri	88.8	.4	3.5	.3	.5	

Rank	State	% of Population for which Mother Tongue is					Reaction
		English	Spanish	German	French	Italian	
16	Kansas	88.4	1.2	4.5	.3	.2	
17	Maryland	87.0	.5	1.6	.4	1.1	
18	Oregon	87.3	.9	3.4	.4	.4	
19	Delaware	87.1	.7	1.3	.4	1.8	
20	Iowa	86.4	.3	5.7	.2	.2	
21	Washington	85.6	1.2	3.1	.6	.5	
21	Wyoming	85.6	3.8	2.8	.3	.5	
21	Florida	85.6	2.2	1.8	.7	1.0	
24	Montana	84.1	.5	4.8	.7	.4	
25	Vermont	83.9	.2	.7	8.1	1.0	
25	Michigan	83.9	.8	2.5	.8	.9	
27	Washington, D.C.	83.8	.8	.8	.7	.4	
28	Nebraska	82.8	.8	6.8	.2	.4	
29	Maine	81.1	.2	.3	12.9	.5	
29	Pennsylvania	81.1	.6	3.5	.2	3.0	
31	Illinois	80.3	2.0	3.8	.4	1.5	
32	Nevada	80.1	2.8	1.8	.7	1.5	
33	Colorado	80.0	8.7	3.6	.4	.8	
34	South Dakota	77.0	.2	10.0	.3	.1	
35	Alaska	76.8	1.1	1.8	.7	.3	
35	California	76.8	8.7	2.2	.8	1.4	
37	Wisconsin	76.5	.6	10.9	.5	.6	
38	New Hampshire	76.4	.2	.6	13.7	.7	
39	Minnesota	76.3	.3	8.1	.7	.3	
39	Ohio	76.3	.5	2.9	.2	1.2	
41	Texas	76.2	14.5	2.0	.8	.2	

Rank	State	% of Population for which Mother Tongue is				
		English	Spanish	German	French	Italian
41	Louisiana	76.2	.7	.4	15.8	.8
43	Massachusetts	75.4	.7	.8	6.0	4.2
44	New Jersey	75.1	2.5	2.7	.5	5.9
45	Connecticut	72.0	1.7	1.7	4.2	6.0
46	Arizona	71.9	13.3	1.9	.5	.6
47	New York	71.4	6.3	2.2	.8	5.7
48	North Dakota	69.3	.2	14.5	.3	.1
49	Rhode Island	68.2	.4	.7	10.4	7.1
50	Hawaii	63.4	1.4	.6	.4	.2
51	New Mexico	54.9	31.9	1.0	.3	.3

Where the Gray Power Lives

Did you hear about the Alaskan Boy Scout who remained on a Fairbanks streetcorner for 19 days and nights waiting for an elderly person he could help across? He never found one, but he did earn a merit badge for downtown camping.

Alaska has very few senior citizens, as you can see from Chart 7. The state with the highest percentage of persons over age 65 is Florida, followed fairly closely by five midwestern states and Rhode Island.

WHERE THE GRAY POWER LIVES
(Ranked by percentage from high to low of citizens 65 and older)

Rank	State	% of total population	Reactions
1	Florida	17.3	
2	Arkansas	13.9	
3	Iowa	13.6	
3	Rhode Island	13.6	
5	South Dakota	13.4	
6	Missouri	13.3	
7	Nebraska	13.2	
7	Pennsylvania	13.2	
9	Kansas	13.1	
10	Massachusetts	12.8	
11	Maine	12.7	
12	North Dakota	12.5	
13	New York	12.4	
13	West Virginia	12.4	
15	Oklahoma	12.3	
16	Wisconsin	12.2	
17	Connecticut	12.0	
17	Minnesota	12.0	
19	New Jersey	11.9	

Rank	State	% of total population	Reactions
19	Oregon	11.9	·
21	Arizona	11.7	
21	Mississippi	11.7	
23	Tennessee	11.6	
24	Alabama	11.5	
25	Kentucky	11.4	
25	Vermont	11.4	
27	New Hampshire	11.3	
28	Illinois	11.2	
29	Ohio	11.1	
30	Indiana	11.0	
30	Montana	11.0	
32	Washington	10.6	
33	North Carolina	10.5	
34	Delaware	10.4	
35	California	10.3	
36	Idaho	10.2	
36	Michigan	10.2	
38	Georgia	9.6	
38	Louisiana	9.6	
38	Maryland	9.6	
38	Texas	9.6	
38	Virginia	9.6	
43	South Carolina	9.5	
44	New Mexico	9.1	
45	Colorado	8.6	
46	Nevada	8.5	

Rank	State	% of total population	Reactions
47	Hawaii	8.3	
48	Wyoming	7.7	
49	Utah	7.5	
50	Alaska	2.9	

Marriage and Divorce Rates

One of the authors was in San Diego recently, looking at real estate and gathering background information for this book. Kristen, the beautiful blonde broker who was acting as his tour guide and financial advisor, was asked about the turnover rates on houses, because it appeared that quite a few were on the market.

"Frankly," she said, "the real estate market here, as in most of southern California, would be impossible except for one thing . . . the famous California lifestyle. Not many get married these days, and those that do are getting divorces almost as fast. Many of these houses are available because of a divorce. Otherwise, owners hang onto their fairly low rate mortgages."

As you look over the figures for marriages on Chart 8, you will see that California is way down in fortieth place. It is a state known for its singles lifestyles, and the trend is spreading across the nation.

Nevada is at the top of the list for marriages, but lest you think that everyone in Nevada either practices polygamy or just loves getting married over and over, keep in mind that Nevada's marriage laws are so permissive that many eager couples travel here for a combination wedding vows, gambling spree, and vacation, not necessarily in that order.

MARRIAGE RATES BY STATE
(Ranked from highest to lowest per 1,000 population)

Rank	State	Rate per 1,000 population	Reaction
1	Nevada	147.4	
2	South Carolina	18.2	
3	Oklahoma	15.4	
4	Idaho	14.8	
5	Wyoming	14.4	
6	Tennessee	13.5	
7	Georgia	13.4	
8	New Mexico	13.1	
9	South Dakota	13.0	
10	Alabama	12.9	
10	Texas	12.9	
12	Hawaii	12.8	
13	Alaska	12.3	
14	Utah	12.2	
15	Arizona	12.1	
16	Washington	12.0	
17	Arkansas	11.9	
18	Colorado	11.8	

Rank	State	Rate per 1,000 population	Reaction
19	Florida	11.7	
20	Virginia	11.3	
21	Mississippi	11.2	
22	Maryland	11.1	
23	Indiana	11.0	
24	Maine	10.9	
24	Missouri	10.9	
26	Vermont	10.5	
26	Kansas	10.5	
28	Montana	10.4	
29	Louisiana	10.3	
30	New Hampshire	10.2	
31	Illinois	9.7	
31	Michigan	9.7	
33	Iowa	9.6	
33	Kentucky	9.6	
35	West Virginia	9.4	
36	Ohio	9.3	
37	North Dakota	9.2	
38	Minnesota	9.1	
39	Nebraska	8.9	
40	California	8.8	
41	Oregon	8.7	
42	Wisconsin	8.4	
43	Connecticut	8.2	
44	New York	8.1	
45	North Carolina	8.0	

Rank	State	Rate per 1,000 population	Reaction
45	Pennsylvania	8.0	
47	Rhode Island	7.9	
48	Massachusetts	7.8	
49	Delaware	7.5	
49	New Jersey	7.5	

Divorce rates in the western and southwestern states are generally higher than those in the rest of the nation. Chart 9 shows comparisons ranked from highest to lowest. Those of you with marital difficulties should note the low divorce rates in Massachusetts and North Dakota . . . do you think it would help if you moved? Perhaps, or it might be cheaper to say you're sorry.

CHART

9

DIVORCE RATES BY STATE
(Ranked from highest to lowest per 1,000 population)

Rank	State	Rate per 1,000 population	Reaction
1	Nevada	16.8	
2	Arkansas	9.3	
3	Alaska	8.6	

Rank	State	Rate per 1,000 population	Reaction
4	Arizona	8.2	
5	New Mexico	8.0	
0	Florida	7.9	
6	Oklahoma	7.9	
8	Wyoming	7.8	
9	Indiana	7.7	
10	Idaho	7.1	
11	Alabama	7.0	
11	Oregon	7.0	
13	Texas	6.9	
13	Washington	6.9	
15	Tennessee	6.8	
16	Georgia	6.5	
16	Montana	6.5	
18	California	6.1	
19	Colorado	6.0	
20	New Hampshire	5.9	
21	Missouri	5.7	
22	Maine	5.6	
22	Mississippi	5.6	
22	Utah	5.6	
25	Hawaii	5.5	
25	Ohio	5.5	
27	Kansas	5.4	
28	Delaware	5.3	
28	West Virginia	5.3	
30	North Carolina	4.9	

Rank	State	Rate per 1,000 population	Reaction
31	Michigan	4.8	
32	South Carolina	4.7	
33	Illinois	4.6	
33	Vermont	4.6	
35	Connecticut	4.5	
35	Kentucky	4.5	
35	Virginia	4.5	
38	Maryland	4.1	
39	Nebraska	4.0	
40	Iowa	3.9	
40	Rhode Island	3.9	
40	South Dakota	3.9	
43	Louisiana	3.8	
44	Minnesota	3.7	
44	New York	3.7	
46	Wisconsin	3.6	
47	Pennsylvania	3.4	
48	New Jersey	3.2	
48	North Dakota	3.2	
50	Massachusetts	3.0	

Where the Boys (and Girls) Are . . . And Their Ages

Looking for companionship? Want to start an all-girls softball team? Whatever your interests, you probably should know about the age and sex characteristics of the places you are considering for relocation. Chart 10 ranks the 82 areas from youngest median age to oldest, with male and female percentages shown for different age groups.

For example, El Paso has the youngest population, with an average (median) age of only 24. Salt Lake City has the highest percentage of children (perhaps because of its cool nights). Very few of Anchorage's citizens are over the age of 50 . . . most retire to "the lower 48" as they say up north.

At the other end of the chart, Tampa has the oldest population, with a median age of nearly 42. Only 21 percent of its residents are children, which is much lower than the rest of the nation. For you single males looking for winsome wives, Portland, Oregon, has many more women than men. Single females looking for eligible bachelors, just look at San Diego.

AGE AND SEX OF POPULATION
(Ranked by median age from youngest to oldest)

Rank	Area*	Median Age	2-17 Children	18-24 Women	18-24 Men	25-34 Women	25-34 Men	35-49 Women	35-49 Men	50-64 Women	50-64 Men	65-over Women	65-over Men	Men Reaction
1	El Paso	24.4	31.6	7.2	7.5	9.0	9.6	8.5	7.5	6.8	6.0	3.8	2.6	
2	Salt Lake City	25.2	32.5	7.1	7.3	8.8	8.3	8.2	7.9	6.4	6.1	4.4	3.0	
3	Biloxi	25.4	28.9	6.7	7.2	8.3	12.2	7.8	7.8	6.7	6.1	5.0	3.3	
4	Austin	26.0	25.8	5.7	6.1	11.9	12.2	8.4	8.6	6.7	5.9	5.3	3.4	
5	Fargo	26.2	24.6	6.7	6.7	12.0	12.0	7.5	7.5	6.7	6.0	6.0	4.5	
6	Anchorage	26.3	30.9	6.9	6.9	8.0	9.7	10.9	11.4	5.7	6.9	1.7	1.1	
7	Baton Rouge	26.3	28.9	6.9	7.1	9.9	9.3	8.9	8.2	7.1	6.3	4.3	3.0	
8	Charleston, S.C.	26.3	29.2	7.3	7.5	8.8	10.8	8.5	8.8	6.8	6.0	4.0	2.5	

Percent of Total Population

Rank	Area*	Median Age	2-17 Children	18-24 Women	18-24 Men	25-34 Women	25-34 Men	35-49 Women	35-49 Men	50-64 Women	50-64 Men	65-over Women	65-over Men	Reaction
9	Corpus Christi	26.6	30.6	7.1	7.4	8.7	8.4	8.1	7.4	7.4	6.5	4.3	3.5	
10	Burlington	26.6	NA	NA	NA	NA	NA	NA	NA	NA	NA	N.A	NA	
11	Columbia	27.0	25.2	6.3	6.3	9.6	13.9	8.8	8.6	7.3	6.5	4.5	3.0	
12	San Antonio	27.0	28.9	6.9	7.1	8.8	10.0	8.3	7.6	7.4	6.3	5.3	3.4	
13	Casper	27.1	27.5	7.2	7.2	8.7	3.7	8.7	7.2	8.7	8.7	4.3	2.9	
14	Norfolk	27.4	26.3	6.6	6.8	8.5	12.5	8.8	8.9	7.3	6.8	4.4	3.0	
15	Houston	27.9	28.1	6.7	6.9	8.7	7.9	9.7	9.4	7.6	7.1	4.7	3.3	
16	Albuquerque	28.0	26.4	7.4	7.6	9.5	8.6	9.3	8.6	7.6	6.9	4.6	3.2	
17	Honolulu	28.0	26.4	6.4	6.7	8.9	11.1	9.6	9.7	7.6	7.2	3.3	3.2	
18	Memphis	28.0	27.5	7.0	7.1	9.1	9.1	9.0	7.9	7.6	6.5	5.7	3.6	
19	Great Falls	28.1	27.4	7.1	8.3	8.3	9.5	9.5	9.5	7.1	7.1	4.8	1.2	
20	Omaha	28.1	27.8	7.2	7.3	8.9	8.0	9.1	8.7	7.2	6.6	5.6	3.5	
21	Boise	28.3	27.0	6.7	6.7	9.2	8.0	8.6	8.6	8.0	6.7	5.5	4.9	
22	Oklahoma City	28.4	25.8	6.5	6.7	9.2	8.8	9.2	8.7	7.8	7.1	6.2	3.9	
23	Raleigh	28.4	23.9	5.8	6.0	11.0	11.6	9.6	9.2	7.5	6.6	5.4	3.5	
24	Columbus	28.5	25.9	6.5	6.7	9.8	9.1	9.3	8.9	7.6	6.9	5.5	3.6	

Percent of Total Population

Rank	Area*	Median Age	2-17 Children	18-24 Women	Men	25-34 Women	Men	35-49 Women	Men	50-64 Women	Men	65-over Women	Men	Reaction
25	Mobile	28.5	28.0	7.2	7.4	8.7	7.8	8.5	7.6	7.8	6.7	6.0	4.3	
26	New Orleans	28.5	27.9	6.9	7.0	8.8	7.8	9.0	8.1	7.9	7.0	5.8	3.7	
27	San Diego	28.5	24.2	6.0	6.2	8.6	13.5	8.6	8.9	7.7	6.9	5.8	3.8	
28	Minneapolis	28.6	26.8	7.0	7.4	9.3	8.0	9.3	9.2	7.1	6.6	5.6	3.6	
29	Grand Rapids	28.7	26.4	7.3	7.5	9.4	8.3	8.7	8.0	7.6	6.8	5.9	4.2	
30	Atlanta	28.8	27.5	6.5	6.7	9.0	8.0	10.2	10.0	7.4	6.8	5.0	3.1	
31	Dallas	28.8	27.0	6.5	6.7	9.0	8.1	9.8	9.5	7.6	6.9	5.5	3.5	
32	Fresno	28.8	27.0	6.8	7.0	9.3	8.7	8.5	7.8	8.0	7.0	5.6	4.2	
33	Sioux Falls	28.8	26.5	6.9	7.8	9.8	7.8	7.8	7.8	7.8	6.9	6.9	3.9	
34	Wichita	29.0	26.1	6.8	7.0	9.1	8.6	8.9	8.4	8.0	7.3	5.7	3.9	
35	Little Rock	29.0	26.8	6.6	6.6	8.7	7.9	9.4	8.7	8.1	7.1	6.0	4.2	
36	Denver	29.1	25.5	7.0	7.2	9.0	8.6	10.0	9.4	7.9	7.3	4.9	3.2	
37	Des Moines	29.1	25.7	6.7	6.7	9.2	8.0	9.2	8.6	8.0	7.0	6.7	4.3	
38	Shreveport	29.1	28.3	6.9	7.2	8.6	7.8	8.9	7.8	8.0	6.6	6.4	3.6	
39	Bakersfield	29.2	27.4	7.1	7.4	8.2	8.2	8.7	8.2	7.9	7.1	5.8	4.2	
40	Louisville	29.4	26.2	6.9	7.1	8.7	8.0	8.9	8.4	8.1	7.4	6.3	3.9	

Percent of Total Population

Rank	Area*	Median Age	2–17 Children	18–24 Women	18–24 Men	25–34 Women	25–34 Men	35–49 Women	35–49 Men	50–64 Women	50–64 Men	65–over Women	65–over Men	Reaction
41	Indianapolis	29.5	26.6	7.0	7.2	8.5	7.9	9.2	8.6	8.0	7.2	5.9	3.8	
42	Sacramento	29.5	23.8	7.0	7.3	9.3	8.8	9.3	8.7	8.5	7.9	5.3	3.9	
43	Las Vegas	29.6	27.1	6.5	6.7	7.8	7.6	10.4	10.4	7.8	7.8	4.1	3.9	
44	Washington, D.C.	29.6	25.3	6.7	6.9	9.1	8.3	10.4	10.0	8.3	7.6	4.5	2.9	
45	Detroit	29.8	25.6	7.1	7.3	8.5	7.8	8.8	8.3	8.8	7.9	5.3	4.1	
46	Akron	29.9	24.6	6.8	7.1	9.7	8.9	8.5	8.0	8.5	7.7	6.1	4.1	
47	Beaumont	30.0	25.7	7.0	7.3	8.6	8.1	8.6	7.8	8.6	7.8	5.9	4.3	
48	Manchester	30.0	27.5	6.4	6.8	8.3	7.5	8.7	8.3	7.9	7.2	6.8	4.5	
49	Nashville	30.0	25.1	6.6	6.7	9.2	8.4	9.5	9.0	8.1	7.1	6.3	4.2	
50	Chicago	30.1	25.8	6.7	6.8	8.2	7.7	9.2	8.7	8.5	7.7	6.4	4.3	
51	Cincinnati	30.1	26.4	7.0	7.2	8.6	7.8	8.9	8.1	8.1	7.1	6.6	4.1	
52	Kansas City	30.1	25.6	6.8	7.1	8.5	7.4	9.5	8.9	8.4	7.5	6.3	4.1	
53	Milwaukee	30.1	25.2	7.0	7.2	8.6	7.8	8.9	8.3	8.3	7.5	6.3	4.5	
54	Phoenix	30.1	26.7	6.7	7.0	8.7	8.2	8.9	8.4	7.9	6.7	6.3	4.9	
55	Tucson	30.2	25.9	6.7	6.8	9.1	9.3	8.4	8.0	8.0	6.7	4.8	4.6	
56	Rochester	30.3	25.5	6.6	6.9	8.9	8.1	9.0	8.6	8.3	7.3	6.6	4.3	

Percent of Total Population

Rank	Area*	Median Age	2-17 Children	18-24 Women	18-24 Men	25-34 Women	25-34 Men	35-49 Women	35-49 Men	50-64 Women	50-64 Men	65-over Women	65-over Men	Reaction
57	St. Louis	30.3	25.6	7.0	7.3	8.5	7.4	9.0	8.3	8.3	7.3	6.9	4.4	
58	Seattle	30.4	23.6	6.6	6.8	9.2	8.2	9.6	9.7	8.3	7.8	5.9	4.1	
59	Wilmington	30.4	25.0	7.0	7.2	8.9	8.3	9.1	8.7	8.5	7.8	5.4	3.9	
60	Tulsa	30.5	25.4	6.6	6.9	8.3	7.3	9.5	8.7	8.3	7.5	7.0	4.5	
61	Portland, Or.	30.6	24.4	6.6	6.8	9.0	7.8	9.0	8.7	8.4	7.5	6.9	4.8	
62	Charleston, W.V.	30.9	23.9	6.6	6.6	8.9	7.7	8.9	8.1	9.7	8.1	6.9	4.6	
63	Portland, Me.	30.9	25.8	6.4	6.9	8.6	8.2	8.2	7.7	8.6	7.3	7.8	4.7	
64	Richmond	30.9	23.0	6.5	6.9	9.5	8.5	9.8	9.2	8.7	7.7	6.4	3.9	
65	Birmingham	31.0	25.2	6.8	6.9	9.0	7.9	8.7	7.7	8.6	7.3	7.3	4.6	
66	Los Angeles	31.1	25.2	6.0	6.1	8.6	8.0	9.4	9.3	8.8	7.8	6.6	4.3	
67	Orlando	31.1	25.4	6.9	7.2	8.1	8.2	9.0	8.1	8.5	7.6	6.8	4.3	
68	Baltimore	31.2	24.2	6.8	7.0	8.6	8.5	9.3	8.8	8.8	8.0	6.1	4.1	
69	Boston	31.2	23.9	6.5	6.8	9.1	8.2	8.9	8.5	8.5	7.5	7.5	4.5	
70	Nassau-Suffolk	31.2	23.2	7.5	7.8	8.0	7.5	9.3	8.0	9.7	9.0	5.8	4.0	
71	Philadelphia	31.4	23.9	6.6	6.9	8.4	8.2	8.9	8.2	9.2	8.1	7.0	4.6	
72	Hartford	31.5	23.6	6.6	6.8	8.9	8.1	9.2	8.9	8.9	8.1	6.5	4.4	

Percent of Total Population

Rank	Area*	Median Age	2–17 Children	18–24 Women	18–24 Men	25–34 Women	25–34 Men	35–49 Women	35–49 Men	50–64 Women	50–64 Men	65→over Women	65→over Men	Reaction
73	Cleveland	31.6	24.4	6.8	6.9	8.5	7.6	9.0	8.2	9.2	8.1	6.7	4.5	
74	San Francisco	31.6	22.4	6.0	6.1	8.9	8.7	9.7	9.7	9.0	8.1	6.7	4.5	
75	Buffalo	31.8	23.7	6.9	7.1	8.8	7.8	8.5	7.8	9.3	8.2	7.2	4.8	
76	Albany	32.0	24.1	6.3	6.6	8.9	8.3	8.4	7.8	8.9	7.8	7.9	5.0	
77	Providence	32.5	23.2	6.3	6.5	8.7	9.0	8.1	7.7	9.3	8.1	8.2	4.9	
78	Newark	32.7	23.2	6.5	6.7	8.0	7.1	9.5	8.5	9.6	8.5	7.2	4.8	
79	New York	33.3	23.1	5.6	5.8	8.4	7.4	9.8	8.8	9.5	7.8	8.5	5.4	
80	Pittsburgh	33.6	21.7	6.6	6.9	8.6	7.7	8.5	7.5	10.3	8.8	8.0	5.4	
81	Miami	35.7	21.7	6.0	6.2	8.1	7.5	9.3	8.2	9.8	8.3	9.2	5.7	
82	Tampa	41.5	21.1	5.8	5.9	7.6	7.2	7.8	7.1	8.7	7.1	13.4	8.2	

*Standard Metropolitan Statistical Area

SRD April 27, 1982 for %
SMM July 27, 1981 for Md. Age

The Religion Factor

Whether or not you regularly attend religious services, this comparison of possible places for you to prosper would not be complete without some review of the pattern of religious affiliations throughout America.

Before you review Charts 11, 12, and 13, please recognize several limitations of the data. For example, actual church membership figures are not readily available. We have reported church attendance data collected by the National Council of Churches. Information for Eastern Orthodox and primarily black churches was not included in their study, but the figures provide some important clues for you.

For the sake of convenience, we have grouped Christians who are not Roman Catholic into Chart 12. This group includes a wide variety of Protestant denominations and the Church of Christ of Latter Day Saints (Mormons). As you know, the information for Utah largely reflects Mormon church attendance. The Jewish population is reflected in Chart 13.

ROMAN CATHOLIC CHRISTIANS
(Ranked from high to low by percentage of total state population)

Rank	State	Percent of total population	Reaction
1	Rhode Island	64.97	
2	Connecticut	41.82	
3	Massachusetts	39.60	
4	New Jersey	38.84	
5	New Hampshire	36.52	
6	New York	35.07	
7	New Mexico	34.21	
8	Louisiana	33.50	
9	Wisconsin	33.40	
10	Illinois	31.76	
11	Pennsylvania	30.94	
12	Vermont	30.52	
13	North Dakota	29.72	
14	Maine	26.56	
15	Minnesota	26.47	
16	Michigan	22.56	
17	California	22.09	
18	Ohio	22.01	
19	Nebraska	21.28	

Rank	State	Percent of total population	Reaction
20	South Dakota	21.20	
21	Hawaii	20.88	
22	Iowa	19.25	
23	Arizona	18.65	
24	Texas	18.17	
25	Montana	18.17	
26	Nevada	18.00	
27	Maryland	17.45	
28	Missouri	17.21	
29	Kansas	15.26	
30	Florida	14.48	
31	Colorado	14.33	
32	Wyoming	14.18	
33	Delaware	13.73	
34	Indiana	13.59	
35	Oregon	12.69	
36	Alaska	10.24	
37	Kentucky	10.23	
38	Washington	9.82	
39	Idaho	8.43	
40	Virginia	5.70	
41	West Virginia	5.46	
42	Oklahoma	4.21	
43	Mississippi	4.12	
44	Utah	4.09	
45	Georgia	3.19	
46	Alabama	3.07	

Rank	State	Percent of total population	Reaction
47	Tennessee	2.76	
48	Arkansas	2.72	
49	South Carolina	2.03	
50	North Carolina	1.72	

CHART
12

CHRISTIANS WHO ARE NOT ROMAN CATHOLICS
(Ranked from high to low by percentage of population of Christian faith, excluding Roman Catholics)

Rank	State	Percent of total population	Reaction
1	Utah	78.8	
2	Oklahoma	51.2	
3	North Dakota	50.7	
4	Vermont	50.6	
5	Missouri	4.96	
6	South Dakota	48.9	
7	Tennessee	47.7	
8	North Carolina	47.0	

Rank	State	Percent of total population	Reaction
9	Alabama	45.3	
9	Kansas	45.3	
9	Idaho	45.3	
12	Kentucky	44.3	
13	Georgia	43.9	
14	Arkansas	42.9	
15	Iowa	41.2	
16	Nebraska	40.8	
17	Minnesota	40.3	
18	South Carolina	38.8	
19	Texas	38.2	
20	Virginia	38.0	
21	Wyoming	33.8	
22	Wisconsin	33.6	
23	West Virginia	34.8	
24	Indiana	30.7	
25	Florida	27.7	
26	Montana	27.6	
27	New Mexico	27.5	
28	Pennsylvania	26.7	
29	Ohio	26.2	
30	Louisiana	24.6	
31	Delaware	24.5	
32	Colorado	24.4	
33	Arizona	24.3	
34	Illinois	23.1	
35	Maryland	22.8	

Rank	State	Percent of total population	Reaction
36	Oregon	22.8	
37	Washington	21.8	
38	Alaska	20.6	
39	Michigan	20.5	
40	Mississippi	19.4	
41	Nevada	19.0	
42	Maine	17.5	
43	Connecticut	15.4	
44	New Hampshire	14.3	
45	California	13.8	
46	New Jersey	13.0	
47	Hawaii	12.5	
48	Rhode Island	11.7	
49	Massachusetts	11.5	
50	New York	11.5	

JEWISH POPULATION
(Ranked from high to low by percent of Jewish population)

Rank	State	Percent of total population	Reaction
1	New York	12.2	
2	New Jersey	5.9	
3	Florida	4.8	
3	Maryland	4.4	
5	Massachusetts	4.2	
6	Pennsylvania	3.5	
7	Connecticut	3.3	
8	California	3.2	
9	Illinois	2.3	
9	Rhode Island	2.3	
11	Nevada	1.8	
12	Arizona	1.7	
13	Delaware	1.6	
14	Missouri	1.5	
15	Ohio	1.3	
16	Colorado	1.1	
16	Virginia	1.1	
18	Michigan	1.0	
19	Minnesota	.9	

Rank	State	Percent of total population	Reaction
20	Georgia	.7	
21	Hawaii	.6	
21	Maine	.0	
21	New Mexico	.6	
21	Wisconsin	.6	
25	Kansas	.5	
25	Nebraska	.5	
25	New Hampshire	.5	
25	Texas	.5	
25	Vermont	.5	
25	Washington	.5	
31	Indiana	.4	
31	Louisiana	.4	
31	Oregon	.4	
31	Tennessee	.4	
31	West Virginia	.4	
36	Iowa	.3	
36	Kentucky	.3	
36	South Carolina	.3	
39	Alabama	.2	
39	Alaska	.2	
39	North Carolina	.2	
39	North Dakota	.2	
39	Oklahoma	.2	
39	Utah	.2	
44	Arkansas	.1	
44	Idaho	.1	

Rank	State	Percent of total population	Reaction
44	Mississippi	.1	
44	Montana	.1	
44	South Dakota	.1	
44	Wyoming	.1	

Directions: Rate only those cities below which are on your Tentative Interest List. Give a 5 to those cities with predominance of (+) ratings on the various charts in this chapter. Give a 3 if a city has only enough (+) marks to remain of interest. Give a 1 to those with few (+) marks. Eliminate from your Tentative Interest List those cities for which you've lost all interest; add additional cities as interest develops and rate them as above.

SUMMARY GRID

		Rating (5, 3 or 1)	Comments
1	Akron, Ohio		
2	Albany, New York		
3	Albuquerque, New Mexico		
4	Anchorage, Alaska		
5	Atlanta, Georgia		
6	Austin, Texas		
7	Bakersfield, California		
8	Baltimore, Maryland		
9	Baton Rouge, Louisiana		
10	Beaumont, Texas		
11	Biloxi, Mississippi		
12	Birmingham, Alabama		
13	Boise, Idaho		
14	Boston, Massachusetts		
15	Buffalo, New York		
16	Burlington, Vermont		
17	Casper, Wyoming		

		Rating (5, 3 or 1)	Comments
18	Charleston, South Carolina		
19	Charleston, West Virginia		
20	Chicago, Illinois		
21	Cincinnati, Ohio		
22	Cleveland, Ohio		
23	Columbia, South Carolina		
24	Columbus, Ohio		
25	Corpus Christi, Texas		
26	Dallas, Texas		
27	Denver, Colorado		
28	Des Moines, Iowa		
29	Detroit, Michigan		
30	El Paso, Texas		
31	Fargo, North Dakota		
32	Fresno, California		
33	Grand Rapids, Michigan		
34	Great Falls, Montana		
35	Hartford, Connecticut		
36	Honolulu, Hawaii		
37	Houston, Texas		
38	Indianapolis, Indiana		
39	Kansas City, Missouri		
40	Las Vegas, Nevada		
41	Little Rock, Arkansas		
42	Los Angeles, California		
43	Louisville, Kentucky		
44	Manchester, New Hampshire		

		Rating (5, 3 or 1)	Comments
45	Memphis, Tennessee		
46	Miami, Florida		
47	Milwaukee, Wisconsin		
48	Minneapolis, Minnesota		
49	Mobile, Alabama		
50	Nashville, Tennessee		
51	Nassau-Suffolk, New York		
52	Newark, New Jersey		
53	New Orleans, Louisiana		
54	New York, New York		
55	Norfolk, Virginia		
56	Oklahoma City, Oklahoma		
57	Omaha, Nebraska		
58	Orlando, Florida		
59	Philadelphia, Pennsylvania		
60	Phoenix, Arizona		
61	Pittsburgh, Pennsylvania		
62	Portland, Maine		
63	Portland, Oregon		
64	Providence, Rhode Island		
65	Raleigh, North Carolina		
66	Richmond, Virginia		
67	Rochester, New York		
68	Sacramento, California		
69	Salt Lake City, Utah		
70	San Antonio, Texas		
71	San Diego, California		

		Rating (5, 3 or 1)	Comments
72	San Francisco, California		
73	Seattle, Washington		
74	Shreveport, Louisiana		
75	Sioux Falls, South Dakota		
76	St. Louis, Missouri		
77	Tampa, Florida		
78	Tucson, Arizona		
79	Tulsa, Oklahoma		
80	Washington, D.C.		
81	Wichita, Kansas		
82	Wilmington, Delaware		

6

WARNING! The Authors Have Determined That Living Here Could Be Hazardous to Your Health

We were meandering along the busy sidewalk one sunny afternoon, people-watching and window shopping, enjoying the peaceful scene. All at once the day was shattered by the strident clanging of a burglar alarm and the piercing wail of approaching sirens.

The reaction of the crowd was nearly instantaneous. Most sprintwalked away from the uproar, keeping their heads low and hardly daring to peek back toward the screeching of tires and slamming of doors. Amazingly, others in the crowd scrambled forward in the direction of the shouting and the sudden explosions of gunshots. And look! There was our friend Judith among them, racing toward the action, ducking low but advancing like a Marine Corps platoon!

When the hubbub had died down and "the perpetrator was apprehended," as the police like to say, Judith rejoined our group, face flushed and eyes flashing with excitement. "I saw it all!" she gloated. "What an adventure! What a terrific place to live! I love this city!"

How Much Risk is Acceptable?

Needless to say, not everyone is like Judith, who turned out to be a closet daredevil. Instead, most of us prefer to avoid such things as robberies, earthquakes, tornadoes, or nuclear accidents, and wouldn't attend even if we received an engraved invitation!

Even if your Prospering Profile, from Chapter 2, does not indicate a high concern for risks and dangers in the environment, the information in the following charts and maps will be extremely useful. It can help you gauge the probability of various kinds of hazards across the nation and decide whether the risks are acceptable to you.

Where the Crooks Live

Almost no one wants to live where there are high crime rates. Certainly we potential victims aren't interested in improved chances to get beat up or stolen from.

Two crime charts are provided here. The first shows crimes of violence against people, and Chart 2 indicates crimes related to property. In both cases we have ranked the areas from least crime to most. The crime champion? A review of both charts show it's probably Miami, with Las Vegas a close second. The area with the least crime appears to be Fargo, with the good honest folk of Albany and Burlington also deserving our applause. Or could it be that their long cold seasons keep the crooks inside watching T.V. by the fire?

CHART

1

WHERE THE VIOLENT CROOKS LIVE
(Violent crime ranked from least to most)

Rank	Area†	# of violent crimes/100,000 People	Reaction
1	Fargo	109	
2	Manchester	140	
3	Sioux Falls	188	
4	Casper	246	
5	Albany	249	
6	Burlington	261	
7	Charleston, W.V.	271	
8	Milwaukee	277	
9	Honolulu	299	
10	Great Falls	307	
11	Portland, Me.	343	
12	Minneapolis	356	
13	Pittsburgh	363	
14	Providence	374	
15	Grand Rapids	378	
16	Salt Lake City	382	
17	Austin	387	

Rank	Area†	# of violent crimes/100,000 People	Reaction
18	Rochester	390	
19	Anchorage	399	
20	Akron	419	
21	Boise	423	
22	Louisville	427	
23	Biloxi	428	
24	Raleigh	438	
25	Wichita	439	
26	Omaha	440	
27	San Antonio	446	
28	Tulsa	468	
29	Cincinnati	470	
30	Richmond	481	
31	Wilmington	482	
32	Indianapolis	485	
33	Buffalo	496	
34	Norfolk	501	
35	Hartford	504	
36	Columbus	513	
37	Nashville	518	
38	El Paso	519	
39	Seattle	520	
40	Philadelphia	529	
41	Beaumont	551	
42	Tucson	561	

Rank	Area†	# of violent crimes/100,000 People	Reaction
43	Chicago	569	
44	San Diego	576	
45	Shreveport	600	
46	Mobile	605	
47	Denver	609	
48	Corpus Christi	611	
49	Birmingham	623	
50	Oklahoma City	633	
51	Boston	648	
52	Houston	674	
52	Phoenix	674	
54	Cleveland	687	
55	Portland, Or.	688	
56	Washington, D.C.	693	
57	Dallas	694	
58	St. Louis	722	
59	Sacramento	725	
60	Memphis	745	
61	Kansas City	752	
62	Albuquerque	765	
63	Bakersfield	777	
64	Little Rock	781	
65	Tampa	784	
66	Detroit	786	
67	Baton Rouge	788	

Rank	Area†	# of violent crimes/100,000 People	Reaction
68	Fresno	846	
69	Charleston, S.C.	852	
70	Newark	857	
71	San Francisco	862	
72	Atlanta	879	
73	Orlando	909	
74	Columbia	916	
75	Las Vegas	1024	
76	Baltimore	1088	
77	New Orleans	1095	
78	Los Angeles	1205	
79	Miami	1373	
80	New York	1497	

†Incorporated City

WHERE THE NON-VIOLENT CROOKS LIVE
(Property crime ranked from least to most)

Rank	Area†	Property crime/100,000 People	Reaction
1	Pittsburgh	2919	
2	Burlington	3013	
3	Albany	3694	
4	Charleston, W.V.	3718	
5	Fargo	3911	
6	Philadelphia	4110	
7	Buffalo	4187	
8	Nashville	4360	
9	Cleveland	4508	
10	Sioux Falls	4604	
11	Milwaukee	4624	
12	Grand Rapids	4633	
13	Louisville	4711	
14	Manchester	4786	
15	Akron	4905	
16	Cincinnati	4988	
17	Indianapolis	5050	

Rank	Area†	Property crime/100,000 People	Reaction
18	Chicago	5071	~
19	Memphis	5079	
20	Beaumont	5132	
21	Mobile	5145	
22	Norfolk	5176	
23	St. Louis	5188	
24	Tulsa	5219	
25	Minneapolis	5313	
26	Providence	5327	
27	Richmond	5422	
28	El Paso	5517	
29	San Antonio	5527	
30	Shreveport	5543	
31	Omaha	5563	
32	Charleston, S.C.	5588	
33	Rochester	5622	
34	Birmingham	5647	
34	Boston	5647	
36	Newark	5688	
37	Boise	5695	
38	Raleigh	5747	
39	Wichita	5790	
40	Hartford	5798	
41	Washington, D.C.	5895	
42	Baltimore	5928	
43	Kansas City	5961	

Rank	Area†	Property crime/100,000 People	Reaction
44	Wilmington	5987	
45	Detroit	6000	
46	Oklahoma City	6104	
47	Corpus Christi	6115	
48	Portland, Me.	6268	
49	Anchorage	6277	
50	Portland, Or.	6291	
51	New York	6308	
52	Columbia	6311	
53	Salt Lake City	6318	
54	Columbus	6384	
55	Great Falls	6418	
56	Little Rock	6438	
57	Casper	6463	
58	Houston	6562	
59	Austin	6601	
59	Los Angeles	6601	
61	San Diego	6604	
62	Tampa	6635	
63	Seattle	6663	
64	Biloxi	6703	
65	New Orleans	6872	
66	Honolulu	6908	
67	Atlanta	6933	
68	Albuquerque	7071	
69	Baton Rouge	7085	

Rank	Area†	Property crime/100,000 People	Reaction
70	Dallas	7094	
71	San Francisco	7356	
72	Denver	7434	
73	Fresno	7494	
74	Bakersfield	7701	
75	Orlando	7781	
76	Tucson	7834	
77	Miami	7926	
78	Sacramento	8087	
79	Phoenix	8340	
80	Las Vegas	8958	

*Standard Metropolitan Statistical Area

Are My Shoes Too Loose or Is This An Earthquake?

You've heard the worriers, who wring their hands and proclaim that pretty soon California is going to start shaking and quaking and will end up by falling off the United States and into the ocean. No one that we know of has started building new beach concessions in the Rockies yet, but no doubt they are under consideration.

And then there are the scoffers, who prefer to believe that the San Andreas fault is only a little crack, hardly worth all the fuss. They sleep serenely, fretting not over the earth's seismic jolts and jiggles.

Now a federal agency has joined the ranks of worriers, predicting that the odds of a major catastrophic earthquake in California in the next 30 years are 50–50. The Federal Emergency Management Agency has issued an alarm and pointed out that the nation is essentially unprepared for the devastation which should be expected in our most populated state.

The shakiest ground in America is in California and western Nevada, with 90 percent of the seismic activity in the United States, not counting Alaska or Hawaii. And the earthquakes here are relatively violent, compared with the rest of the nation.

Not only California is threatened by earthquakes, however. Washington and Oregon also have a lot of high intensity quakes, particularly around Puget Sound. Alaska has greater earthquake activity than any other state, but few of the shocks have caused severe damage because there are relatively few highly populated areas.

The western mountain region has had much quake activity, but many of the jolts have occurred in sparsely populated areas. An earthquake near Yellowstone National Park in 1959 caused an avalanche which killed 28 people and blocked the Madison river, forming a new lake.

Usually the flat interiors of continents are less earthquake prone than other parts of the earth. For some unknown reason, this is not true for the central United States. Relatively frequent quakes, and big ones at that, have been recorded in the Upper Mississippi and Ohio Valleys.

The northeastern states, including New York and Connecticut and those northeast of them, contain zones of relatively high earthquake frequency. Happily, the other eastern states experience only a moderate amount of low-level quake activity.

Map Number 1 shows the distribution and intensity of earthquakes throughout the United States. Chart 3 reflects the earthquake hazard level for our areas.

Distribution of Earthquakes of Extreme Intensity

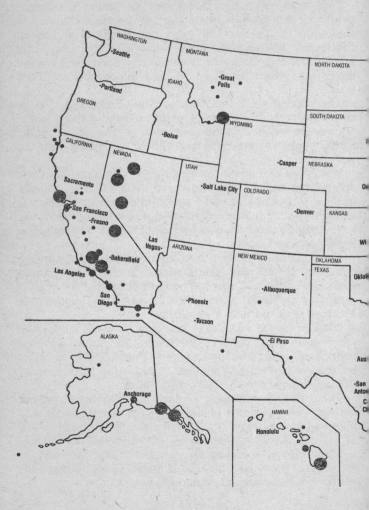

MAP 1

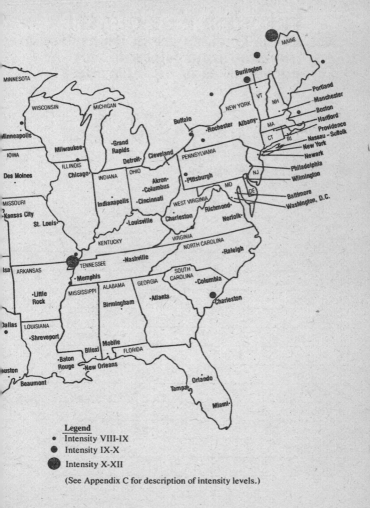

Legend
- Intensity VIII-IX
- ● Intensity IX-X
- ⬤ Intensity X-XII

(See Appendix C for description of intensity levels.)

FREQUENCY OF QUAKES
Not all the Quakers are in Pennsylvania
(Ranked from fewest to most earthquakes of all intensities)

Legend
☆   Virtually no quakes
☐   Quakes are rare
◆   Moderate number of quakes
●   Frequent earthquakes

Rank	Area*	Hazard Level	Reaction
1	Austin	☆	
1	Biloxi	☆	
1	Corpus Christi	☆	
1	Houston	☆	
1	Miami	☆	
1	Orlando	☆	
1	San Antonio	☆	
1	Tampa	☆	
9	Akron	☐	
9	Baltimore	☐	
9	Baton Rouge	☐	
9	Beaumont	☐	
9	Birmingham	☐	

Rank	Area*	Hazard Level	Reaction
9	Boise	☐	
9	Charleston, W.V.	☐	
9	Chicago	☐	
9	Cleveland	☐	
9	Columbus	☐	
9	Dallas	☐	
9	Des Moines	☐	
9	Detroit	☐	
9	El Paso	☐	
9	Fargo	☐	
9	Grand Rapids	☐	
9	Hartford	☐	
9	Kansas City	☐	
9	Las Vegas	☐	
9	Little Rock	☐	
9	Milwaukee	☐	
9	Minneapolis	☐	
9	Mobile	☐	
9	Nashville	☐	
9	Nassau-Suffolk	☐	
9	Newark	☐	
9	New Orleans	☐	
9	New York	☐	
9	Norfolk	☐	
9	Omaha	☐	
9	Philadelphia	☐	
9	Pittsburgh	☐	

Rank	Area*	Hazard Level	Reaction
9	Raleigh	□	
9	Richmond	□	
9	Shreveport	□	
9	Sioux Falls	□	
9	Tulsa	□	
9	Washington, D.C.	□	
9	Wilmington	□	
48	Albany	◆	
48	Albuquerque	◆	
48	Atlanta	◆	
48	Burlington	◆	
48	Cincinnati	◆	
48	Denver	◆	
48	Fresno	◆	
48	Indianapolis	◆	
48	Louisville	◆	
48	Manchester	◆	
48	Oklahoma City	◆	
48	Phoenix	◆	
48	Portland, Me.	◆	
48	Portland, Or.	◆	
48	Providence	◆	
48	Sacramento	◆	
48	St. Louis	◆	
48	Tucson	◆	
48	Wichita	◆	
67	Anchorage	●	

Rank	Area*	Hazard Level	Reaction
67	Bakersfield	●	
67	Boston	●	
67	Buffalo	●	
07	Charleston, W.V.	●	
67	Columbia	●	
67	Great Falls	●	
67	Honolulu	●	
67	Los Angeles	●	
67	Memphis	●	
67	Rochester	●	
67	Salt Lake City	●	
67	San Diego	●	
67	San Francisco	●	
67	Seattle	●	

*Standard Metropolitan Statistical Area

The Pollution Solution

The sneakiest kinds of pollution are the most dangerous. The junked car abandoned on the side of the highway, used tissues blowing like snow across the vistas of America, and cigarette butts and dog poo on the sidewalks . . . unsightly yes, but not the pollution which can be extremely hazardous. The dangerous pollution is invisible.

Pollution is not something which was invented by man, by the way. Volcanoes, forest fires, wind erosion, and caterpillar droppings, not to mention elephants, have always dirtied up the world. But with industrialization came a fantastic increase in polluting byproducts. Approximately 90% of today's air pollution, for example, is due to man's factories, automobiles, and energy use.

How do we avoid it if it cannot be seen? By relying on the agencies which measure the various pollutants across our nation, and making our selection of places to prosper based on this vital information.

Try Not To Breathe Too Often...

George was a vigorous and handsome visitor to the Los Angeles basin and having a wonderful time meeting the famous California girls. Understandably, he was very sorry to have to tell his hosts that he'd better not go to the beach after all. "I think I'm coming down with something," he explained. "I feel kind of headachy, my eyes are watering, and when I breathe deeply my lungs hurt."

"Oh, you're all right!" they chuckled. "It's only the smog. Just try not to breathe too often."

Air pollution sure does get in the way of having fun and feeling good. Even more important, evidence is piling up that it is a major contributor to lung and breathing diseases, and can intensify and aggravate respiration and heart problems an individual already has.

We have provided air pollution information for different areas in Charts 4 and 5. Five types of pollutants are included in the charts because studies indicate their relationship to health disorders. The five pollutants and their sources are shown in Chart 4 and more completely discussed in the Appendix at the end of the book.

Air Pollution Emissions in the United States

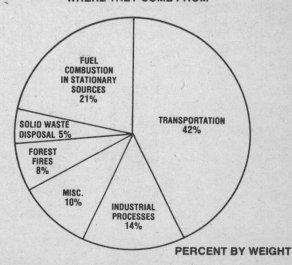

WHAT THEY ARE

OXIDES
15%

HYDRO-
CARBONS
15%

CARBON
MONOXIDE
47%

PARTICULATES
13%

NITROGEN
OXIDES
10%

WHERE THEY COME FROM

FUEL
COMBUSTION
IN STATIONARY
SOURCES
21%

SOLID WASTE
DISPOSAL 5%

FOREST
FIRES
8%

MISC.
10%

TRANSPORTATION
42%

INDUSTRIAL
PROCESSES
14%

PERCENT BY WEIGHT

AIR POLLUTION RATINGS
(Ranked alphabetically)

Legend
☆ = very good
○ = reasonable
◇ = marginal
● = health hazard

Area†	Nitrogen Dioxide	Ozone Oxident	Sulfur Dioxide	Carbon Monoxide	Suspended Particulate	Reaction
Akron	○	○	◇	☆	◇	
Albany	NA	NA	NA	NA	☆	
Albuquerque	☆	☆	☆	○	○	
Anchorage	NA	NA	NA	◇	○	
Atlanta	☆	NA	○	NA	○	

Area†	Nitrogen Dioxide	Ozone Oxidant	Sulfur Dioxide	Carbon Monoxide	Suspended Particulate	Reaction
Austin	☆	☆	☆	NA	○	
Bakersfield	◇	●	○	☆	●	
Baltimore	☆	☆	○	☆	●	
Baton Rouge	☆	●	☆	NA	○	
Biloxi	NA	NA	NA	NA	☆	
Birmingham	○	●	NA	☆	●	
Boise	NA	NA	○	●	●	
Boston	◇	NA	○	●	●	
Buffalo	☆	NA	◇	NA	◇	
Burlington	NA	☆	○	NA	NA	
Casper	NA	NA	☆	NA	◇	
Charleston, S.C.	NA	NA	○	NA	○	
Charleston, W.V.	☆	☆	○	NA	○	
Chicago	◇	☆	○	●	●	
Cincinnati	○	●	○	☆	◇	
Cleveland	◇	☆	○	◇	●	

Area†	Nitrogen Dioxide	Ozone Oxident	Sulfur Dioxide	Carbon Monoxide	Suspended Particulate	Reaction
Columbia	☆	NA	☆	NA	○	
Columbus	◇	○	○	○	◇	
Corpus Christi	☆	☆	☆	NA	◇	
Dallas	○	☆	☆	NA	◇	
Denver	◇	☆	○	●	●	
Des Moines	☆	NA	☆	●	●	
Detroit	○	☆	○	●	◇	
El Paso	☆	☆	○	☆	●	
Fargo	☆	NA	☆	☆	○	
Fresno	○	○	☆	●	●	
Grand Rapids	◇	NA	○	NA	○	
Great Falls	NA	NA	NA	◇	○	
Hartford	○	◇	○	◇	○	
Honolulu	NA	NA	☆	NA	○	
Houston	○	◇	☆	NA	●	
Indianapolis	○	◇	○	◇	◇	

Area†	Nitrogen Dioxide	Ozone Oxident	Sulfur Dioxide	Carbon Monoxide	Suspended Particulate	Reaction
Kansas City	☆	●	☆	☆	●	
Las Vegas	☆	NA	NA	NA	○	
Little Rock	☆	○	☆	NA	◇	
Los Angeles	●	●	○	●	●	
Louisville	○	●	○	●	●	
Manchester	☆	☆	○	NA	○	
Memphis	◇	●	NA	◇	◇	
Miami	NA	☆	☆	NA	○	
Milwaukee	○	☆	◇	☆	◇	
Minneapolis	○	☆	○	●	◇	
Mobile	NA	●	○	NA	◇	
Nashville	○	☆	○	○	○	
Newark	○	NA	○	☆	◇	
New Orleans	○	☆	☆	NA	○	
New York	○	☆	◇	☆	○	
Norfolk	☆	●	○	☆	○	

Area†	Nitrogen Dioxide	Ozone Oxident	Sulfur Dioxide	Carbon Monoxide	Suspended Particulate	Reaction
Oklahoma City	☆	☆	☆	NA	◇	
Omaha	○	☆	○	☆	◇	
Orlando	☆	NA	☆	NA	○	
Philadelphia	◇	☆	◇	○	◇	
Phoenix	☆	☆	☆	●	●	
Pittsburgh	NA	◇	●	●	●	
Portland, Me.	☆	NA	○	NA	○	
Portland, Or.	○	☆	○	●	○	
Providence	○	☆	◇	●	●	
Raleigh	☆	NA	○	NA	○	
Richmond	☆	○	○	☆	○	
Rochester	☆	○	◇	NA	○	
Sacramento	○	◇	○	◇	●	
Salt Lake City	○	●	○	●	●	
San Antonio	☆	☆	☆	NA	○	
San Diego	◇	○	☆	☆	◇	

Area†	Nitrogen Dioxide	Ozone Oxident	Sulfur Dioxide	Carbon Monoxide	Suspended Particulate	Reaction
San Francisco	○	☆	☆	NA	○	
Seattle	◇	☆	○	●	◇	
Shreveport	☆	NA	☆	☆	○	
Sioux Falls	☆	NA	☆	NA	○	
St. Louis	☆	○	○	◇	●	
Tampa	☆	☆	○	NA	◇	
Tucson	☆	☆	☆	●	◇	
Tulsa	◇	●	○	☆	●	
Washington, D.C.	○	◇	○	●	◇	
Wichita	NA	NA	○	○	○	
Wilmington	○	NA	◇	NA	●	

Nitrogen Dioxide
☆ = < 50
○ = 51-75
◇ = 76-99
● = 100 +

Ozone Oxident
☆ = < 160
○ = 161-200
◇ = 201-234
● = 235 +

Sulfur Dioxide
☆ = < 11
○ = 12-50
◇ = 51-80
● = 81 +

Carbon Monoxide
☆ = < 4
○ = 5-6
◇ = 7-10
● = < 10

Suspended Particulate
☆ = < 35
○ = 36-60
◇ = 6-74
● = 75 +

And Don't Drink the Water

Not long ago a river which flows (or should we say oozes) into Lake Erie was declared a *fire hazard*, it was so polluted. Imagine explaining to an insurance company that,

"I'd like to file a claim, please. Robert Smith lost his life in a boating accident. Pardon? No, he didn't drown, actually. He, uh . . . he was smoking and he . . . well, he fell in the river and was burned to a crisp."

During the drought in the northeast in 1980–81, more than half of the water in the Passaic River in New Jersey was *sewage*! The water authorities claimed that by putting four times as much chlorine in the water as usual they were able to make it fit for drinking. It probably made an excellent lawn fertilizer as well!

Water pollution in America is such that you should give careful consideration to an area's resources before deciding whether it is your best place to prosper. No one knows for sure what the long term effects of the various chemicals in water supplies really are. And as we use more water all the time, water conservation and pollution will become increasingly important issues.

The water pollution information most useful to you likely pertains to drinking water. Chart 6 shows the rankings of areas by the suspected cancer causing pollutants in the potable water.

DRINKING WATER POLLUTANTS— SUSPECTED CARCINOGENS
(Ranked from least to most micrograms per liter of water sampled)

Rank	Area†	Micrograms/ liter	Reactions
1	Fresno	.4	
2	Baton Rouge	2	
3	Boston	5	
4	Portland, Me.	7	
5	Providence	8	
6	San Antonio	13	
7	Albuquerque	15	
7	Des Moines	15	
9	Boise	16	
10	Milwaukee	16	
11	Memphis	17	
12	Portland, Or.	20	
13	Buffalo	23	
14	Nashville	24	
15	Wichita	27	
16	Sacramento	29	
17	Detroit	34	

Rank	Area†	Micrograms/liter	Reactions
17	Kansas City	34	
17	Richmond	34	
20	Hartford	36	
21	Denver	39	
22	Casper	41	
23	Little Rock	42	
24	Pittsburgh	43	
24	Salt Lake City	43	
25	Cleveland	49	
25	Los Angeles	49	
27	Chicago	50	
27	Tulsa	50	
29	St. Louis	51	
30	Manchester	60	
31	Wilmington	64	
32	Baltimore	65	
33	Grand Rapids	69	
34	Atlanta	75	
34	Birmingham	75	
36	Las Vegas	76	
37	San Francisco	78	
38	Dallas	79	
38	Sioux Falls	79	
40	Indianapolis	82	
41	Minneapolis	90	
42	Burlington	91	
43	San Diego	97	

Rank	Area†	Micrograms/ liter	Reactions
44	Washington, D.C.	110	
45	Omaha	120	
46	Phoenix	130	
47	Louisville	150	
47	Norfolk	150	
49	Charleston, S.C.	200	
49	Oklahoma City	200	
51	Columbus	210	
52	Tampa	230	
53	Houston	250	

†Incorporated Cities

Doing the Twist: Tornadoes

Tornadoes are awesome. They are the most violent winds on the earth, with speeds at the center up to 300 miles per hour! In 1975 a Mississippi tornado carried a home freezer more than a mile. In 1931 a Minnesota tornado carried an 83 ton railroad car and its 117 passengers 80 feet (at no extra charge). In 1925 a single twister traveled across Missouri, Illinois, and Indiana at about 60 miles per hour and killed 689 people. And in 1974 a super outbreak of 148 tornadoes whipped across a 13 state area from Michigan to Alabama within a few hours, killed over 300 people, injured over 6,000, and caused $600 million in damage!

What are the chances of a tornado striking an area? In the far west, practically zero. And even in the areas most frequently subject to tornadoes, it's only about once every 250 years! One reason is that although tornadoes, also called cyclones, are powerful, they are not really very large. On the average, tornado paths are only a quarter of a mile wide and rarely travel more than fifteen miles. Their usual speed is about 30 miles per hour, but the bigger and faster they are, the more devastating. The months with the most twisters are April, May, and June, and they are most likely on the Gulf Coast and midwest.

Chart 7 shows the tornado incidence in America for a recent 25 year period.

TORNADO DANGER RATINGS
(Ranked from least to most danger)

Legend
☐ = Scarce
○ = Low
◆ = Medium
● = High

Rank	Area†	Hazard Level	Reaction
1	Anchorage	None	
2	Bakersfield	☐	
2	Boise	☐	
2	Great Falls	☐	
2	Honolulu	☐	
2	Las Vegas	☐	
2	Los Angeles	☐	
2	Portland, Or.	☐	
2	San Diego	☐	
2	San Francisco	☐	
2	Seattle	☐	
12	Albany	○	
12	Buffalo	○	
12	Charleston, W.V.	○	
12	El Paso	○	

Rank	Area†	Hazard Level	Reaction
12	Fresno	○	
12	Nassau-Suffolk	○	
12	New York	○	
12	Phoenix	○	
12	Portland, Me.	○	
12	Providence	○	
12	Rochester	○	
12	Salt Lake City	○	
12	Tucson	○	
12	Washington, D.C.	○	
26	Baltimore	◆	
26	Burlington	◆	
26	Denver	◆	
26	Louisville	◆	
26	Minneapolis	◆	
26	Norfolk	◆	
26	Philadelphia	◆	
26	Pittsburgh	◆	
26	Raleigh	◆	
26	Richmond	◆	
36	Akron	●	
36	Albuquerque	●	
36	Atlanta	●	
36	Austin	●	
36	Baton Rouge	●	
36	Beaumont	●	
36	Biloxi	●	

Rank	Area†	Hazard Level	Reaction
36	Birmingham	●	
36	Boston	●	
36	Charleston, S.C.	●	
36	Chicago	●	
36	Cincinnati	●	
36	Cleveland	●	
36	Columbia	●	
36	Columbus	●	
36	Corpus Christi	●	
36	Dallas	●	
36	Des Moines	●	
36	Detroit	●	
36	Fargo	●	
36	Grand Rapids	●	
36	Hartford	●	
36	Houston	●	
36	Indianapolis	●	
36	Kansas City	●	
36	Little Rock	●	
36	Manchester	●	
36	Memphis	●	
36	Miami	●	
36	Milwaukee	●	
36	Mobile	●	
36	Nashville	●	
36	Newark	●	
36	New Orleans	●	

Rank	Area†	Hazard Level	Reaction
36	Oklahoma City	●	
36	Omaha	●	
36	Orlando	●	
36	San Antonio	●	
36	Shreveport	●	
36	Sioux Falls	●	
36	St. Louis	●	
36	Tampa	●	
36	Tulsa	●	
36	Wichita	●	
36	Wilmington	●	

†Incorporated City

284

The Mighty Hurricanes

In 1972 Hurricane Agnes killed 122 people and did two *billion* dollars worth of damage between North Carolina and New York. Best way to avoid the hurricane devastation which booms into the gulf and east coast states? Crawl into a closet . . . in North Dakota.

Map 2 indicates the relative frequency of destructive hurricanes over a period of fifty years and Chart 8 reflects the hurricane hazard level for 81 of our areas.

Number of Times During Fifty Year Period
Destruction was Caused by Hurricanes

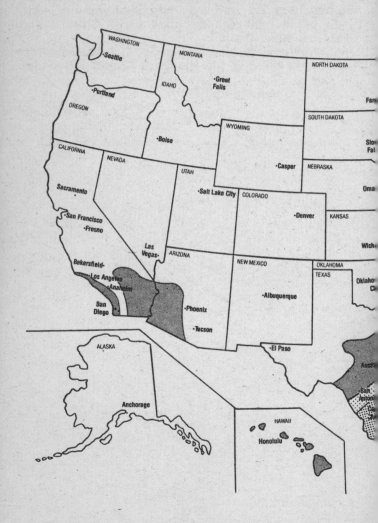

MAP 2

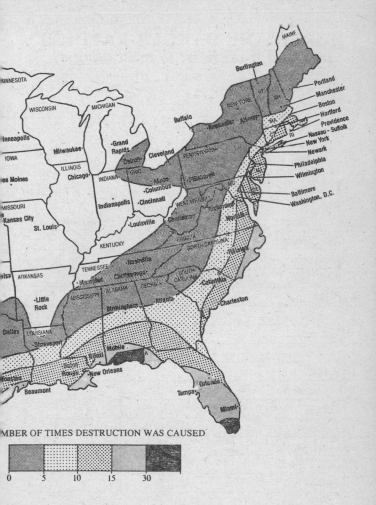

NUMBER OF TIMES DESTRUCTION WAS CAUSED

0   5   10   15   30

HURRICANE DANGER RATINGS
(Ranked from least to most danger)

Legend
☆ = No hurricanes
□ = Rarely significant
○ = Moderately significant
◆ = Major significance
● = Extreme significance

Rank	Area†	Hazard Level	Reaction
1	Albuquerque	☆	
1	Anchorage	☆	
1	Bakersfield	☆	
1	Boise	☆	
1	Chicago	☆	
1	Cincinnati	☆	
1	Columbus	☆	
1	Denver	☆	
1	Des Moines	☆	
1	El Paso	☆	
1	Fresno	☆	
1	Grand Rapids	☆	
1	Great Falls	☆	
1	Indianapolis	☆	

Rank	Area†	Hazard Level	Reaction
1	Kansas City	☆	
1	Las Vegas	☆	
1	Louisville	☆	
1	Milwaukee	☆	
1	Minneapolis	☆	
1	Oklahoma City	☆	
1	Omaha	☆	
1	Phoenix	☆	
1	Portland, Or.	☆	
1	Sacramento	☆	
1	Salt Lake City	☆	
1	San Francisco	☆	
1	Seattle	☆	
1	Sioux Falls	☆	
1	St. Louis	☆	
1	Tucson	☆	
1	Wichita	☆	
33	Akron	☐	
33	Buffalo	☐	
33	Burlington	☐	
33	Charleston, W.V.	☐	
33	Cleveland	☐	
33	Detroit	☐	
33	Fargo	☐	
33	Honolulu	☐	
33	Los Angeles	☐	
33	Memphis	☐	

Rank	Area†	Hazard Level	Reaction
33	Nashville	□	
33	Pittsburgh	□	
33	Rochester	□	
33	San Diego	□	
47	Albany	○	
47	Atlanta	○	
47	Austin	○	
47	Baltimore	○	
47	Birmingham	○	
47	Dallas	○	
47	Little Rock	○	
47	Manchester	○	
47	Portland, Me.	○	
47	San Antonio	○	
47	Shreveport	○	
47	Washington, D.C.	○	
59	Boston	◆	
59	Charleston, S.C.	◆	
59	Columbia	◆	
59	Hartford	◆	
59	Newark	◆	
59	Nassau-Suffolk	◆	
59	New York	◆	
59	Philadelphia	◆	
59	Raleigh	◆	
59	Richmond	◆	
59	Wilmington	◆	

Rank	Area†	Hazard Level	Reaction
59	Baton Rouge	●	
70	Beaumont	●	
70	Biloxi	●	
70	Corpus Christi	●	
70	Houston	●	
70	Miami	●	
70	Mobile	●	
70	New Orleans	●	
70	Norfolk	●	
70	Orlando	●	
70	Providence	●	
70	Tampa	●	

Ben Franklin Should Have Lived in Tampa

Are you one of those bravest of all souls who can go calmly about your business amidst the crackling flashes and tumultuous booming of an honest-to-Fred rip-roaring thunderstorm right over your head? Are nature's pyrotechnics exciting for you?

Or are you like most of us? We count the seconds between lightning and thunder, measuring the approach of what might be that final electrifying experience. We laugh a little louder in our conversations, at the same time edging away from the windows and anything that looks suspiciously like an electric appliance. And the quick deals we try to make with God . . . "God, I won't cheat on my taxes any more. Just don't let the lightning hit this house! Especially this bed I'm hiding under."

Thunderstorm dangers are not restricted to lightning, by the way. Very strong winds, heavy rainfall, and hailstorms also are destructive. While almost no one has been killed by being hailed to death, hailstorms can be extremely damaging to crops and paint.

The number of days of thunderstorms, ranked by area, is shown in Chart 9. The west coast has the fewest, and the Gulf Coast has the most.

NUMBER OF DAYS OF THUNDERSTORMS
(Ranked from fewest to most)

Rank	Area†	# of Days	Reactions
1	Anchorage	1	
2	San Francisco	2	
3	Bakersfield	3	
3	San Diego	3	
5	Fresno	5	
5	Sacramento	5	
7	Los Angeles	6	
7	Seattle	6	
9	Honolulu	7	
9	Portland, Or.	7	
11	Las Vegas	13	
12	Boise	15	
13	Nassau-Suffolk	18	
13	New York	18	
15	Boston	19	
16	Phoenix	20	
16	Portland, Me.	20	
18	Providence	21	
19	Baltimore	24	

Rank	Area†	# of Days	Reactions
19	Manchester	24	
21	Newark	25	
22	Burlington	27	
22	Great Falls	27	
24	Albany	28	
24	Hartford	28	
24	Tucson	28	
24	Washington, D.C.	28	
28	Rochester	29	
29	Buffalo	30	
29	Fargo	30	
29	Wilmington	30	
32	Corpus Christi	32	
33	Detroit	33	
34	Pittsburgh	35	
34	San Antonio	35	
36	Columbus	36	
36	Chicago	36	
36	El Paso	36	
36	Minneapolis	36	
36	Norfolk	36	
41	Grand Rapids	37	
41	Milwaukee	37	
41	Richmond	37	
44	Cleveland	38	
44	Denver	38	
46	Akron	39	

Rank	Area†	# of Days	Reactions
47	Austin	40	
48	Dallas	41	
48	Salt Lake City	41	
50	Philadelphia	42	
51	Albuquerque	43	
51	St. Louis	43	
53	Charleston, W.V.	45	
53	Raleigh	45	
55	Sioux Falls	47	
55	Indianapolis	47	
57	Atlanta	50	
57	Kansas City	50	
57	Memphis	50	
60	Oklahoma City	51	
60	Omaha	51	
62	Cincinnati	52	
62	Columbia	52	
62	Louisville	52	
62	Nashville	52	
66	Tulsa	53	
66	Wichita	53	
68	Des Moines	55	
69	Little Rock	56	
70	Charleston, S.C.	58	
70	Shreveport	58	
72	Houston	59	
73	Beaumont	63	

Rank	Area†	# of Days	Reactions
74	Birmingham	65	
75	Miami	71	
76	New Orleans	73	
77	Baton Rouge	80	
77	Biloxi	80	
79	Orlando	85	
80	Mobile	86	
81	Tampa	91	

†Incorporated City

The Nuclear Reactor Factor

The potential danger from nuclear power reactors and the storage of nuclear waste is, as you know from reading bumper stickers, very controversial. Our intention is not to add to the debate, but to show you where the possible hazards are and let you make your own choices.

Map 3 shows the locations of nuclear power reactors in the United States. Map 4 identifies active and inactive storage sites for commercial and government nuclear waste and shows nuclear weapons storage. We'll have to ask you to keep the locations a secret.

Nuclear Power Reactors in the United States

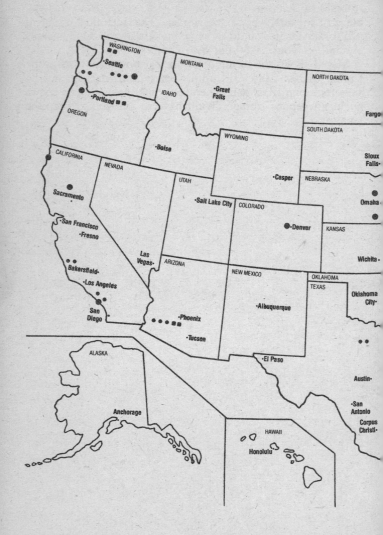

MAP 3

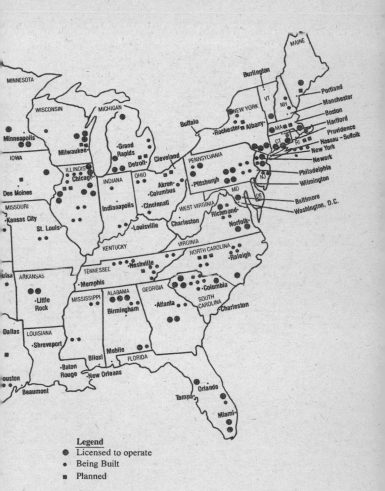

Legend
- Licensed to operate
- Being Built
- Planned

Nuclear Weapons Locations in the United States

Whidbey Is. Air Station
Trident Sub Base
McChord AFB
Portland International Airport
Great Falls Int. Airport
Fairchild AFB
WASHINGTON
Hanford Reservation Weapons Material (United Nuclear/Rockwell)
OREGON
MONTANA
Malmstrom AFB
Minot AFB
NORTH DAKOTA
SOUTH DAKOTA
Ellsworth AFB
IDAHO
Idaho Lab. Weapons Material (Exxon)
WYOMING
Kingsley Field
Mountain Home AFB
Sierra Army Depot
CALIFORNIA
NEVADA
UTAH
Travis AFB
Mather AFB
Concord Weapons Station
Weapons Design
Alameda Naval Air Station
Livermore Lab (Univ. of Calif.) Weapons Design
Castle AFB
Fresno Air Terminal
Moffett Field Air Station
Lemoore Naval Air Station
Nevada Test Site
Nellis AFB
George AFB
Norton AFB
ARIZONA
Long Beach Station and Seal Beach Weapons Station
March AFB
San Diego Naval Base and North Island Air Station
Davis Monthan AFB
Hill AFB
COLORADO
F. E. Warren AFB
NEBRASKA
Rocky Flats Plant Weapons Production (Rockwell)
KANSAS
McConnell
NEW MEXICO
Los Alamos Lab (Univ. of Calif.) Weapons Design
Kirtland AFB
Sandia Lab (Western Electric) Weapons Design
Cannon AFB
OKLAHOMA
TEXAS
Tinker
Ft. S
Pantex Plant (Mason & Hanger) Nuclear Weapons Assem
Dyess AFB
ALASKA
Galena Airport
Eielson AFB
King Salmon Airport
Elmendorf AFB
Adak Naval Station
Kelly AFB
Pearl Harbor Naval Base
West Loch Weapons Storage
Hickham AFB
Barbers Pt. Air Station
HAWAII
Waikele Weapons Storage

MAP 4

Loring AFB
MAINE
...rks AFB
...or Field
K. I. Sawyer AFB
WISCONSIN
MICHIGAN
Wurtsmith AFB
Plattsburgh AFB
Brunswick Air Station
NEW YORK
VT
NH
Pease AFB
Griffiss AFB
MA
Otis AFB
MINNESOTA
IOWA
ILLINOIS
Selfridge ANG Base
Niagara Falls Intl. Airport
Seneca Army Depot (Storage
CT
RI
New London Sub Base
OHIO
INDIANA
Ashtabula Plant (Reactive Metals) Weapons Material
Mound Lab. (Monsanto) Weapons Production
Portsmouth Plant (Goodyear) Weapons Material
PENNSYLVANIA
McGuire
NJ
DE
MD
Earle Weapons Station
Atlantic City Airport
MISSOURI
Kansas City Plant (Bendix) Weapons Production
Fernald Plant (National Lead) Weapons Material
KENTUCKY
WEST VIRGINIA
Yorktown Naval Weapons Station
Langley AFB
Oceana Naval Air Station
Whiteman AFB
Paducah Plant (Union Carbide) Weapons Material
VIRGINIA
Norfolk Naval Base
TENNESSEE
Y-12 Plant (Union Carbide) Weapons Production
NORTH CAROLINA
Seymour Johnson AFB
Blytheville AFB
SOUTH CAROLINA
Little Rock AFB
ALABAMA
GEORGIA
Savannah River Plant (Dupont) Weapons Production
Carswell AFB
ARKANSAS
LOUISIANA
Robins AFB
Charleston AFB
Charleston Naval Base and Weapons Station
Barksdale AFB
MISSISSIPPI
Moody AFB
King's Bay Sub. Base
...ton AFB
Jacksonville Intl. Airport
Mayport Naval Station
Cecil Field N.A.S.
Jacksonville Air Station
Tyndall AFB
FLORIDA
MacDill AFB
Pinellas Plant (General Electric) Weapons Production
Homestead AFB

Key:

⚓ Navy

✈ Army

▮ ICBM Missile Base and Field

⚛ Nuclear Weapons Design and Production (Dept. of Energy)

☢ Radioactive Waste Burial Ground

✈ Air Force

SUMMARY GRID

Directions: Rate only those cities below which are on your Tentative Interest List. Give a 5 to those cities with predominance of (+) ratings on the various charts in this chapter. Give a 3 if a city has only enough (+) marks to remain of interest. Give a 1 to those with few (+) marks. Eliminate from your Tentative Interest List those cities for which you've lost all interest; add additional cities as interest develops and rate them as above.

		Rating (5, 3 or 1)	Comments
1	Akron, Ohio		
2	Albany, New York		
3	Albuquerque, New Mexico		
4	Anchorage, Alaska		
5	Atlanta, Georgia		
6	Austin, Texas		
7	Bakersfield, California		
8	Baltimore, Maryland		
9	Baton Rouge, Louisiana		
10	Beaumont, Texas		
11	Biloxi, Mississippi		
12	Birmingham, Alabama		
13	Boise, Idaho		
14	Boston, Massachusetts		
15	Buffalo, New York		
16	Burlington, Vermont		
17	Casper, Wyoming		

		Rating (5, 3 or 1)	Comments
18	Charleston, South Carolina		
19	Charleston, West Virginia		
20	Chicago, Illinois		
21	Cincinnati, Ohio		
22	Cleveland, Ohio		
23	Columbia, South Carolina		
24	Columbus, Ohio		
25	Corpus Christi, Texas		
26	Dallas, Texas		
27	Denver, Colorado		
28	Des Moines, Iowa		
29	Detroit, Michigan		
30	El Paso, Texas		
31	Fargo, North Dakota		
32	Fresno, California		
33	Grand Rapids, Michigan		
34	Great Falls, Montana		
35	Hartford, Connecticut		
36	Honolulu, Hawaii		
37	Houston, Texas		
38	Indianapolis, Indiana		
39	Kansas City, Missouri		
40	Las Vegas, Nevada		
41	Little Rock, Arkansas		
42	Los Angeles, California		
43	Louisville, Kentucky		
44	Manchester, New Hampshire		

303

		Rating (5, 3 or 1)	Comments
45	Memphis, Tennessee		
46	Miami, Florida		
47	Milwaukee, Wisconsin		
48	Minneapolis, Minnesota		
49	Mobile, Alabama		
50	Nashville, Tennessee		
51	Nassau-Suffolk, New York		
52	Newark, New Jersey		
53	New Orleans, Louisiana		
54	New York, New York		
55	Norfolk, Virginia		
56	Oklahoma City, Oklahoma		
57	Omaha, Nebraska		
58	Orlando, Florida		
59	Philadelphia, Pennsylvania		
60	Phoenix, Arizona		
61	Pittsburgh, Pennsylvania		
62	Portland, Maine		
63	Portland, Oregon		
64	Providence, Rhode Island		
65	Raleigh, North Carolina		
66	Richmond, Virginia		
67	Rochester, New York		
68	Sacramento, California		
69	Salt Lake City, Utah		
70	San Antonio, Texas		
71	San Diego, California		

		Rating (5, 3 or 1)	Comments
72	San Francisco, California		
73	Seattle, Washington		
74	Shreveport, Louisiana		
75	Sioux Falls, South Dakota		
76	St. Louis, Missouri		
77	Tampa, Florida		
78	Tucson, Arizona		
79	Tulsa, Oklahoma		
80	Washington, D.C.		
81	Wichita, Kansas		
82	Wilmington, Delaware		

7

Quality of Life

For many people, the most important factor in choosing a place to prosper is the "quality of life" possible there. They value a certain quality of lifestyle and cultural opportunity more than weather, money, safety, or population characteristics.

When you think about it, how *well* we live may be more important than how *long* we live.

But a problem is apparent. The judgment of quality is up to each person. We do not have absolute measures of the quality of life which each place offers. We can measure inches of rainfall or incomes earned, but can not measure cultural qualities in the same way.

Each place in America is unique. Each of the 82 areas we have described in this book has much to offer . . . but what it has may not be good for you.

Similarly, each place has a unique quality of life. Some of them are culturally rich with the performing arts, museums, educational and research facilities, architectural wonders, and treasures of all sorts. These are usually, although not always, the largest and oldest of our cities.

Other regions are rich in natural beauty and recreational opportunity. For some of us, the quality of life we value offers miles of sparkling beaches and crystal clear water, or the timbered vistas of a mountain range, or wonderful rolling hills and farmlands

America has it all. Whether you enjoy the hard-driving excitement of an industrial giant, or the easy informality of a smaller area, the variety of lifestyles is marvelous.

Our intention here is to introduce you to some of the highlights and flavor of each of our 82 places to prosper. Of course, we realize that no matter how carefully presented, no summary can capture all of the cultural advantages and disadvantages of a region. Our genuine hope is that these descriptions will provide important clues and guidelines for your selection process. We have tried to be as fair and as accurate as possible, so that the impressions you gain from them will be representative of what the areas have to offer.

As you review the following descriptions, give your Tentative Interest Areas a rating of 5, 3 or 1 in the Reaction Column. Then place the ratings in the Summary Grid at the end of the chapter.

Akron, Ohio

Reaction_____

As the home base of Firestone, Goodyear, Goodrich, and General, you might guess that Akron's major industry is rubber processing. It also is known as one of the largest trucking centers in the nation. As a tire and transportation hub, perhaps it is natural that the All-American Soap Box Derby is held here.

Akron is located 30 miles south of Lake Erie on the Ohio-Eric Canal. Portgage Lakes State Park, Akron Art Institute, the Thomas Performing Arts Center, and the Akron Symphony Orchestra are major contributors to Akron's cultural life. The Cleveland Orchestra makes its summer home here, as well.

The surrounding countryside is rolling and green, and the University of Akron, Kent State University, and the Firestone

Conservatory of Music are found in this northern Ohio region.

Albany, New York

The state capital has been undergoing a renovation of much of its downtown area, with the new Empire State Plaza and new highway and bridge construction enhancing the city. The Hudson River and Erie Canal have contributed much to its economic development, but the business of governing the state of New York is the basis of Albany's strength.

This is an old and historic region, with many of the early mills and industries shut down and empty. Its major urban renewal projects, however, have transformed parts of Albany back into the attractive and pleasant city it once was. The countryside is beautiful, with dairy and crop farming amidst rolling hills near the Adirondack Mountains.

Albuquerque, New Mexico

Nestled over a mile high in the mountains, Albuquerque is surrounded by timbered slopes and lovely vistas. The air is dry and clear, with plenty of sunshine and definite seasons. And largely because of the favorable climate and gorgeous scenery, many newcomers have taken up residence here.

The long-term business climate is almost as favorable because of many reseach laboratories. The largest is Sandia Laboratories, which is engaged in nuclear research and weapons development. Many other companies specialize in electronics research.

Recreational facilities are nearby, with skiing slopes and the Cibal State Forest offering outdoor fun. Albuquerque has its own symphony orchestra, five museums, and is the home of two universities. The area is building up rapidly, but still retains its mountain city charm.

Anchorage, Alaska

Alaskans are proud of their frontier-style culture and a ruggedly individualistic approach to life. With fewer than one person per square mile in the state, and Anchorage a sprawling and enormous city, the philosophy of living uncrowded and close to the land is popular. As in days of yore, hunters and trappers still rendezvous in Anchorage, and there is much talk of government interference in Alaskans' right to develop timberlands, mineral deposits, fishing waters, and oil sites.

Anchorage has weather patterns much like those of the northeastern United States, and is an important transportation and trading center. Its airport is one of the busiest in the country, and its seaport is open year-round.

With the natural riches of Alaska, including oil discoveries and the Alaska pipeline, Anchorage has developed rapidly and continues to do so today. It has a community college, psychiatric institute, the annual Fur Rendezvous, enough new shopping centers to rival many of the areas in "the lower 48," and a developing cultural base.

Atlanta, Georgia

Ninety percent of Atlanta was destroyed in the Civil War, but since that time its residents have been dedicated to its regrowth and success. Today it is the southeast's leading commercial, industrial, and distribution center. Its financial success is an accomplished fact, with both a major national financial district and one of the busiest airports in the nation.

At the same time, the region has maintained a deep interest in cultural excellence. It is an international city in every sense, with a superb convention center, a modern and elegant downtown area, well respected cultural arts, and 29 higher education facilities. Its parks are famous, and its entertainment variety is wonderful. For the sports enthusiast, this is the home of the Braves (baseball), Falcons (football), Hawks (basketball), and Flames (hockey).

Atlanta has been growth oriented for more than a century,

and most of its homes and buildings are relatively new and modern. Vitality and enthusiasm are as much a part of the region as its rolling plateaus and pine woods. It is an ultra-sophisticated oasis in the midst of easy-going rural Georgia.

Austin, Texas

Reaction_____

The capital of Texas was built around two lakes which lie in the heart of the city, and next to the Colorado River. This is an area with lovely homes and a very attractive downtown area. The broad tree-lined avenues are illuminated at night by mercury vapor lights which were installed on tall towers in 1895. The residents are proud of their bluish "moonlight glow" from the past.

Ranching, dairy, poultry, cotton, and grain production are mainstays of the local economy. Recent additions of such industries as the manufacture of electronic products and pleasure boats have boosted the business outlook dramatically to one of the most positive in the country.

Several colleges, the L. B. Johnson Presidential Library, and a number of museums and art galleries add to the unique culture of this area.

Bakersfield, California

Reaction_____

The discovery of oil around the turn of the century helped Bakersfield develop, and oil continues to play an important part in this area's economy. In addition, a quarter of California's wine comes from the region's vineyards, and the sunny climate also produces cotton and grain. It is an important transportation center as well.

Stated succinctly, this is a friendly western city, near the Sequoia National Forest, with an emphasis on informal outdoor living, and a thriving agricultural region surrounding it.

Baltimore, Maryland

Reaction_____

Baltimore has been involved in extensive urban renewal programs for many years, and the quality of life is steadily improving. This is the home of more than fifteen colleges and universities, including Johns Hopkins University and Medical School, the University of Maryland Professional School, and the Peabody Conservatory of Music.

Baltimore is an extremely varied city, with many historical sites and museums, all facets of the performing arts, and new civic center facilities and theaters.

As an important transportation hub, with one terminus of the famous Baltimore and Ohio Railroad and the fourth largest seaport in the nation, Baltimore is a busy industrial and commercial metropolis. Major industries include metals, chemicals, food processing, petroleum, and aircraft parts. It is struggling with the problems faced by so many of the old industrialized regions of the north, but its location on Chesapeake Bay and proximity to the warmer climates of the south enhance its economic outlook.

Baton Rouge, Louisiana

Reaction_____

Probably the major cultural boast of this industrial center (petroleum, chemicals, and cement) is the sumptuous capitol building . . . which some say is a shrine to Huey Long, whose grave is located in a front garden. The building is constructed of 26 kinds of marble and various stones, and it feature a fine art exhibit and lovely gardens.

Two major universities are located here: Southern University and Louisiana State University. This is a busy Mississippi seaport, with nearby historic plantations, museums, and art galleries.

Beaumont, Texas

Reaction_____

This is not a large city, but we have predicted it to do well in the next decade. It is home to Mobil Oil Company's largest refinery, and is a producer of chemicals, synthetic rubber, forest products, ships, and oil equipment.

Beaumont is an important inland port and is located on a deep ship channel connected to the Intracoastal Waterway.

As an industrial region, very near Houston, Beaumont has been able to use the facilities and programs of its giant neighbor. Its own cultural attractions include a major theme/amusement park, several museums, La Marr University, and such events as the South Texas State Fair, Spindletop Boom Days, and the Arts and Crafts Festival. With its anticipated growth, however, one might expect an even greater emphasis on cultural development of its own.

Biloxi, Mississippi

Reaction_____

Located right in the center of what is often called "America's Riviera," Biloxi has 25 miles of lovely coastline on the Gulf of Mexico. It is an area of tropical sunshine and ocean breezes, high humidity, and casual outdoor living. The picturesque beauty of ancient mossy oaks, magnolias and camellias, historic preservations, lovely gardens, and attractive new resorts is diminished by the high level of pollution in the Gulf around Biloxi.

Fishing, boating, hunting, golfing ... outdoor activities of all sorts are found in Mississippi. This is a leading shrimp and oyster processing center, and much commercial fishing is done here. The federal government spends an enormous amount of money in Mississippi, and Keesler Air Force Base is located in Biloxi.

Birmingham, Alabama

Reaction_____

This is an iron and steel producing city, once known as "the Pittsburgh of the South." Iron ore, coal, and limestone all are mined near this industrial city, and the huge (60 tons) cast iron statue of Vulcan, god of the forge, can be seen here as a reminder of the area's rich resources.

But Birmingham is also a modern, progressive city with

opera, ballet, theater, and the clear intention of maintaining and improving its cultural life. A large zoo, museum of art, several colleges and universities, gardens and state parks all contribute to the welfare of the region.

Boise, Idaho

Reaction

When you live in Boise, which takes its name from the French word meaning trees, you live close to nature. The Boise National Forest provides wonderful opportunities for nature enthusiasts, with water sports and hiking trails aplenty. Principal industries include lumber, naturally, along with mobile home and reaction vehicle production, sugar beets, and fruit processing. Abundant hydroelectric power has benefited growth in this area.

The Bogus Basin Ski Area is a major vacation attraction, and various state and city parks add to the pleasure of outdoor living. Boise State University is located here, and a symphony orchestra is supported. This is a friendly western city with a small-town down-home atmosphere, and its clean and natural environment makes it a nice place to live.

Boston, Massachusetts

Reaction_____

New England's largest city is one of the nation's finest financial and trading centers. More than fifty insurance companies have their home offices here. Its excellent colleges and universities and financial institutions are well known. In terms of dollars invested, the largest industry is health care . . . which is considered to be exceptional. Needless to say, the regions' medical schools are held in high regard.

Does Boston have much culture? The area was once known as "the Athens of America!" Its love affairs with its Boston Pops Orchestra, the Boston Symphony, and theater and ballet companies are almost scandalous.

The Boston area parks, including the famous Boston Common, beaches and harbor islands are excellent. Recreational opportunities abound, and if you really like exercise, try the

Boston Marathon. Sports fans are as partisan and enthusiastic here as those anywhere, with a long history of supporting a variety of pennant-winning teams.

The only cultural drawback is the unfortunate fact that many Bostonians are unable to pronounce their "r's." Perhaps it is something in the watah.

Buffalo, New York

Reaction_____

Quick. What is the second largest city in the state of New York? And did you know it is an extremely important transportation hub? When the Erie Canal opened, and then the St. Lawrence Seaway, Buffalo became a world port. The railroad center is one of the largest in the nation.

Buffalo's industries have been encouraged by the available hydroelectric power from the Niagara River, and among other industries it became the world's largest grain milling center. Its largest employer now is the State University at Buffalo.

Buffalo's culture is not limited to honeymooning under the mist of Niagara Falls, by any means. It has an excellent philharmonic orchestra, over 100 nightclubs, a variety of museums, and an impressive ring of parks. Professional sports teams include the Buffalo Bills (football) and the Sabres (hockey).

Because of the economic slump in the industrial north, Buffalo has lost a considerable number of residents. However, its people are determined to revitalize and recapture its past vigor and pride.

Burlington, Vermont

Reaction_____

A small city nestled in the beautiful mountain scenery of Vermont, Burlington offers a combination of New England traditions and a very pleasant base from which to enjoy some of the finest scenery in the world.

Parks, recreation areas, Lake Champlain, and a wonderful choice of ski slopes make Burlington a splendid choice for the outdoors-oriented individual. Dairying and logging are important to the economy, as is tourism. The University of Vermont was established here in 1791 and has a lovely campus.

Vermont is extremely interested in keeping its environment ecologically balanced and clean, and recent renovation and renewal in Burlington is a part of that effort.

Casper, Wyoming

Reaction_____

Casper is a small town, but as you have observed in various charts provided in earlier chapters, this region is growing rapidly. The reasons? Oil was discovered here in 1890, and oil and mineral deposits continue to enrich the area. The energy crunch has brought added prosperity to this region of coal, uranium, and bentonite.

The elevation of Casper is nearly one mile, located next to the Platte River and near the wilderness paradise of the Rocky Mountains. Needless to say, hunting, fishing, and other outdoor recreations are an important part of the lifestyle of this central Wyoming region.

Charleston, South Carolina

Reaction_____

Filled with dignified pre-Civil War homes, with the lovely countryside dotted with numerous old plantations and world famous gardens, Charleston still has the charm and cultivated manners of the old south.

The aristocratic traditions continue in the preservation of Old Charleston, with the Dock Street Theatre, Old Slave Mart Museum, and a wonderful array of carefully restored homes and churches still maintained along its lovely winding streets.

Charleston's economy is linked to its excellent harbor, but a diversified list of businesses and industrial plants are located here. Both Air Force and Naval bases are established in the area, as well as Army and Coast Guard facilities. Many tourists come to admire Cypress Gardens, assorted historic monuments, marvelous plantations and parks, and superb sightseeing. Numerous annual events celebrate art and beauty in various forms.

Charleston, West Virginia

Reaction_____

Charleston is the capital of the state and a trade center for the Great Kanawha Valley, an area rich in natural resources, including lumber, coal, oil, natural gas, and, of all things, brine. It is ranked high among the country's centers of chemical and glass production.

Among the area's cultural resources are its lovely physical setting, a variety of parks both large and small, the State Science and Culture Center, and Sunrise, which is a complex of buildings devoted to an art gallery, children's museum and planetarium, and a garden center.

Even though Charleston is relatively small, it has a symphony orchestra, a light opera guild, and theater group. Several colleges are located in this lovely region.

Chicago, Illinois

Reaction_____

This is an industrial giant, built on the manufacturing might of 13,000 or so factories, the largest rail center in the nation, one of the busiest airports, access to the ocean via the St. Lawrence Seaway and the Great Lakes, mills and processing plants for the bounty of the Great Plains, and an ethnic mix of residents which lends even more spice and flavor to this blend of power.

And yet it is refined power, with cultural niceties and modern beauty. There are nearly 500 parks in Chicago, and the lakefront along Lake Michigan is a fringe of green parkland for miles. The arts are important here, with a world-renowned orchestra, opera, galleries and museums of all kinds, zoos, planetariums . . . the list is almost endless.

Chicago is one of the major educational centers in the nation, and boasts enormous capacity for conventions and trade shows. It is a major financial center and marketplace, and its cosmopolitan style combined with its vitality makes this area worth your careful consideration as a place to prosper.

Cincinnati, Ohio

Reaction_____

As the place where the Environmental Protection Agency has its headquarters, Cincinnati has been undergoing renovations and redevelopment in its downtown and riverfront areas and improving even more what has long been a lovely and thriving city.

The industries of Cincinnati are highly diversified, including bedding manufacturing, piano construction, soap, playing cards, radar equipment, and a great variety of sundry products. Several universities and colleges are located in this region, including the University of Cincinnati.

Cincinnati maintains a convention and exposition center, sports facilities including those for the Reds (baseball) and Bengals (football), and several museums and galleries. As you might expect, the region also supports a symphony and the ballet. Parks and scenic drives add to the beauty of the region.

Cleveland, Ohio

Reaction_____

The economy of Cleveland has depended on its location amidst so much of the manufacturing and commerce of the nation, and on the iron, steel, and automobile industries. In addition to being a major industrial city, Cleveland has a large convention center, a network of 17,500 park acres called "the Emerald Necklace," and some lovely residential areas.

As one of the industrial cities of the north losing population, Cleveland has been struggling to retain its economic viability in the face of higher energy costs and economic bad times. It is Ohio's largest city, however, and retains an enormous reservoir of financial strength and skilled workers.

Columbia, South Carolina

Reaction_____

The broad avenues of Columbia were originally intended to reduce the spread of malaria, but they add a lot of the charm to the lovely city of Columbia. The area is dotted with lakes and set in the wooded center of South Carolina.

Well over a hundred state and federal agencies are located here, comprising a substantial portion of the economic base of the region. Many retired persons make their homes in Columbia, enjoying the mild climate, several museums, and a variety of cultural facilities. A philharmonic orchestra, ballet, choral society, and the like are supported, and several colleges and the very large University of South Carolina are located here as well. The people here are proud of their historic traditions and southern lifestyle.

Columbus, Ohio

Reaction_____

This is an attractive state capital, located in the center of the state, with wide avenues, many parks, and one of the largest universities in the country, Ohio State University. This last is almost a city in itself.

Coal mining, aircraft assembly, printing, and manufacturing of all sorts are part of the economic strength of the area. However, the biggest enterprises are the state government itself and education, with several other colleges somehow sharing the space with Ohio State U.

The area supports its own symphony, theater companies, ballet, and various museums. In addition to several medical centers and hospitals, a children's hospital is located here. Columbus resident typically are sports enthusiasts and followers of the "Big Ten" college athletic conference. This is a highly populated region but it retains much of the charm of a small town.

Corpus Christi, Texas

Reaction_____

This area is an industrial and livestock center, but because of its fine harbor it is also a resort area, with fishing, swimming, and various water sports. Many tourists visit the region, enjoying the Corpus Christi Museum, the important

Naval Air Station, and the excellent beaches and fishing of Padre Island. This 110-mile stretch of beachfront has seen rapid construction of high-rise condominiums and a wide variety of beach homes, but the beachcombing for shells, driftwood, and assorted flotsam remains exciting

The federal government adds to the economic well-being of the area with its various programs, and oil-related industries, aluminum plants, and commercial fishing also contribute to its commercial life.

An art museum, symphony, and little theater, plus activities related to the two major colleges located here, augment Corpus Christi's cultural dimensions.

Dallas, Texas

Reaction_____

Cosmopolitan, somewhat formal, urbane and sophisticated, Dallas is not a cowboy town. It is, rather, a modern center of trade, finance, transportation, manufacturing, and a giant among America's cities. Within a 50 mile radius of the city are over 25 colleges and universities providing services to over 200,000 students. Its medical facilities are both numerous and highly regarded.

Dallas considers itself to be the cultural center of Texas . . . if not the nation. It offers ballet, opera, symphony, museums, and a variety of theaters, along with the diverse programs one would expect of a cultural leader. As a convention site, Dallas deserves a high rating, with three huge convention halls and supportive hotels and services in abundance. Sports and recreation? Also plentiful and varied.

This is a well-dressed area, as befits one of the nation's fashion and clothing manufacturing centers. In addition, Dallas is a thriving transportation center, with oil, aerospace, insurance, and finance thrown in for good measure.

The city has valued the arts and cultural pursuits since its early days, and its breadth and depth of cultural opportunity are the fruits of this long-standing effort.

Denver, Colorado

Reaction_____

With a dry, mild, and mile-high climate, proximity to the splendor of the Rocky Mountains, and a vigorously growing economy, Denver is a city with an exciting and dynamic quality of life. Innumerable educational, cultural, and recreational facilities make this a busy and multi-dimensional metropolis.

Aerospace, the Atomic Energy Commission, a federal mint, food processing, the Coors Brewery, the Federal Solar Energy Research Institute, and many other varied and fascinating industries add to the excitement and diversified strength of this burgeoning region. It is a thriving vacation center, located close to the Denver Mountain Park System, with a zillion things to see and do. Several major medical research centers are located here, as well.

Des Moines, Iowa

Reaction_____

Located near the center of the United States, Des Moines is middle America in every sense. This prairie city, surrounded by rolling rich loam, reflects the agricultural base on which is was founded, with pleasant and hard working residents.

It is the capital of Iowa, with a towering 23-carat dome on the Capitol Building. It was even more impressive when gold was over $800 an ounce!

The home offices of more than fifty insurance companies are located in Des Moines, and it has a fairly active industrial base for a city of this size. A symphony, several colleges and universities, a convention center, and a love of flowers are all found here, along with a whopping state fair in August.

Detroit, Michigan

Reaction_____

This is "Motor City," home of General Motors, Ford, Chrysler, and American Motors. And the labor counterpart to these giants, the UAW, placed its international headquarters here too.

Other important industries include machine tools, iron products, industrial chemicals, pharmaceuticals, and much more.

Interestingly, this is one of the few places in America where you will see Canada if you look south.

Art museums, auto museums (naturally), a newly developed 75-acre civic center complex with convention facilities, a symphony, and the institute of art are all part of the recent cultural efforts this area has made to offest the city's earlier singleminded emphasis on growth and production. Numerous recreation areas are near at hand.

Unemployment has been extremely high, and Detroit has been losing population like many of the other industrialized cities of the north. It is not possible to say when this trend will be slowed or reversed, but one should not assume that the former status of these older cities is irretrievable.

El Paso, Texas

Reaction_____

More than 400 manufacturing plants are located here, with oil refineries, cement plants, a copper smelter and copper refinery, cotton processing plants, and clothing manufacturers, among others.

As a border town, El Paso residents are as likely to speak Spanish as English, and traffic to and from Mexico is an accepted part of life. Clearly, El Paso is influenced by a Spanish style of life. It is a sunny area with low humidity and a low cost of living which makes it a popular retirement area. It is located at 3700 feet in the mountains, with interesting scenery and quite a range in weather.

Outdoor sports are emphasized in this climate, and there are few days when one cannot play tennis or golf. The El Paso Symphony provides a full concert season, and a large park system is maintained.

Fargo, North Dakota

Reaction_____

Did you know there are quite a few Red River Valleys in the United States? Well, Fargo is located in one of the nicest

Red River Valleys you will ever care to visit. It is a small city, clean as a whistle, safe as your mother's arms, with many residents of German descent, thrifty and industrious. North Dakota State University is located here, and Bonanzaville, U.S.A. is a reconstruction of the nineteenth century farm era.

Many parks, campsites, and recreational facilities are provided in the city, and farming and farm products help keep the economy humming.

Fresno, California

Reaction_____

This thriving area is in the heart of the famous San Joaquin Valley, sometimes referred to as "California's Garden of Eden." The region's agricultural production is incredible, including fruit, grain, and vegetables, and it is not an accident that one of the world's largest wineries and the largest dried fruit packing plant are located here.

Three national parks (Yosemite, Sequoia, and King Canyon) are nearby. Recently a downtown shopping mall was created, and community theater, opera, ballet, and philharmonic orchestra presentations are not infrequent here. California State University has a campus in Fresno. Outdoor living? Very popular, because any region which can grow such terrific grapes has to have a wonderful climate.

Grand Rapids, Michigan

Reaction_____

Of course, this area is known best for its furniture manufacturing. In addition, it has been an important convention center for many years. It is located about 100 miles from the shores of Lake Michigan, and only 15 miles from two skiing areas.

Grand Rapids is the site of fifty parks, zoological gardens, and several museums, as well as three colleges. The surrounding countryside is green, tranquil, and lovely.

Great Falls, Montana

Reaction_____

The Big Sky Country's lifestyle is based on the great outdoors, ranching, hunting, fishing, construction, farming, and the other pursuits close to the hearts of rugged individual-ists everywhere. Great Falls reflects much of that philosophy.

The city itself is almost incidental to the wonderful land surrounding it. There are towering mountains, canyons to explore, meadows and forests, all beckoning you to hike and camp or take advantage of splendid scenic drives. If you are an urban cowboy yearning for the wide open spaces but would like to locate in an interesting small city, you should give consideration to moving to Great Falls.

Incidentally, a major Strategic Air Command base (Malmstrom AFB) is here, which is the center of the largest interballistic missile complex in the free world.

Hartford, Connecticut

Reaction_____

Hartford has long been known for its many insurance companies and cultural excellence. Its recent, and highly acclaimed, urban redevelopment program has added to its attractiveness and desirability. The Hartford Civic Center and other new buildings in the downtown area include facilities for many cultural events.

One of the nation's largest art museums, several colleges, a children's museum, and a variety of historic sites add cultural and recreational richness. Jai-alai is a recent addition to the sports scene. In addition to the major contribution of the insurance business, a wide variety of other industries are represented in Hartford.

Honolulu, Hawaii

Reaction_____

Perhaps the first thing you notice upon arrival in Honolulu is the wonderful overpowering aroma of pineapples. Then one becomes aware of the other exotic odors and vivid colors of the tropics and its rich variety. The people themselves, tourists and residents alike, are an exciting mix of various races and countries, and all are garbed in hues to rival the flowers found everywhere. Restaurants feature exciting island and oriental dishes such as mahi-mahi (dolphin), shishimi (raw tuna), and, of course, poi.

323

Hotels have gone up at a prodigious rate, and the streets and beaches are generally crowded. The area's largest industry is the military complex, with seven bases scattered across the area. Other commercial contributions come from tourism, sugar cane, and pineapple.

Honolulu's residents are deeply concerned about preserving the Polynesian heritage of the islands, and a variety of museums and cultural centers are maintained. There are several hospitals, the University of Hawaii, and a special center for international students and researchers located in "Hono." But mostly it is an island paradise, with swimming, surfing, sailing, fishing, and, for the less active, sun-tanning, always part of the Honolulu scene.

Houston, Texas

Reaction_____

The fastest growing large city in the nation, with an economic outlook which is superb, Houston has an excellent chance of becoming what many of its supporters call its destiny: the most important city in America.

Houston's list of thriving industries and businesses is long and varied, with petrochemical manufacturing and other oil related industries leading the way. In addition, it supports more than 80 research centers exploring medicine, aerospace, oceanography, and much, much more.

Twenty-eight major universities are located here, with five medical schools. Its harbor is ranked number three in tonnage shipped, with only New York and New Orleans ahead. It is a space exploration headquarters, with the Lyndon B. Johnson Space Center located nearby.

Lifestyle? High, wide, and handsome. Taxes are relatively low and zoning laws are loose, so that building and investment are booming. In fact, just about everything in Houston is booming. This is a lively, sophisticated city with a wide variety of cultural interests represented. Two famous sports centers support professional teams, and five major convention and exhibit halls attract many conventions.

Of course, opera, ballet, and all the rest are supported proudly by this dynamic supercity of the present and future.

Indianapolis, Indiana

Reaction_____

Indianapolis is both the commercial and geographical center of Indiana. Its leading industries include grain markets, livestock markets and meat processing, pharmaceuticals, paper, airplane and automobile parts, and a variety of electronic manufacturing.

It is indisputable that its main claim to fame is the Indianapolis 500 automobile race, but several colleges and universities, over 13,000 acres of parklands, a zoo, museum of art, and the nation's largest children's museum all add much more to the region's cultural depth. The Indiana Pacers (professional basketball) make this their home.

Kansas City, Missouri

Reaction_____

Kansas City, Missouri, and Kansas City, Kansas, are located just across the Mississippi River from each other. Both are major industrial centers, with grain milling, food processing, petroleum refining, automobile production, and the like strengthening their mutual economies. This area also is a leading grain and livestock market for the middle west.

Kansas City, Missouri, is larger and as such has more cultural attractions and resources. Both have invested much in urban renewal in recent years and have improved their downtown areas significantly.

A very interesting variety of museums, a major theme park, several colleges, historic sites, philharmonic orchestra, and art galleries are maintained.

Las Vegas, Nevada

Reaction_____

Of course, this city built in the desert is best known for "The Strip," with its all-day and all-night gambling and glittering nightclubs. Las Vegas also is becoming known for its fantastic growth. It has a hot, dry climate, but almost every building is air-conditioned. This major entertainment area has much recreation to offer besides gambling, including golf, fishing, water sports, hunting, riding, and other popular outdoor activities.

Nellis Air Force Base is located here because it is almost always "CAVU" (excellent visibility) for flying. A number of ghost towns also are located here because they have no choice.

Little Rock, Arkansas

Reaction_____

The Arkansas River flows between Little Rock, on one bank, and North Little Rock on the other. Both are picturesque, clean, and hospitable cities, with excellent fishing, boating, and other water sports right at their doorsteps. Little Rock is the state capital, and federal investment includes an Air Force base and National Guard training center.

This culturally-oriented region supports a symphony, convention center, art center, a major campus of the University of Arkansas, and a variety of recreational facilities.

Little Rock's modern, optimistic lifestyle makes it a region worth considering as your possible place to prosper in America.

Los Angeles, California

Reaction_____

Hollywood! Excitement! A marvelous climate which has pulled people in from everywhere. So many, in fact, that urban sprawl, choked freeways and sometimes choking citizens, have made LA a big city in every sense. There are about 11 million people in the greater Los Angeles area, with an ethnic mix and cultural diversity as great as any city in America.

All manner of cultural opportunities are found here, from an abundance of major-league sports teams to excellent symphonies, museums, art galleries, theatre and ballet. The number of colleges and universities boggle the mind, and there are over 25 daily newspapers and 16 television stations.

Neighborhoods vary from the "homes of the stars" and other mansion dwellers to tacky and rundown slum areas. L.A. also has what must be among the biggest and most boring housing developments in the world, with miles and miles of the same tract houses and shopping centers repeated over and over.

Industry? A solid future, with aerospace and related fields leading the way. The entertainment industry is not kaput by any means, and the original Disneyland, Marineland, and Knotts Berry Farm continue to help attract millions of tourists.

A hint: the quality of life is better outside the "Smog Alley" created by offshore winds blowing from Los Angeles toward San Bernardino and Riverside to the east.

Louisville, Kentucky

Reaction_____

Southern in its manners and social graces, Louisville is more midwestern in its approach to business and industry. It blends a serious approach to culture with a vigorous effort to attract enterprise. It also blends half of the world's whiskey in the nine distilleries located here.

Tobacco, paint and varnish, synthetic rubber, and home appliances are produced here, with oil refineries and meat packing plants adding to the positive business outlook for this region.

Louisville is committed to supporting the arts, and conducts a public subscription fund to subsidize the highly regarded Louisville Orchestra, ballet, theater and art groups, opera, and a variety of additional cultural efforts.

The social event of the year is, of course, the annual running of the Kentucky Derby. Mint juleps, anyone?

Manchester, New Hampshrie

Reaction_____

New Hampshire is a beautiful state, justly famous for its marvelous scenery, abundant natural resources, and resort areas. At the same time, its people are also famous for their tenacity and pride. The residents of the small city of Manchester and its surrounding area can be proud of their home and their efforts to keep it economically alive.

The area refused to quit when economic hard times came

during the depression, and the spirit of independence and self-sufficiency lives on. More than 200 industries have been encouraged to establish their plants in this fairly small and conservative New England region. Most is "clean industry," such as electronics, attracted to the area by its highly motivated and skilled work force. The state's tax incentives and general "business climate" are also prime reasons for the state's recent economic strength.

Manchester remains a lovely region, however, with a variety of small art galleries, quaint restaurants, and the charm of old New England.

Memphis, Tennessee

Reaction_____

Its location on the Mississippi River makes Memphis a major port of entry for all kinds of goods, and it also is an important marketing center for four states. One third of the nation's cotton is traded here, along with an impressive amount of agricultural and livestock products. It is a focal point of many railroads, and home for more than 800 industrial plants.

Recreationally and culturally, Memphis is the home of a repertory theater, ballet, symphony, and opera. Its Acadamy of Arts and art gallery provide much in the way of cultural entertainment.

Memphis State University and a dozen or so other colleges add more cultural depth, and its medical facilities are highly regarded.

This is a modern metropolis, with southern style and charm, and a diversified economy capable and willing to invest in cultural excellence. In a number of competitions, Memphis frequently has been named as the cleanest, or safest, or quietest, or otherwise most desirable city in America. Its quality of life is recognized as outstanding.

Miami, Florida

Reaction_____

For years New Yorkers have almost automatically moved to the Miami area when they retired, so that some of Miami looks and sounds much like New York City. More recently, Cuban refugees have made a major part of downtown Miami into a Little Havana, and make up about half of the population.

These changes have produced a many faceted place, with great glitter and wealth in beachfront areas and abject poverty and slums behind the rows upon rows of hotels, motels, luxury homes, and restaurants.

More than 3500 manufacturing firms, including many clothing manufacturers, are located here, with many exports going to Latin America. It's also a major agricultural area.

The cultural emphasis here has been geared toward tourism, with horse racing, jai-alai, and approximately 60 nightclubs and theater-restaurants, 100 art galleries, the Seaquarium, Orange Bowl and Miami Dolphins professional football team, and an emphasis on informal outdoor living.

As you might expect from a well established retirement area, medical facilities are numerous and health care is regarded as excellent. Other costs of living are much more reasonable, although you can live as luxuriously and expensively here as in any other place in America.

Milwaukee, Wisconsin

Reaction_____

Think of Milwaukee and one generally thinks of breweries, for this is the world's largest brewer of beer. However, its major industry is the generating and transmitting of electrical power. In addition, it is the major port on the St. Lawrence Seaway. Other major industries include grains, diesel and gasoline engines, and construction equipment.

Higher education also is big business here, with around 50,000 college students in the area. Opera, symphony, ballet, and an art center are supported, and a convention center, performing arts center, and 13,000 acres of parkland are part of the cultural makeup of Milwaukee.

And so are sports. College sports are actively supported in this area, and professional baseball, basketball, and football games are played here.

Minneapolis/St. Paul, Minnesota

Reaction_____

They are the lovely twin cities of the north, separated by the Mississippi River, but joined by a common vigor, beauty, cleanliness, and economic strength. Both Minneapolis and St. Paul are major cities in their own right, but they complement each other well.

St. Paul is a dignified terraced city with lovely homes and many nearby lakes. Minneapolis is famed for its park system, with 153 parks within its borders! Both have thriving industries which have not felt recessions as much as other places, and both are centers for agricultural marketing.

A symphony orchestra, fine stores, a variety of theaters, museums, and art galleries, and a wide choice of nightlife activities make this region culturally diverse and exciting. Hunting and fishing are close at hand, and major league professional sports teams are supported enthusiastically. A number of highly regarded colleges and universities make their homes here.

Mobile, Alabama

Reaction_____

Picturesque historical landmarks have been preserved from the early 1800s, with their distinctly French and Spanish influence. Ten days of Mardi Gras and handsome old mansions with iron grillwork balconies invite a comparison with New Orleans, but Mobile is decidedly an industrially-oriented city as well. It is the only seaport in Alabama, with shipping and shipbuilding among the major industries. Paper, chemicals, paints, textiles, and aircraft engines also are manufactured here, attracted in large measure by the relatively low salaries. We should add that costs of living also are commensurately low as well.

Cultural opportunities are not abundant, with Cypress Creek Country Club often mentioned as a highlight, along with excellent restaurants and a real effort to maintain a first-class symphony and theater. It is not a large city, however, and lacks the resources to develop the variety of fine arts facilities, universities, medical centers, parks, and so forth which are so much a part of large metropolitan regions. But keep in mind that Mobile is part of the rising south, and appears to have every intention of further improving its cultural programs in the near future.

Nashville, Tennessee

Reaction_____

Nashville has several nicknames . . . it is known as the country music capital of America, ranking first in the recording of country music. It has also been called the "Athens of the South," and has an exact replica of the Greek Parthenon housing a magnificent art gallery. Clearly, it deserves both titles.

This is a city of enormous wealth and power, and much investment money has been spent for civic renovation and improvement. At the same time, this combination investment banking center and manufacturing giant has retained much of the charm, beauty, and sophistication of the old south.

Other industries are major and varied, giving this lovely old state capital a powerful economic base. More than a dozen colleges and universities are here, and the old gracious homes and lush countryside of the region are beautiful. Can we close this description of Nashville without mentioning the Grand Ole Opry and Opryland U.S.A.? Apparently not.

Nassau-Suffolk, New York

Reaction_____

It is not a coincidence that so many of the super-rich of days gone by built their mansions on Long Island. Close to the cultural and financial excitement of New York City, these two counties still retain much of their open-fields-and-woods charm. The strict zoning laws have kept houses spaced and even the polite industry, such as electronics and publishing, has been separated from residential areas.

The north shore of Long Island in particular retains its "old money" atmosphere, with large manicured estates and horse farms amidst the towering oaks. High rise apartments and condominiums have been excluded from most Nassau and Suffolk villages.

No large city has emerged in Nassau or Suffolk Counties, even though 2.6 million people live here. Mass transportation remains a problem, with most people having to depend on automobiles to get around. Commuting to New York City is facilitated by the extraordinarily busy Long Island Railroad. Cultural facilities are not abundant, although many colleges and universities are found on Long Island and take up some of the slack. Manhattan is only a short distance away, however.

The economy of Nassau-Suffolk has been excellent throughout the current recession, with unemployment rates only around six percent. The Atlantic Ocean and Long Island Sound provide a popular playground and help to keep temperatures relatively moderate throughout the year. Eastern Long Island, especially the Hamptons, is high on everyone's list for fashionable summer living.

Newark, New Jersey

Reaction_____

The Newark area is a major insurance center and very active manufacturing region. It is New York City's smaller sister, with many of the same strengths and liabilities. A wide diversity of products pour out of its factories, including chemicals, plastics, beer, leather goods, and automobile parts. Because many businesses have left the area, however, recent years have seen Newark making a significant urban renewal effort to lure major corporations back. Excellent strides have been made toward this end. It is one of the leading manufacturing cities in the nation, with much remaining strength.

Northern New Jersey is extremely lovely, with beautiful old homes, famous vegetable farming, and wonderful scenery. Only a short distance from Newark's suburbs is a distinctly rural region and outdoor recreational opportunities. And do not overlook the fact that all of the cultural opulence of Manhattan is only a short distance away.

New Orleans, Louisiana

You probably already know about New Orleans jazz, the famous French Quarter, the lovely wrought-iron balconies on the wonderfully preserved French and Spanish buildings, its old world charm, and, of course, Mardi Gras.

But in addition, New Orleans is a cosmopolitan and prosperous city. It has an extremely busy harbor, second only to New York City in dollar values of tonnage shipped. The population includes Creoles, who are descendants from original French and Spanish colonists, Cajuns, whose Acadian ancestors were forced to flee from Nova Scotia and settled here, and lots of just plain folks, including many retirees, who discovered that New Orleans is an exciting and lovely place to live and prosper.

This is a leading industrial, financial, and oil center, with a marvelous culture and style all its own. The quality of the air and water is excellent, and the nearby countryside is beautiful. Universities include Loyola, Tulane, Louisiana State University, and Xavier.

New York City, New York

In a word, awesome. Incredible diversity, ranging from some of the poorest slums in the nation to extraordinary opulence and wealth. Anyone who knows the greater New York area probably loves it or dislikes it intensely. It is at the same time both crowded and dirty and cosmopolitan and chic. It is culturally rich with some of the greatest museums and theaters in the world, but its cultural treasures go unnoticed and unvisited by the majority of its residents.

It is losing population rapidly . . . more rapidly than most of the other old industrial areas. Yet it remains a behemoth among cities, still the financial leader, pacesetter in the world of the performing arts, possessor of the magnificent art galleries, skyscrapers, its own university system, and so much more.

The future of "The Big Apple" is uncertain. Its detractors

contend it will fall of its own weight, that the quality of life has deteriorated beyond rescue. Crime, grime, pollution, corruption, carelessness, rudeness, and more are cited as reasons for its certain demise. On the other hand, others argue that its crime rates are not as high as many other areas, its people are busy but not rude, and pollution statistics are nowhere as dire as found in other places. The water quality, for example, has been described as excellent, and air quality is generally regarded as not nearly as bad as many other areas.

In sum, whether the New York City area has high or low quality depends on your own judgment. If you thrive on excitement, adventure, diversity, challenge, and constant change, you may find this region has much of what you are seeking. On the other hand, it might have too much of what you would prefer to avoid.

Norfolk, Virginia

Reaction_____

Norfolk is a splendid example of the resurgence of the south, based on a combination of military spending, industrial initiative, and respect for its cultural heritage. This region has one of the finest natural harbors in the world and is the home of the navy's Atlantic Fleet. The military presence in Norfolk is considerable, with 36 military commands headquartered here.

The shipping industry is extremely important, as you might guess with such a harbor, and manufacturing also contributes much to the area's wealth. Among its many enterprises are seafood processing plants and the production of farm implements and fertilizer.

Excellent colleges, 25 miles of good beaches, and a number of historical restorations are part of the culture of Norfolk, with symphony, ballet, opera, and theater encouraged and supported by the area's population.

Oklahoma City, Oklahoma

Reaction_____

Thriving, bustling, growing, Oklahoma City was literally established in a day as a result of the great land rush, and its economic strength today is almost as impressive. The city was settled on a prairie in the middle of the state, but underneath the prairie sod lay oil. Today, even the Capitol lawn has oil wells on it.

Oklahoma City sprawls over a wide area, with major financial, commercial, and industrial activity. Besides oil production and oil field equipment manufacturing, livestock, cotton, food processing, tire manufacturing, and a variety of other diversified industries are located in the region. Tinker Air Force Base and the FAA Aeronautic Center are maintained here as well.

Cultural development has followed economic growth, with major convention facilities, a variety of excellent science centers and museums, symphony, excellent medical facilities, and a fine zoo. In brief, Oklahoma's prosperity is bringing new programs and facilities to an already impressive quality of life.

Omaha, Nebraska

Reaction_____

This midwestern region is an educational leader, with at least nine colleges and universities in residence. Much of the grain produced in America is marketed here, and it is one of the biggest meatpacking and livestock marketing centers in the world.

The headquarters of the Strategic Air Command is located near Omaha, and the region also is known for lead smelting and the manufacturing of farm implements. Father Flanagan's famous Boys Town is located just west of the city.

The Orpheum, Omaha's performing arts center, presents ballet, symphony, and opera performances, and the 1,300 acre Fontenelle Forest provides nature trails along woodlands, marshes, lakesides, and prairie terrain.

The "Ak-Sar-Ben" Civic Organization (Nebraska spelled

backward) is a 60,000 member group which sponsors many of the area's cultural and entertainment events.

Orlando, Florida

Central Florida is often called the ''retirement belt,'' because so many retirees have discovered its charm and beauty. This is lake and hill country . . . in fact, there are more than 50 lakes within Orlando's city limits! Needless to say, therefore, Orlando is lovely, open, green, and parklike, and the countryside around it is diverse and interesting.

Of course, this is the home of Disney World, with Sea World, Barnum and Bailey Circus World, Kennedy Space Center, and a multitude of other attractions located not too far away. Art galleries, the Florida Symphony, a planetarium, and so forth add more traditional cultural opportunities, but for the most part, Orlando's emphasis is on pleasant outdoor living.

The region's economic growth has been excellent, with tourism supplemented by aerospace, defense, and electronics industries and a bustling transportation system.

Philadelphia, Pennsylvania

Reaction_____

From a business and financial standpoint, Philadelphia has an enormous amount going for it. It is the largest petroleum refining center on the east coast, and has the largest freshwater port in the world. Its economy also is based on diverse industries such as publishing, printing, shipbuilding, chemicals, machinery, and textiles. It also is a leader in international cargo and a major financial center.

More than fifty colleges and universities and six medical schools are located here. Almost one hundred hospitals and a sixteen-acre research complex, called the University City Science Center, are found in Philadelphia.

As you might expect of an area which twice was the capital of a newly developing nation, Philadelphia offers many cultural opportunities. Symphony orchestra, museums of art and science, a zoo, botanical gardens, ballet and opera companies, 8000 acres of parks, nearby beaches and mountains, and the home of several major league teams... this is a place with cultural diversity and depth.

Phoenix, Arizona

Reaction_____

Phoenix has been built on a flat desert, but due to intense irrigation of the surrounding farmland, the desert has been caused to bloom. In the same manner, Phoenix itself has bloomed into a large metropolis, attracting industry and retirees alike.

This is a resort and retirement area, where the sun shines warmly almost every day. In the summer it shines too warmly, with a daily average of 86 degrees... during the day the average high temperature reached is 105 degrees. Not to fear, however, because almost the entire city has been air-conditioned. The humidity is very low, moreover, and many bring their sinus, asthma, arthritis, and other health problems here for possible relief.

A number of electronics and research firms have located here, and the abundant sunshine does wonders for the cotton, lettuce, melon, citrus fruit, and vegetable crops in the region.

Phoenix has a symphony orchestra, art museum, and other museums preserving some of the area's history, but for the most part this is a sun-loving, fun-loving region which loves informal, outdoor patio living by the pool.

Pittsburgh, Pennsylvania

Reaction_____

Steeltown, U.S.A., is how most people think of Pittsburgh, and many movies and the long reign of the football champion Pittsburgh Steelers have solidified this common perception.

Yes, the area serves western Pennsylvania's mines, and one-fifth of the nation's steel is produced here. But it has experienced a remarkable improvement in its quality of life, with a dramatic reduction of air pollution, transformation of deteriorated areas into clean and modern centers, and the development of lovely parks where industrial blight existed.

The civic revitalization program cost three billion dollars and required community planning and pride. The area has a greatly diversified industrial strength, many research and testing laboratories, and America's largest inland river port. All things considered, we are very happy they didn't take famous architect Frank Lloyd Wright seriously when, after he was asked his advice as to what should be done with Pittsburgh, he replied, "Abandon it."

Pittsburgh's cultural personality is not quite a match for its industrial power but it is rich in opportunity. It has hill-climbing trollies, a symphony orchestra, opera, ballet, a planetarium, a number of highly regarded museums, well-respected universities and colleges, fine medical facilities, and many parks among other cultural delights. Sports fans just might be more enthusiastic here than in any other region.

Portland, Maine

Reaction_____

The waves crashing against a rocky beach, wilderness adventures beckoning in the distance, seafood dinners which are out of this world, and New England charm all add up to the marvelous city of Portland. This area attracts many tourists, and for good reason. The beautiful Casco Bay is dotted with islands, and the fishing and sailing boats add to the ocean vistas.

This is an old city, with fine historic sites and well preserved homes. It is a place which seems almost designed for strolling along the lovely streets and poking into quaint shops and art galleries. The University of Maine has one of its campuses here, and the economy has been remarkably robust.

Portland, Oregon

Reaction_____

This beautiful area is frequently cited as one of the most desirable places to live in America. It is surrounded by superb scenery, with mountain peaks floating ethereally in the distance, the lush and verdant Willamette Valley, forests, water-falls, lakes and streams all within easy reach. The public beaches in Oregon have to be seen to be believed, and the ecologically-minded residents insist on a clean and pollution-free environment.

This "City of Roses," as it is known, has a thriving industrial base, but relatively cheap hydroelectric power from the Columbia River keeps the air pollution level low. Its deepwater port and shipyards contribute a great deal to the area's economy.

The northwest will continue to grow, and Portland's obvi-ous destiny is to add even more economic and cultural strength. Several colleges, a medical school, various muse-ums and art galleries, a symphony orchestra, and the Opera Association add to the cultural depth. Professional sports teams are enthusiastically, but very politely, supported. Portland is a lovely place to live, with people proud of their tradition of being nice neighbors.

Providence, Rhode Island

Reaction_____

About one third of the state's population lives in Provi-dence, and the silverware and jewelry industries have employed a goodly number of its residents. The area is an important producer of hardware, various kinds of machine tools, and rubber and oil products.

Recently Providence has fallen on difficult economic times, with silver price fluctuations causing havoc with the jewelry and silverware industries. As one of the old established industrial cities, it has suffered from population loss recently and is projected to continue the outflow of residents.

Cultural highlights include Brown University, which is the seventh oldest college in the nation, the well respected Rhode Island School of Design, and a variety of homes preserved for historical purposes. The best known annual event is the "Rhody Roundup," a bicycle ride around the area followed by various recreational activities. In brief, Providence retains a distinctly small-town and old-wealth flavor, somewhat isolated from mainstream USA, with nostalgia for its early prominence as one of the first settlements in what became America. An indication of its interest in preserving the culture and charm of yesteryear is the fact that Rhode Island is the home of the Americas Cup Races for yachts.

Raleigh, North Carolina

Reaction_____

Although this region has a fairly large population, it has the appearance and demeanor of a small town. It is pleasant and charming, with few tall buildings and much of the natural beauty for which North Carolina is justly famous. More recently, however, Raleigh has been gaining economic momentum, with electronics, food processing, and research facilities for the chemical and textile industries.

The city and surrounding region is more suburban than urban, and the many colleges and universities in the area enhance its very pleasant atmosphere. The climate is moderate, costs are not high, medical facilities are excellent, and as a consequence many retired persons have relocated to North Carolina's state capital.

Richmond, Virginia

Reaction_____

Richmond, the capital of Virginia, is rich in history and proud of its role in both the Revolutionary War and the Civil War. The region is an excellent example of the new south, blending a modern industrial aggressiveness with its deep cultural heritage. It reflects new architectural trends and still retains much of the flavor of the old south.

The tobacco industry is extremely important to this area, of course, and it and the chemical industry are the region's largest employers. Printing, publishing, and the production of paper, textiles, machinery, and aluminum also contribute to the area's wealth.

The area boasts a wide variety of restored plantations, gardens, churches, monuments, homes, and in Williamsburg

340

a whole town from the early 1600s has been preserved. History buffs enjoy Richmond very much. In addition, a symphony orchestra, several universities, and the beautiful Fine Arts Museum add cultural depth to the lovely region.

Rochester, New York

Reaction_____

The area is an industrial and cultural center, with Eastman Kodak, Bausch and Lomb, Xerox, and other technical-scientific companies both bringing employment and supporting the arts. The Eastman School of Music, Eastman Theater, and Eastman House of Photography are prime examples.

Rochester is a highly respected health care center, with Memorial Hospital among the notables of the nation. Educational facilities include the University of Rochester, Rochester Institute of Technology, and several others. Its symphony orchestra, the Rochester Philharmonic, also is well regarded. The Rochester Museum and Science Center is impressive.

The city is located in the midst of fruit and truck farming, with the Genesee River winding through the lovely rolling countryside.

Sacramento, California

Reaction_____

A missile development center, two important Air Force Bases, and such natural resources as timber, oil, natural gas, and a location making it an important transportation center have Sacramento's supported economy growth. This state capital is inland, but is connected to the Pacific Ocean by a deepwater channel. Also, it is a very important marketplace for the prolific farms of the Sacramento Valley.

Several colleges and a division of the California State University are located here, along with two law schools. Fort Sutter is maintained as a museum, and the Sacramento Science Museum, Crocker Art Gallery, and the William Land Park are other cultural sites. It is often called the "Camellia Capital of the World."

St. Louis, Misouri

The strength and beauty of America's "Gateway to the West" are exemplified by the startling sight of its 630 foot stainless steel Gateway Arch looming over the city. It is a busy cultural, industrial, and commercial center, with many government facilities located here . . . several army bases, the Postal Service Data Processing Center, and an air force base. It is second only to Detroit in the number of automobiles produced. Its location at the juncture of the Mississippi and Missouri Rivers makes it a major port. The zoo is famous, and the museums, theaters, opera, symphony, planetarium, and restored historic sites provide cultural depth. Recent renovation and new construction in the downtown and riverfront areas have enhanced the quality of the city.

Four major universities and several other smaller colleges are a part of the impressive cultural picture of St. Louis.

Salt Lake City, Utah

One of the loveliest and best planned cities in the nation, the capital of Utah is industrious and energetic and proud of its heritage. As you are probably aware, the state and this region are populated primarily by members of the Church of Jesus Christ of Latter Day Saints. The area is dominated by Temple Square, and a new Center for the Cultural Arts recently has been completed.

This region is growing rapidly, and a variety of business and industrial enterprises have been attracted to this bustling city. The violent crime rate is low, and the residents are pleasant, responsible citizens. The Utah Symphony Orchestra, ballet, art galleries, theater company, major ski areas, and a location amidst the topographical splendor of Utah's great outdoors make Salt Lake City a real contender for your place to prosper.

San Antonio, Texas

Reaction_____

This is a large city, actually, but San Antonio has retained a small-town flavor despite its growth. It has a clean atmosphere and attractive homes, a quiet lifestyle, and the Alamo situated right smack-dab in the center of this beautiful old city.

The federal government is the largest employer, with several Air Force and Army bases and military medical facilities. A variety of other industries, including tourism, contribute to the area's vitality.

One of the nation's largest medical centers, the University of Texas at San Antonio, and five other universities and colleges are found here. Professional basketball and football teams have franchises here. The annual Livestock Exposition and Rodeo and the Fiesta San Antonio are exciting and remind residents of the area's multi-dimensional cultural heritage, including Mexican, Spanish, Indian and early American roots.

The area surrounding San Antonio is fairly flat, but a short distance away is the wild and wooly hill country where the late Lyndon Johnson's ranch is located. Finally, San Antonio offers many interesting and well preserved homes and museums for your exploration, and historical sites abound. And what other city has the Texas Ranger Museum?

San Diego, California

Reaction_____

It's a navy-oriented city, half an hour's drive from Mexico, with a balmy year-round climate, an expensive mecca for the wealthy retired, growing rapidly with "polite industry" and relatively little pollution, lush with flowers and palms . . . sound wonderful? It is.

The beautiful hook-shaped harbor is home to the 11th Naval District, with ships of all sizes constantly coming and going. One out of every ten retired naval officers settles in San Diego, which is quite a commentary on its desirability.

After all, the officers have seen much of what the rest of the world has to offer, and they choose San Diego.

A Spanish influence is everywhere, with red tile roofs and graceful porticos. Industries include aerospace and aircraft production, various research programs, electronics, shipbuilding, tuna fishing, oceanography, and tourism with a capital T.

San Diego is much like Los Angeles and San Francisco used to be, relatively uncrowded and with very little smog. It hasn't become big-city yet. The major cultural attraction probably is the 100-acre zoo, with a wide variety of other parks, art galleries, missions, museums, the restored Old Town section, Sea World, and many tourist-oriented facilities. Oh yes, opera, ballet, and symphony can be found here, along with major-league sports teams. The colleges and universities could be called major-league too.

Medical facilities are abundant, as you might expect in a retirement area.

P.S. The earthquake fault line misses this area, and tornadoes, hurricanes, thunderstorms, and hailstones are as rare as ducks' teeth. Snow has never been recorded here.

San Francisco, California

Reaction_____

San Francisco is so startlingly dramatic in its diversity and beauty that we often forget that it is one of America's major centers of finance, commerce, and transportation. It fairly reeks of culture, and the ongoing debate with New Yorkers as to which area has the better symphonies, theaters, operas, museums, and so forth continues with gusto and much local pride. There can be no discussion about which city is cleaner, however.

The greater San Francisco region has a dazzling array of options. Neighborhoods range from Nob Hill to Chinatown, Fisherman's Wharf to the financial district, the Embarcadero to North Point Pier . . . and on and on. Nearly everyone loves San Francisco and its environs.

The area is quite sunny, but if you still find San Francisco and Oakland a bit too cool and foggy, only a few miles to the south you will find much sunnier and drier regions, such as Palo Alto, San Jose, and Santa Clara.

From the famous precipitous hills, over which the equally famous cable cars have been rattling through the years, the views are magnificent. Sightseeing, even for long-time residents, is a never ending delight, the restaurants are diverse and renowned for their excellence, the bridges inspire poetry, a bay surrounds three sides of the city . . . well, let's just say that it may not be the best place for you to live and prosper, but without doubt you should plan to visit it at least a few times.

Living costs are very high, it's crowded, some areas are becoming run down, the traffic problems are getting worse, but even with these, we would have to consider the quality of life and cultural dimensions of San Francisco to be in a class by themselves.

Seattle, Washington

Reaction_____

Overlooking Puget Sound, with Olympic and Cascade mountain peaks surrounding it, Seattle is a scenic wonder. Few other cities in the world can compete with its natural beauty. Green and lush, with traditionally friendly and open people, this northwestern metropolis has an outstanding future. It is a major gateway to the orient, with many natural resources and assets.

However, Seattle has had "boom and doom" economic cycles for the past several decades, and it is once again on the low end of the curve. Airlines and the housing industry have been battered by the current recession, and Seattle depends on Boeing and its timber resources. The economy is more diversified than it has been in the past, however, so the area has not been as hard hit as in previous years.

Seattleites have been shocked and angry about dramatic increases in their traditionally low electric rates, but their costs are still below those of most of the nation.

The residents are justifiably proud of their cultural excellence, with buildings left intact and functioning from the

1962 World's Fair. They house opera, symphony, art exhibits, a marvelous science center, museum of flight, and a startling variety of restaurants. The view from the Space Needle is breathtaking. The University of Washington is one of the leaders in the country, and many other colleges and universities with their own specialties are located here.

Many compare this clean and exciting city to San Francisco, for both have colorful waterfronts, a dedication to cultural excellence, cool climates, and enough diversity to satisfy anyone.

Shreveport, Louisiana

Reaction_____

Shreveport is an industrialized city, manufacturing telephone equipment, batteries, oilfield equipment, electrical transformers and the like, and processing lumber in great quantities. As do so many southern cities, Shreveport has a military base nearby (Barksdale Air Force Base).

Numerous parks, an annual art festival called the Red River Revel, and the Louisiana State Fair are part of the cultural offerings of Shreveport. Flower lovers will appreciate the emphasis on horticulture, with the American Rose Center, Barnwell Memorial Garden and Art Center, and the beauty of the surrounding countryside.

Sioux Falls, South Dakota

Reaction_____

This is a major wholesale and retail trading market for the state, as well as a major meat packing center. As you might assume, much of its economy depends on agriculture, but a surprise is the Earth Resource Observation Systems Center which is located here. It is the international center for photography of the earth from aircraft and space vehicles.

Several colleges add cultural depth, and the city has over fifty parks. Although there really are not many people in this region, they do make an outstanding effort to support their symphony, zoo, community playhouse, fine arts association, and other programs designed to round out the quality of life in Sioux Falls.

Tampa, Florida

Reaction_____

Tampa itself is a large industrial city, with some of the pollution and congestion that manufacturing, beer brewing, cigar making, and phosphate production would bring to any area. But this enterprise is necessary for the economic growth of the area, and close by are the well-known retirement areas of St. Petersburg, Sun City, Sarasota, Venice, and the other sun spots on the west coast of Florida.

Cultural facilities in the region include the Florida Gulf Coast Symphony, local community theaters, Busch Gardens, and a fine library system. Most of the lifestyle revolves around the marvelous beaches, fishing and boating, shuffleboard, and just generally enjoying the consistently warm and sunny days for which Florida is famous.

Excellent medical care is available, living costs are fairly low, and several colleges are located in the region. The terrain itself is fairly flat with many housing tracts, so the scenic charm of this area depends on its miles of lovely beaches and the fantastic vista of the Gulf of Mexico filling the horizon.

Tucson, Arizon

Reaction_____

This town has been exploding in population in the last several years, and retirees have been leading the influx of newcomers. It is known as a healthy environment; the place to take your sinuses when clogged. At the same time it is a cosmopolitan place, with its own museum of art, symphony, ballet and light opera company, and plans for the future.

Copper, cattle, aircraft, and cotton are the major ingredients in the relatively small industrial picture. The scenery is magnificent, if you enjoy desert sunsets, mountain ranges shimmering in the distance, and being near a wonderful national forest.

The air quality is not what one might hope, however, with increased traffic and industrial pollution creating smog. Water levels are dropping due to extensive use, and wells must be driven deeper all the time. One consequence is that Tucson's citizens are not as eager to encourage others to join their population. It must be suspected that retired persons will continue to move to Tucson, however, because for people who enjoy a dry sunny climate and outdoor western lifestyle, it has much to offer.

Tulsa, Oklahoma

Reaction_____

With the recent completion of the Arkansas River Navigation System, Tulsa now has access to both the Gulf of Mexico and the Great Lakes. This is adding more prosperity to an already thriving region.

Major employers include many oil and oil-related companies, American Airlines, and McDonnell-Douglas Aircraft. Although oil is a vital part of the area's economy, Tulsa has long made it a policy to pursue cultural excellence rather than boom-town profits, and as a result, the quality of life here is splendid. Concerts, a variety of museums and art centers, two major universities, many parks, and a clean and attractive environment make Tulsa a lovely place to live with an excellent economic outlook.

Washington, D.C.

Reaction_____

As you might imagine, the biggest industry in the nation's capital is the government itself. Approximately a third of a million people work for Uncle Sam in Washington, and no one knows how many lobbyists, trade association employees, journalists, and the like live in Washington because the power base of the nation is here.

The city was planned and developed around 1800, and its beautiful monuments and buildings are well known. Just about any major cultural pursuit imaginable can be found in several important auditoriums and a variety of centers. Art galleries, museums, beautiful parks, marvelous zoological gardens, excellent restaurants and a plethora of nightclubs are available.

Many respected colleges and universities, major research

and diagnostic health centers, and government agencies of every ilk add much to the region. Professional sports are represented by the Redskins (football), Bullets (basketball), and Capitals (hockey).

Finally, in a word, Washington, D.C. is unique. There is no other place like it in the world.

Wichita, Kansas

Reaction_____

This is the place where the three major private aircraft manufacturers compete, and the air is busy with Cessnas, Pipers, and Beechcraft flying into and out of their various airports. McDonnell Air Force Base also is located here.

Many oil companies, grain mills and elevators, and livestock marketing facilities also buoy the economy.

A variety of museums and art galleries, several colleges and universities, a planetarium, and symphony are among the cultural attractions of Wichita.

Wilmington, Delaware

Reaction_____

Wilmington has been an important transportation and industrial center since the early days in American history. It is a major producer of chemicals and has been known as the "Chemical Capital of the World."

Several colleges and the Delaware Law School are located here, and a variety of historical sites and museums are maintained. However, the most popular pastime in this area might be horse racing, with college football also closely followed.

The region is a blend of city and country living, with Philadelphia's excellent cultural programs and facilities located a few short miles away.

Directions: Rate only those cities below which are on your Tentative Interest List. Give a 5 to those cities for which you had a strongly positive reaction from reading the descriptive paragraphs; give a 3 if you had a moderately positive response; and a 1 if you retained little interest after reading the paragraphs. Eliminate from your Tentative Interest List those cities for which you lost all interest.

SUMMARY GRID

		Rating (5, 3 or 1)	Comments
1	Akron, Ohio		
2	Albany, New York		
3	Albuquerque, New Mexico		
4	Anchorage, Alaska		
5	Atlanta, Georgia		
6	Austin, Texas		
7	Bakersfield, California		
8	Baltimore, Maryland		
9	Baton Rouge, Louisiana		
10	Beaumont, Texas		
11	Biloxi, Mississippi		
12	Birmingham, Alabama		
13	Boise, Idaho		
14	Boston, Massachusetts		
15	Buffalo, New York		
16	Burlington, Vermont		
17	Casper, Wyoming		
18	Charleston, South Carolina		

		Rating (5, 3 or 1)	Comments
19	Charleston, West Virginia		
20	Chicago, Illinois		
21	Cincinnati, Ohio		
22	Cleveland, Ohio		
23	Columbia, South Carolina		
24	Columbus, Ohio		
25	Corpus Christi, Texas		
26	Dallas, Texas		
27	Denver, Colorado		
28	Des Moines, Iowa		
29	Detroit, Michigan		
30	El Paso, Texas		
31	Fargo, North Dakota		
32	Fresno, California		
33	Grand Rapids, Michigan		
34	Great Falls, Montana		
35	Hartford, Connecticut		
36	Honolulu, Hawaii		
37	Houston, Texas		
38	Indianapolis, Indiana		
39	Kansas City, Missouri		
40	Las Vegas, Nevada		
41	Little Rock, Arkansas		
42	Los Angeles, California		
43	Louisville, Kentucky		
44	Manchester, New Hampshire		
45	Memphis, Tennessee		

		Rating (5, 3 or 1)	Comments
46	Miami, Florida		
47	Milwaukee, Wisconsin		
48	Minneapolis, Minnesota		
49	Mobile, Alabama		
50	Nashville, Tennessee		
51	Nassau-Suffolk, New York		
52	Newark, New Jersey		
53	New Orleans, Louisiana		
54	New York, New York		
55	Norfolk, Virginia		
56	Oklahoma City, Oklahoma		
57	Omaha, Nebraska		
58	Orlando, Florida		
59	Philadelphia, Pennsylvania		
60	Phoenix, Arizona		
61	Pittsburgh, Pennsylvania		
62	Portland, Maine		
63	Portland, Oregon		
64	Providence, Rhode Island		
65	Raleigh, North Carolina		
66	Richmond, Virginia		
67	Rochester, New York		
68	Sacramento, California		
69	Salt Lake City, Utah		
70	San Antonio, Texas		
71	San Diego, California		
72	San Francisco, California		

		Rating (5, 3 or 1)	Comments
73	Seattle, Washington		
74	Shreveport, Louisiana		
75	Sioux Falls, South Dakota		
76	St. Louis, Missouri		
77	Tampa, Florida		
78	Tucson, Arizona		
79	Tulsa, Oklahoma		
80	Washington, D.C.		
81	Wichita, Kansas		
82	Wilmington, Delaware		

8

The Final Analysis

You have made many important decisions and judgments in your life.

One of the most crucial choices you will ever make is your choice of your personal place to prosper. America is a wonderland of opportunity. There are so many exciting potential locations. Our purpose in this book has been to help you make the best selection possible for you as an individual.

As you have made discoveries of facts and predictions for 82 different areas, you have made judgments. Your judgments have been about the places themselves, and about your own potential happiness and prosperity in those areas.

The purpose of this chapter is to put your personal values together with your judgments about the different locations. This process we call "The Final Analysis."

We have made every effort to make the Final Analysis an easy-to-follow process which takes only a few minutes. After all, we wouldn't let you down now, in the final chapter, when you are so close to finding your best places to prosper.

The Final Analysis Chart has been developed for your convenience. As you can see, all of the 82 areas are listed. In addition, we have included columns for each of the chapters in which you made judgments.

You also will note that bonus point columns have been included. The bonus points will come from your own Prospering Profile, which you discovered in Chaper 2.

Summarizing very briefly, the Final Analysis, using the Final Analysis Chart, will give you a score for each of the places on your Tentative Interest List.

The score will include your ratings from each chapter and bonus points taken from your Prospering Profile. The places with the highest total scores will be your best choices for prospering locations.

For your convenience, we have outlined in detail the easy steps which make up the Final Analysis and provided a sample Final Analysis Chart.

The Easy Steps

1. Your Tentative Interest List of places to prosper probably has suffered through a number of additions and deletions. In Column A of the Final Analysis Chart which follows, place a checkmark for those areas which are still on your Tentative Interest List. These are the regions which will get most of your attention in the Final Analysis.

As you will note, the first five areas have been checked in our *sample* Final Analysis, but you, no doubt, will have a different and probably a longer list of places under consideration.

2. Look again at your Prospering Profile in Chapter 2. Your profile represents the relative values you placed on five factors: Economics, Weather, Population, Risks and Hazards, and Quality of Life.

Give 5 bonus points to the factor which is highest in your Prospering Profile. Give 4 points to the next highest factor, 3 points to the third highest, and 2 points to the next-to-lowest factor. The lowest factor on the Prospering Profile receives 1 bonus point. In the event of a tie between factors, see the footnote below.[1]

On our *sample* Prospering Profile in Chapter 2, we have the five factors rated in the following order:

1. Economic factors—5 points
2. Risks and hazards—4 points
3. Population—3 points
4. Quality of life—2 points
5. Weather—1 point

3. Place the bonus points for each factor in the bonus point column (Column B) in the Final Analysis Chart. In our sample, Economy was the highest factor, so 5 points were awarded in the bonus column for Economy. That is, 5 bonus points were given to each place on the Tentative Interest List.

In the same manner, give 4 points for the next highest factor. In our sample, we have given 4 bonus points to Risks & Hazards for each city on our Interest List. Then put 3 points, 2 points, and 1 point in the appropriate bonus point columns, as we have done in the sample Final Analysis Chart.

4. As you remember, you scored or rated the places on your Tentative Interest List as you discovered more about them in each chapter. Your scores were then recorded in the Summary Grid at the end of each chapter.

Transfer the scores from the Summary Grid at the end of Chapter 3 to the Final Analysis Chart. Put the scores in the score column for Chapter 3. Then transfer the scores from the Summary Grid at the end of each of the other chapters and enter them in the appropriate score columns for each factor.

5. All you have to do now is multiply column B × column C for each chapter on a separate piece of paper. Now *add* up the

---

[1]In the event of a tie for first place, give 5 bonus points to each, with the next highest considered in third place with 3 points. If there is a tie for second place, give both 4 points and 2 points to the next highest. In case of a tie for third place, give each 3 points and award 1 point for last place. If there is a tie for fourth place, give the two tying factors 2 points each.

five numbers for your total score. It's easy. See the Sample Final Analysis Chart on the next page.

The areas can be ranked by scores and their rankings entered in the "Best Places" column. Our sample, based on alphabetical order, shows that Akron earned the highest score, followed by Albuquerque, Austin, Bakersfield and Beaumont.

But Should You Really Move?

Your own personal list of best places to prosper in America is now in front of you. You have made discoveries and learned a great deal about the opportunities which exist in other areas in our nation, and you have made many, many judgments and decisions to come up with your personal list.

And yet, you might very well be hesitant. You very likely have questions which need to be answered. After all, it is an extremely large step from (a) deciding where you would like to go, and (b) actually packing your socks and toothbrush.

Your hesitation, and even perhaps a wee bit of anxiety, is normal and natural. After all, you have a genuine investment in the place where you now live, and changing locations can be anxiety-provoking.

Let us consider the factors relating to your possible move, and see if some of your concern can be reduced. It would be wonderful if you could make the move with the knowledge that you had thought it over and really knew that it was the best action you could take.

You have an investment in your present location. And your investment is much more than financial. You are, in fact, a living part of the community you now call home.

You know many people and they know you. You have an identity, and you also have a role to play where you now live. Your investment also includes knowing where to shop, which restaurants you like best, the plans you have been making with friends and neighbors, your church membership, and so much more.

If you move to another place, even one which is clearly better than where you are now, you will have to find a new residence, meet new friends, and generally start over with much of what you now can take for granted.

357

SAMPLE FINAL ANALYSIS CHART

Column A	Tentative Interest Areas	Chapter 3 Economics B Bonus Points	Chapter 3 C Scores from Summary Grid on Page 112	Chapter 4 Weather B Bonus Points	Chapter 4 C Scores from Summary Grid on Page 156	Chapter 5 Population B Bonus Points	Chapter 5 C Scores from Summary Grid on Page 206	Chapter 6 Risks & Hazards B Bonus Points	Chapter 6 C Scores from Summary Grid	Chapter 7 Quality of Life B Bonus Points	Chapter 7 C Scores from Summary Grid on Page 293	Total	Your Best Places
✓ 1	Akron	5	5	1	5	3	3	4		2	3	65	1
2	Albany												
✓ 3	Albuquerque	5	5	1						2	5	59	2
4	Anchorage												
5	Atlanta								3				
✓ 6	Austin	5				3	3	4	3	2	3	47	3
✓ 7	Bakersfield	6			3	3	5	4	1	2	3	43	4
8	Baltimore												
9	Baton Rouge												
✓ 10	Beaumont	5	3	1	5	3	3	4	1	2	5	43	4
11	Biloxi												

SAMPLE COMPUTATIONS

	Chapter 3	Chapter 4	Chapter 5	Chapter 6	Chapter 7	Total
Akron	$5 \times 5 = 25$	$1 \times 5 = 5$	$3 \times 3 = 9$	$4 \times 5 = 20$	$2 \times 3 = 6$	
	$25 +$	$5 +$	$9 +$	$20 +$	$6 =$	65

FINAL ANALYSIS CHART

Column A	Tentative Interest Areas	Chapter 3 Economics		Chapter 4 Weather		Chapter 5 Population		Chapter 6 Risks & Hazards		Chapter 7 Quality of Life		Total	Your Best Places
		B Bonus Points	C Scores from Summary Grid on Page 134	B Bonus Points	C Scores from Summary Grid on Page 188	B Bonus Points	C Scores from Summary Grid on Page 247	B Bonus Points	C Scores from Summary Grid on Page 302	B Bonus Points	C Scores from Summary Grid on Page 350		
1	Akron												
2	Albany												
3	Albuquerque												
4	Anchorage												
5	Atlanta												
6	Austin												
7	Bakersfield												
8	Baltimore												
9	Baton Rouge												
10	Beaumont												

Column A	Tentative Interest Areas	Chapter 3 Economics B Bonus Points	C Scores from Summary Grid on Page 134	Chapter 4 Weather B Bonus Points	C Scores from Summary Grid on Page 188	Chapter 5 Population B Bonus Points	C Scores from Summary Grid on Page 247	Chapter 6 Risks & Hazards B Bonus Points	C Scores from Summary Grid on Page 302	Chapter 7 Quality Life B Bonus Points	C Scores from Summary Grid on Page 350	Total	Your Best Places
11	Biloxi												
12	Birmingham												
13	Boise												
14	Boston												
15	Buffalo												
16	Burlington												
17	Casper												
18	Charleston, S.C.												
19	Charleston, W.V.												
20	Chicago												
21	Cincinnati												
22	Cleveland												
23	Columbia, S.C.												

Column A Tentative Interest Areas	Chapter 3 Economics B Bonus Points	C Scores from Summary Grid on Page 134	Chapter 4 Weather B Bonus Points	C Scores from Summary Grid on Page 188	Chapter 5 Population B Bonus Points	C Scores from Summary Grid on Page 247	Chapter 6 Risks & Hazards B Bonus Points	C Scores from Summary Grid on Page 302	Chapter 7 Quality Life B Bonus Points	C Scores from Summary Grid on Page 350	Total	Your Best Places
24 Columbus												
25 Corpus Christi												
26 Dallas												
27 Denver												
28 Des Moines												
29 Detroit												
30 El Paso												
31 Fargo												
32 Fresno												
33 Grand Rapids												
34 Great Falls												
35 Hartford												
36 Honolulu												

Column A	Tentative Interest Areas	Chapter 3 Economics B Bonus Points	Chapter 3 Economics C Scores from Summary Grid on Page 134	Chapter 4 Weather B Bonus Points	Chapter 4 Weather C Scores from Summary Grid on Page 188	Chapter 5 Population B Bonus Points	Chapter 5 Population C Scores from Summary Grid on Page 247	Chapter 6 Risks & Hazards B Bonus Points	Chapter 6 Risks & Hazards C Scores from Summary Grid on Page 302	Chapter 7 Quality Life B Bonus Points	Chapter 7 Quality Life C Scores from Summary Grid on Page 350	Total	Your Best Places
37	Houston												
38	Indianapolis												
39	Kansas City												
40	Las Vegas												
41	Little Rock												
42	Los Angeles												
43	Louisville												
44	Manchester												
45	Memphis												
46	Miami												
47	Milwaukee												
48	Minneapolis												
49	Mobile												

Column A	Tentative Interest Areas	Chapter 3 Economics		Chapter 4 Weather		Chapter 5 Population		Chapter 6 Risks & Hazards		Chapter 7 Quality Life		Total	Your Best Places
		B Bonus Points	C Scores from Summary Grid on Page 134	B Bonus Points	C Scores from Summary Grid on Page 188	B Bonus Points	C Scores from Summary Grid on Page 247	B Bonus Points	C Scores from Summary Grid on Page 302	B Bonus Points	C Scores from Summary Grid on Page 350		
50	Nashville												
51	Nassau-Suffolk												
52	Newark												
53	New Orleans												
54	New York												
55	Norfolk												
56	Oklahoma City												
57	Omaha												
58	Orlando												
59	Philadelphia												
60	Phoenix												
61	Pittsburgh												
62	Portland, Me.												

363

Column A Tentative Interest Areas	Chapter 3 Economics		Chapter 4 Weather		Chapter 5 Population		Chapter 6 Risks & Hazards		Chapter 7 Quality Life		Total	Your Best Places
	B Bonus Points	C Scores from Summary Grid on Page 134	B Bonus Points	C Scores from Summary Grid on Page 188	B Bonus Points	C Scores from Summary Grid on Page 247	B Bonus Points	C Scores from Summary Grid on Page 302	B Bonus Points	C Scores from Summary Grid on Page 350		
63 Portland, Or.												
64 Providence												
65 Raleigh												
66 Richmond												
67 Rochester												
68 Sacramento												
69 Salt Lake City												
70 San Antonio												
71 San Diego												
72 San Francisco												
73 Seattle												
74 Shreveport												
75 Sioux Falls												

Column A Tentative Interest Areas	Chapter 3 Economics		Chapter 4 Weather		Chapter 5 Population		Chapter 6 Risks & Hazards		Chapter 7 Quality of Life		Total	Your Best Places
	B Bonus Points	C Scores from Summary Grid on Page 134	B Bonus Points	C Scores from Summary Grid on Page 188	B Bonus Points	C Scores from Summary Grid on Page 247	B Bonus Points	C Scores from Summary Grid on Page 302	B Bonus Points	C Scores from Summary Grid on Page 350		
76 St. Louis												
77 Tampa												
78 Tucson												
79 Tulsa												
80 Washington, D.C.												
81 Wichita												
82 Wilmington												

Boiling down all your questions about moving or staying put, they might best be reduced to this one key question:

Is It Worth the Risk?

Any time we make changes, of course, we also accept a certain level of risk. When we think about changing the living room decor, or joining a new group, or changing jobs, we automatically evaluate the risks involved. Then we decide whether the potential benefits are worth making the change.

Of course, moving to another place usually causes more anxiety and concern than just deciding to change the wallpaper and drapes. But in just the same way that making small changes can bring benefits, so can making big changes bring even bigger payoffs.

For some people, any change is difficult. Their security needs are so strong that even small decisions are made with extreme reluctance. When it comes to moving, they might even approach panic, and start to stammer, "Oh, we couldn't do that. After all, the kids are in school. And our roots are here. No, it just isn't for us."

Most of us make excuses when it comes to making important decisions, and we rationalize by proclaiming ourselves to be "careful" and "conservative by nature." The problem is, it is too easy to miss out on the wonderful opportunities of life by not making decisions and appropriate changes.

The greatest part of the anxiety involved in moving comes from fear of the unknown. A variety of questions spin through our heads when we think of pulling up stakes and moving to a new home:

Will I be able to find a good job?

Can I find people who will like me and accept me?

What are the schools like?

Will I be able to get a new mortgage?

Can I transfer my lines of credit?

What will happen to our old friendships?

These and so many other questions are important and legitimate. Even if the place we call home is a dead-end, at least it is a familiar dead-end. We often hang on to old ways and places much longer than we need to, however.

Much of the unknown can be learned rather easily. Think again about all the information contained in this book. You have learned a great deal already about new places to prosper. With this knowledge, you have an excellent headstart on getting the information you should have before you actually call the moving company. In fact, by this time you already have more accurate information about some important aspects of life in your "Best Places" than most people who have lived there for many years.

To help you make the decision to move or not with as little anxiety and trepidation as possible, we have outlined some useful steps.

Hello, Reference Librarian

Of all the invaluable sources of help in this world, reference librarians surely must rank near the top of the list. Furthermore, we have found them to be among the most pleasant and effective professionals on earth.

Just imagine! The library holds the accumulated information possessed by mankind. This includes the facts and knowledge you need about your newly identified places to prosper. And the reference librarians will help you find that information, quickly and easily. Just tell them what you would like to know, and if the information is available, they will amaze and delight you with their information retrieval talents. When using the library, be certain to refer to our extensive bibliography at the end of this chapter.

Dear Chamber of Commerce

If you write a letter to the chambers of commerce for the city areas in which you are interested, you might just be deluged with material. Ask for a "newcomer's pack" or for general information and specific answers to your questions. You will receive maps, colorful brochures, business trend outlines, costs of living information, real estate brochures, cultural events descriptions, and all kinds of goodies welcoming you to the area.

You might even find that the information is so enticing and helpful that your anxiety will begin to melt away immediately. This knowledge at the very least will help give you a more complete picture of the places you are considering.

Hi. I'm A Visitor

The most informative step of all is to actually visit the places you are considering as your best new location. Yes, it costs money, but even a brief visit will help you fill in the information gaps. It also will help you form impressions about the people, quality of life, business outlook, and so forth. Besides, you can consider it a vacation and adventure rolled into one.

We suggest that you plan to use a car during your visit, unless you are going to one of the few cities which has excellent public transportation. Anticipate some frustration in finding your way around. Give yourself plenty of time to get from one place to another and expect to get lost occasionally. After all, you cannot gather accurate impressions if you are rocketing around town and missing what you came to see.

May we also suggest that you look over the business areas, several different residential areas, and generally try to get a cross-section of the different places in the region. In addition, travel into the countryside to get an impression of the "lay of the land," and see whether you like the scenery.

An excellent strategy for learning about new locations is a simple one: ask the natives. For example, you should spend a few hours with a real estate salesperson. He not only will help you learn about the real estate market, he also will provide you with invaluable insights about the area and what's doing there.

Strike up conversations with people you meet and ask their opinions. You will be pleasantly surprised at how open and friendly most people are if you ask them for help. Even in large metropolitan areas, where everyone seems to be too busy and important, you will find just about everyone willing to assist you.

Ask the questions you would like answered. What are the newest economic or political developments? Recent tax trends? What is happening with the schools? Cultural and recreational opportunities? Best places to live?

If you have special questions about your career or business opportunities, the chamber of commerce can be a splendid asset. If you write to them before your visit, they can help arrange meetings with professionals with the specialized information you might like to have before making your final relocation decision.

Other useful sources of information and insights include places of worship, branches of the company for which you or a friend might be employed, fraternal or service organizations such as Lions Club or Rotary Club, professional groups related to your area of expertise, or just plain knowing somebody who will arrange an introduction to a knowledgeable person in the new place.

You never know . . . not only will you learn amazing and wonderful things about the areas you are considering, you are almost sure to meet some amazing and wonderful people too.

Don't Burn Your Bridges

A funny thing often happens when people relocate to find a better way of life. They make the move, get settled, start to prosper, and then get a call from someone back in the place they just left.

The message frequently is something like: "We are setting up a new program and wonder if you would be interested in managing it for us." Can you believe it? A new and golden opportunity back where you came from!

It is a nice problem to have. But keep one thing in mind, please. You will not have the chance to benefit from your old relationships and place if you leave it in the wrong way. What is the wrong way? It is giving the impression to the people you are leaving behind that the place is not good enough for you. By implication, this means that you are rejecting the place and the people. This is burning your bridges.

When you decide to move, explain it in positive terms. But be sure to tell others that you are making the move with mixed feelings, because you enjoy (a) your present location and the people very much, and (b) perhaps temporarily, because you have to try it out and may decide to return at the earliest opportunity. This approach should help to retain friendships and keep doors open for future possibilities.

Telling Family and Friends

Before you tell your uncles, cousins, bowling buddies, or others in your life, try to anticipate how your announced decision will affect them. You might expect that some will be envious, others will be happy for you, and not a few will resent the change in you and the implied rejection of them.

Knowing this in advance, we suggest that your strategy follow these steps:

1. Decide whom you would really like to retain as friends or close relatives.

2. Make an agreement with them that this is possibly an opportunity for them as well, and you will act as scout for the group. If the new place provides better chances to prosper, you want them to consider joining you or at least visiting you there. Explain that if unforeseen circumstances make a return appropriate, you very much want to be welcomed back.

3. Share with them the decision-making process you have learned in this book, and encourage them to give some thought to finding their own best place to prosper . . . perhaps in the same area where you will be.

4. Reassure them that they are an important part of your life and you fully intend for them to remain so. Some concrete plans for keeping in touch and getting together will show that you are concerned about their feelings and genuinely care about continuing the relationship.

5. Ask for their help in making the transition. By asking for their advice and views, you will involve them in the decision-making process. When they give this assistance,

370

they will have made a psychological investment in your future and as such will be much more likely to continue to be supportive and caring.

6. When you discuss the possibility of an impending move with your children, keep the steps outlined above in mind. Depending upon the ages of your youngsters, you can expect them to be good problem solvers and probably surprisingly supportive. To the extent possible, allow them the privilege and responsibility of sharing the selection process with you and making judgments about the desirable and undesirable features of the places under consideration.

In Conclusion

Whether or not you decide that a move is in your best interests, you have made some wonderful discoveries . . . both about yourself and about the remarkable opportunities available in America.

Whatever your decision, you will make it as an informed and thoughtful person. And the charts and predictions will be extremely useful as references for subsequent planning for your life and that of your family and friends.

Please keep in mind that your prosperity in life depends upon your willingness to think about cause and effect, and then to try to make things happen rather than wait for things to happen to you.

Most of what occurs can be influenced by our efforts, and this includes living life to its fullest.

In sum, there are some splendid places in America where you can live more successfully and happily. We have tried to help you find the ones best for you to prosper. But regardless of where you live, remember that prospering is in large measure an attitude and a style of life. It involves an effort to discover the marvelous offerings of our world and then to enjoy them to the fullest.

We hope that we have helped you make those discoveries.

Bibliography

THE RELOCATION BIBLIOGRAPHY

(Used with permission of The Reference Committee, Reference and Adult Services Section, New York Public Library Association.)

Climate

Climates of the States. James Ruffner and Frank Blair, eds. Detroit, Mi., Gale Research, 1977. 2v.

Traveling Weatherwise in the U.S.A. Edward Powers and James Witt. New York, Dodd, Mead, 1972.
Over 150 charts, giving the weather characteristics of cities all over the U.S., as well as 50 pages of maps discussing weather patterns and local conditions in each weather area.

Weather Almanac. Ruffner and Bair. 2nd ed. Detroit, Mi., Gale Research, 1977.
A reference guide to weather and climate of the U.S. and its key cities. Includes reference data on storms and weather extremes. Also includes world climatological highlights.

Weather Atlas of the United States. U.S. Environmental Data Service, Detroit, Mi., Gale Research 1968 reprint 1975. Original title **Climate Atlas of the United States.**
Depicts climate of U.S. in terms of distribution and variation of such climate measures as temperature, precipitation, wind, barometric pressures, relative humidity, etc.

Weather Handbook. Conway and Liston. Rev. ed. Atlanta, Ga., Conway Research, 1977.
A summary of weather statistics for principal cities throughout the U.S. and around the world. Charts & maps.

Crime

Almanacs
CBS News Almanac
Information Please Almanac
World Almanac and Books of Facts
These give crime rates by state: totals.

America's 50 Safest Cities. David Franke. New Rochelle, N.Y., Arlington House, 1974.
Gives crime rates for all communities with a population of 50,000 or more; number of offenses in each crime category for 1970–71. Read introduction for best use of materials.

Crime in the United States. Washington, D.C., U.S. Department of Justice, Federal Bureau of Investigation, G.P.O.
Annual. Includes all communities of 25,000 or more in population. This is the root source of all information on the subject.

Statistical Abstract of the United States. Washington, D.C., U.S. Census Bureau, Department of Commerce, G.P.O.
Annual. Crime for 48 cities: police protection and fire protection.

Sourcebook of Criminal Justice Statistics. Michael J. Hindelang et al., Criminal Justice Research Center. Albany, N.Y., Washington, D.C., U.S. Department of Justice, G.P.O.
   Annual. Statistical coverage of criminal justice system, public attitudes, crime in selected cities.

Safe Places: East of the Mississippi. David Franke and Holly Franke, N.Y., Warner Books, 1973.

Cultural/Recreational

American Art Directory. 47th. ed. New York, Bowker, 1978.
   Title and frequency vary. Covers museums, art organizations, universities and colleges having art departments and museums of their own, art schools and classes in the United States, Canada and abroad. In addition there are sections listing state art councils; art magazines; newspapers carrying art and their critics; traveling exhibitions with booking agencies and type of material and their sources and children's and junior museums.

The American Music Handbook. Christopher Pavlakis, New York, Free Press, 1974.
   Intends to bring together information on all areas of organized musical activity in the United States. About 5,000 entries for service organizations and institutions, performing groups and ensembles, music societies, schools of music, music libraries and archives.

Campground and Trailer Park Guide. New York, Rand McNally & Co.
   Annual. Covers the United States and Canada. Maps are accompanied by tables giving information on size, elevation, facilities, activities, etc.

Dance Magazine. New York, Danad Publishing Co.
   Regular feature, Domestic Reports, provides information on a wide variety of dance activities in communities across the country.

Folk Dance Directory. Raymond La Barbara, ed. Brooklyn, N.Y., New York Folk Dance Association.

Annual. National listing of folk, square and round dancing with a classified directory.

Festivals U.S.A. and Canada. New York, Washburn.

Festivals are described under such groupings: agricultural festivals, beauty pageants, drama festivals, music festivals, sports festivals.

High Fidelity (magazine)—"Musical America" edition. New York, A.B.C. Leisure Magazines Inc.

The "Musical America" edition carries 32 extra pages which cover current music performances, music centers, and performing artists for those with a special interest in "live" music.

The Musician's Guide. Gladys S. Field, New York, Music Information Service, 1972.

Irregular. Offers directory information on music associations, competitions, awards, etc., education; libraries and publications; festivals; unions; and the music industry and trade.

National Directory for the Performing Arts and Civic Centers. Dallas, Tx., Handel & Co.

Annual. A listing by state, then by city, of performing arts organizations, with information on management, purpose, income sources, etc. College and university facilities are listed only when such institution has the major performance house for a surrounding area.

National Register of Historic Places. Washington, D.C., National Park Service.

Biennial. Describes places designated as national historic landmarks or preserved by the National Park Service with name, location, historical connection, etc. Geographical arrangement by state, then county.

New Woman's Survival Sourcebook. Susan Rennie and Kirsten Grimstad, eds., new York, Alfred A. Knopf. 1975.

A catalog of information on feminist communications, art, self-health, children, learning, self-defense, work, justice, and organizations and women's centers.

The Official Museum Directory: United States, Canada, Washington, D.C., Skokie, Il., American Association of Museums and National Register Publishing Co.
Provides information on 6,657 museums of art, history and science in four main sections: 1) institutions by state and province, 2) by name alphabetically, 3) by director and department heads alphabetically and 4) by category.

Opera News (magazine) New York, Metropolitan Opera Guild.
Two regular features provide information on the quantity and quality of operatic activity around the country. The U.S. Calendar lists operas (with casts) currently being performed by local opera companies nationwide.

Woodall's Trailering Parks and Campgrounds Directory. Highland Park, Il.
Annual. Covers United States, Canada and Mexico. Includes suggestions on planning trips.

Education

American Trade Schools Directory. Queens Village, N.Y., Croner, 1974.
Subject & geographical listings.

American Art Directory. See: Cultural/Recreational.

College Guide for Students with Handicaps. See: Handicapped.

Directory of Educational Programs for The Gifted. Lavonne B. Axford, N.J., Scarecrow, 1971.
Listing is by state. Includes both public and private institutions and summer programs.

The Directory for Exceptional Children. See: Handicapped.

The Directory of Facilities for the Learning-Disabled and Handicapped. See: Handicapped.

Directory of Public Elementary & Secondary Schools in Selected Districts. Enrollment and Staff by Racial/ Ethnic Groups. Washington, D.C., U.S. Dept. of Health, Education and Welfare. Office of Civil Rights, 1972.

Directory of Schools and School Systems. Syracuse, N.Y., Gaylord Bros. 7 vols.

Annual. All states and the District of Columbia are covered and are arranged alphabetically. Each state is sub-arranged by county. Within the county the list is by school district giving all public and parochial elementary and secondary schools. Information included is name and function of all chief officers and address, telephone, grades covered and enrollment of all schools.

Ed Fac Career School Directory: Business, Paraprofessional, Correspondence, Technical & Trade. Pekin, Il., Ed. Fac Publishing Co.

Arranged by state with subject headings such as hairdressing, real estate and floral designs.

Educational Directory. Washington D.C., U.S. Office of Education. G.P.O.

Annual. A useful annual varying in format and contents. In four parts: State government, public school systems, higher education, and education associations.

A Handbook of Private Schools. Boston, Ma., Porter Sargent Publications Inc.

Annual.

Jewish Education Register and Directory. New York, American Association for Jewish Education.

A general section on various phases of Jewish education is followed by the directory, which includes educational agencies, schools, libraries, museums, summer camps, etc. Covers the United States and Canada.

Guide to Middle State Schools in Delaware, District of Columbia, Maryland, Puerto Rico, Canal Zone, Virgin Islands and Overseas. Philadelphia, Pa. Middle State Assn. of Colleges and schools, 1978.

Guide to Middle States Schools in New Jersey. Philadelphia, Pa., Middle States Assn. of Colleges and Schools, 1978.

Guide to Middle States Schools in New York. Philadelphia, Pa., Middle States Assn. of Colleges and Schools, 1978.

Guide to Middle States Schools in Pennsylvania. Philadelphia, Pa., Middle States Assn. of Colleges and Schools, 1978.

> Guide books list special programs, test data, grades and rank, and post-secondary plans of students.

Lovejoy's Career and Vocational School Guide. Clarence E. Lovejoy, 5th. ed. New York, Simon & Schuster, 1978.

> Directory of institutions training for job opportunities.

Musicians Guide. See: Cultural/Recreational.

The New York Times Guide to Suburban Public Schools. Long Island, Westchester, Rockland, Connecticut, New Jersey. Maeroff and Buder. New York, Quadrangle/The N.Y. Times Book Co., 1976.

> Gives descriptions and statistical information on school districts.

Official Guide to Catholic Educational Institutions and Religious Communities in the United States. New York, Catholic Institutional Directory Co.

> Annual. A directory of catholic universities, colleges, junior colleges, nursing schools, secondary boarding schools, and religious orders for men and women in the U.S. Includes information on admission requirements, courses offered, facilities, costs.

Patterson's American Education. Mount Prospect, Il., Education Directories.

> Annual. A comprehensive list of public and private schools, colleges, universities and other special schools in two main parts: school systems, arranged by states then by towns; directory of schools, colleges and universities classified by specialty. Includes officers of state, county and city educational systems, etc., and a list of educational associations.

Private Independent Schools. Wallingford, Conn., Bunting. Annual. Gives fairly lengthy descriptions of a large selection of private schools and brief listings of others. Includes a list of educational associations.

Registry of Private Schools for Children with Special Educational Needs. See: Handicapped.

Employment Information

Ad Search: The National Want Ad. Newspaper. Milwaukee, Wi., Leibherr.
Weekly. Photocopies of want ads from 67 major U.S. newspapers.

College Placement Annual. Bethlehem, Pa., College Placement Council, Inc.
Annual. Lists occupational needs of corporate and government employers who recruit college graduates.

Digest of Executive Opportunities. New Canaan, Ct. General Executive Services Inc.
Weekly.

Directory of Private Employment Agencies. Washington, D.C., National Employment Association.

Federal Job Information Centers Directory. Washington, D.C., U.S. Civil Service Commission. G.P.O.

Finding a Job: A Resource for the Middle-Aged and Retired. Garden City, N.Y., Adelphi University Press, 1978.
Lists state and non-profit employment agencies on a state basis.

Occupations in Demand at Job Services Offices. Washington, D.C., U.S. Department of Labor. Employment and Training Administration, U.S. Employment Service. G.P.O.
Monthly bulletin. Identifies occupations for which large numbers of job openings were listed with public employment service computerized job banks during previous month.

Handicapped

Access Guide Directory. Rehabilitation International USA, 20 W 40th St. N.Y., 10018.
> Annual. Directory of 275 handbooks to cities and transportation facilities throughout world. Free to disabled, handicapped and elderly persons.

The College Guide for Students with Disabilities. A Detailed Directory of Higher Education Services, Programs and Facilities Accessible to Handicapped Students in the U.S. Elinor Gollay, Cambridge, Ma., Abt Associates, 1976.
> Arranged geographically.

Directory of Agencies Serving the Visually Handicapped in the U.S. 20th. ed. New York, American Foundation for the Blind, 1978.

Directory of Facilities for Learning-Disabled and Handicapped. Careth Ellinson and James Cass. New York, Harper & Row, 1972.
> Includes "analytical descriptions of diagnostic facilities . . ., as well as descriptions of remedial, therapeutic and developmental programs." Listing is by states of the U.S. and the provinces of Canada. Index by names of institutions, and lists of facilities in major cities.

Directory for Exceptional Children. Boston, Ma., Porter Sargent Publications Inc., 1978.
> Gives information on public and private schools and treatment centers for the emotionally disturbed and socially maladjusted; psychiatric guidance clinics; facilities for orthopedic and neurological handicaps; facilities for the mentally retarded; schools for the blind, the partially sighted, the deaf and hard of hearing; speech and hearing clinics, etc. Includes list of associations, foundations and societies.

Public Welfare Directory: 1977–78. Michele Moore. Chicago, Il., American Public Welfare Association.
> Annual. Information concerning basic programs, practices and staff of all public welfare and related public agencies in the U.S. and Canada.

Registry of Private Schools for Children with Special Educational Needs. Baltimore, Md., National Educational Consultants, 1971.

Arranged alphabetically by state. Index by type of disability served. Updating supplements are issued annually.

Health

American Dental Directory. Chicago, Il., American Dental Association.

Annual. A geographical and alphabetical listing of dentists.

American Medical Directory. Littleton, Ma. PSG Publishing, 1979 5v.

A register of physicians of the U.S., Canal Zone, Puerto Rico, Virgin Islands, certain Pacific Islands, and U.S. physicians located temporarily in foreign countries, who possess a degree of Doctor of Medicine or Doctor of Osteopathy from an approved medical school. Arranged geographically.

Directory of Medical Specialists. Chicago, Il., Marquis Who's Who Inc.

Annual. American Specialty Boards certified physicians.

Guide to Health Care Field. Chicago, Il., American Hospital Association.

Annual. Center source of information on health care institutions, medical organizations, agencies, educational programs in the health field.

Handbook and Directory of Nursing Homes and Other Facilities for the Aged Within a 50-mile Radius of New York City. Edkman and Furman. New York, Basic Books Inc., 1975.

National Directory of Private Social Agencies. Queens Village, N.Y., Croner.

Loose-leaf, up-dated monthly. Has subject and geographical listing.

U.S. Guide to Nursing Homes. Dan Greenberg. New York, Grosset & Dunlap, 1973.

East, West and Midwest editions. By state, then city. Includes points to consider in choosing a home.

Moving and Home Purchase

Condominiums: How To Buy, Sell, and Live in Them. Genevieve Gray. New York, Barnes and Noble Books, 1976.
Legal, financial and other aspects of condominium ownership.

Do-It-Yourself Moving. George Sullivan. New York, Macmillan, 1973.

The Fannie Mae Guide to Buying, Financing and Selling Your Home. Curt Tucker. Garden City, N.Y., Doubleday, 1978.
Covers financing, housing market, law etc. for houses, condominiums, and co-operatives.

How To Move Your Family Successfully. Tucson, Az., H.P. Books, 1979.

Home for Sale by Owner. Gerald M. Steiner. Chicago, Ill., Ana-Doug Publishing, 1976.
Legal and financial information and practical tips on home selling.

Religion

American Jewish Organization Directory. Margaret F. Goldstein, ed. 10th. ed. New York, Frenkel Mailing Service, 1978.
Lists Jewish organizations, schools, synagogues and Israeli institutions in the U.S. and Canada.

Jewish Travel Guide. Sidney Lightman, ed Jewish Chronicle Publications 25 Furnival St., London, England. No American Distributors, European Publisher's Representatives, Inc. and British Publications, Inc., 11-03 46th Ave., Long Island City, New York, 11101.
Lists organizations and synagogues in U.S. as well as Great Britain and Israel. U.S. section less complete than American Jewish Organization Directory.

The Official Catholic Directory. New York, P.J. Kenedy & Sons.

Annual. Lists Archdioceses and clergy in U.S., territories and overseas missions. Arranged alphabetically by diocese and clergy. Parishes, missions and parochial schools within diocese.

Note: Most Protestant denominations have their own directories. A sample is included. Consult your minister for the directory for your church if it is not included on this list.

Directory of Churches—Conservative Baptist Association of America. Wheaton, Ill., Conservative Baptist Association of America.

Annual. Geographically arranged directory.

Directory Unitarian Universalist Association. Boston, Ma., Unitarian Universalist Association.

Annual. Geographically arranged directory.

The Episcopal Church Annual Including the Polish National Catholic Church of America and Canada. New York, Morehouse-Barlow Co.

Annual. Alphabetical list of dioceses and churches within diocese.

Mennonite Yearbook. Scottdale, Pa., Mennonite Publishing House.

Annual. Regional directory.

Year Book and Directory of the Christian Church. (Disciples of Christ) Indianapolis, Ind., The Christian Church.

Annual. Geographically arranged directory.

Yearbook Lutheran Church of America. Philadelphia, Pa., Board of Publications of the Lutheran Church of America.

Annual. Geographical Directory of churches.

Yearbook United Church of Christ. New York, United Church of Christ.

Annual. Geographical Directory of churches.

Retirement

National Directory of Retirement Residences: Best Places To Live When you Retire. Noverre Musson. Rev. ed., New York, Fell, 1973.
State by state directory. Factors to consider in choosing.

Sunbelt Retirement: The Complete State-by-State Guide to Retiring in the South and the West of the U.S. New York, E. P. Dutton, 1978.
Summarizes climate, cost of housing, food and cultural advantages by state with brief description of major cities.

Woodall's 1978 Retirement Communities Directory. New York, Grosset and Dunlop, 1978.

Guide to Retirement Living. Paul Holter. Chicago, Rand McNally & Co. 1973.
Lists retirement communities, condominiums, apartments and trailer parks.

Where To Retire on a Small Income. Norman D. Ford, Greenlawn, N.Y., Harian, 1978.

SOURCES

CHAPTER 3

Chart

1. Standard Rate & Data Service, June 12, 1982.
2. Survey of Current Business, U.S. Dept. of Commerce, April, 1982.
3. Chase Econometrics/Interactive Data Corporation, Regional Forecasts, State and Metropolitan Areas, Vol. II, Spring 1982.
4. Chase Econometrics/Interactive Data Corporation, Regional Forecasts, State and Metropolitan Areas, Vol. II, Spring 1982.
5. Chase Econometrics/Interactive Data Corporation, Regional Forecasts, State and Metropolitan Areas, Vol. II, Spring 1982.
6. U.S. Dept. of Commerce & Labor, May, 1982.
7. Chase Econometrics/Interactive Data Corporation, Regional Forecasts, State and Metropolitan Areas, Vol. II, Spring 1982.

8. U.S. Dept. of Commerce & Labor, 1982.
9. Chase Econometrics/Interactive Data Corporation, Regional Forecasts, State and Metropolitan Areas, Vol. II, Spring 1982.
10. Chase Econometrics/Interactive Data Corporation, Regional Forecasts, State and Metropolitan Areas, Vol. I, July 1980.
11. Federal Home Loan Bank Board, 1982.
12. U.S. Census Bureau, 1980
13. Bureau of Census, U.S. Dept. of Commerce
14. U.S. Dept. of Labor, April, 1982.
15. U.S. Dept. of Labor, April, 1982.
16. U.S. Dept. of Labor, April, 1982.
17. U.S. Dept. of Labor, September, 1981.
18. U.S. Dept. of Labor, September, 1981.
19. U.S. Dept. of Labor, September, 1981.
20. U.S. Dept. of Energy, 1981.
21. AFT, Dept. of Research & Education, Research Service, Inc., 1980.
22. U.S. Dept. of Labor, Bureau of Labor Statistics, 1981.
23. U.S. Dept. of Labor, Bureau of Labor Statistics, 1981.
24. U.S. Dept. of Labor, Bureau of Labor Statistics, 1981.
25. U.S. Dept. of Labor, Bureau of Labor Statistics, 1981.
26. U.S. Dept. of Labor, Bureau of Labor Statistics, 1981.
27. U.S. Dept. of Labor, Bureau of Labor Statistics, 1981.
28. U.S. Dept. of Labor, Bureau of Labor Statistics, 1981.

CHAPTER 4

Chart

1. U.S. Dept. of Commerce, Comparative Climatic Data for U.S. Through 1980.
2. U.S. Dept. of Commerce, Comparative Climatic Data for U.S. Through 1980.
3. National Weather Service and Comparative Climatic Data, 1978.
4. U.S. Dept of Commerce, Comparative Climatic Data for U.S. Through 1978.
5. U.S. Dept. of Commerce, Climatography of the U.S.,

No. 60 and National Oceanic and Atmospheric Administration, 1978.
6. U.S. Dept. of Commerce, National Oceanic and Atmospheric Administration and Comparative Climatic Data for U.S. Through 1978.
7. U.S. Dept of Commerce, Comparative Climatic Data for U.S. Through 1978.
8. U.S. Dept of Commerce, Comparative Climatic Data for U.S. Through 1978.
9. U.S. Dept of Commerce, Comparative Climatic Data for U.S. Through 1978.
10. U.S. Dept of Commerce, Comparative Climatic Data for U.S. Through 1978.

CHAPTER 5

Chart
1. U.S. Bureau of the Census, 1980
2. Chase Econometrics/Interactive Data Corporation, Regional Forecasts, State & Metropolitan Areas, Vol. 11, Spring, 1981.
3. U.S. Bureau of the Census, 1970, 1980.
4. U.S. Bureau of the Census, 1980.
5. U.S. Bureau of the Census, 1980.
6. U.S. Bureau of the Census, 1970.
7. U.S. Bureau of the Census, 1981.
8. U.S. Bureau of the Census, 1981.
9. U.S. Bureau of the Census, 1981.
10. Standard Rates and Data, April 27, 1982. Sales and Marketing Management: July 27, 1981.
11. National Council of Churches, 1977.
12. National Council of Churches, 1977.
13. National Council of Churches, 1977.

CHAPTER 6

Chart
1. U.S. Federal Bureau of Investigation, 1980.
2. U.S. Federal Bureau of Investigation, 1980.
3. National Oceanic and Atmospheric Administration, 1979.

4. National Air Pollution Control Administration, HEW, 1968.
5. U.S. Environmental Protection Agency, 1979.
6. U.S. Environmental Protection Agency, 1979.
7. National Oceanic and Atmospheric Administration, 1979.
8. United States Weather Bureau.
9. United States Weather Bureau.

Map
1. National Oceanic and Atmospheric Administration, 1979.
2. United States Weather Bureau.
3. United States Department of Energy, 1979.
4. Center for Defense Information, 1982.

Appendix A

A standard metropolitan statistical area always includes a city (cities) of specified population, which constitutes the central city, and the county (counties) in which it is located. A standard metropolitan statistical area also includes contiguous counties when the economic and social relationships between the central and contiguous counties meet specified criteria of metropolitan character and integration. A standard metropolitan statistical area may cross state lines. In New England, standard metropolitan statistical areas are composed of cities and towns instead of counties.

SMSA—Counties Included in SMSA
1. **Akron, Ohio** Portage, Summit
2. **Albany—Schenectady—Troy, N.Y.** Albany, Montgomery, Rensselaer, Saratoga, Schenectady

3. **Albuquerque, N. Mexico** Bernalillo, Sandoval
4. **Anchorage, Alaska** Anchorage Census Division
5. **Atlanta, Georgia** Butts, Cherokee, Clayton, Cobb, DeKalb, Douglas, Fayette, Forsyth, Fulton, Gwinnett, Henry, Newton, Paulding, Rockdale, Walton
6. **Austin, Texas** Hays, Travis, Williamson
7. **Bakersfield, Calif.** Kern
8. **Baltimore, Maryland** Baltimore City, Anne Arundel, Baltimore, Carroll, Hartford, Howard
9. **Baton Rouge, Louisiana** Ascension, East Baton Rouge, Livingston and West Baton Rouge Parishes
10. **Beaumont-Port Arthur-Orange, Texas** Hardin, Jefferson, Orange
11. **Biloxi-Gulfport, Miss.** Hancock, Harrison, Stone
12. **Birmingham, Alabama** Jefferson, St. Clair, Shelby, Walker
13. **Boise City, Idaho** Ada
14. **Boston, Mass.; Boston, Lowell-Brockton; Lawrence-Haverhill** Essex, Middlesex, Norfolk, Plymouth, & Suffolk, Mass.; Rockingham, N.H.
15. **Buffalo, N.Y.** Erie, Niagara
16. **Charleston, S.C.** Berkeley, Charleston, Dorchester
17. **Charleston, W.V.** Kanawha, Putnam
18. **Chicago, Ill.** Cook, DuPage, Kane, Lake, McHenry, Will
19. **Cincinnati, Ohio-Ky.-Ind.** Clermont, Hamilton, Warren Counties, Ohio; Boone, Campbell, Kenton Counties, Kentucky; Dearborn County, Indiana
20. **Cleveland, Ohio** Cuyahoga, Geauga, Lake and Medina Counties
21. **Columbia S.C.** Lexington, Richland
22. **Columbus, Ohio** Delaware, Fairfield, Franklin, Madison, Pickaway Counties.
23. **Corpus Christi, Texas** Nueces, San Patricio.
24. **Dallas-Ft. Worth, Texas** Collin, Dallas, Denton, Ellis, Hood, Johnson, Kaufman, Parker, Rockwall, Tarrant, Wise
25. **Denver-Boulder, Colo.** Adams, Arapahoe, Boulder, Denver, Douglas, Gilpin, Jefferson
26. **Des Moines, Iowa** Polk, Warren

27. **Detroit, Mich.** Lapeer, Livingston, Macomb, Oakland, St. Clair, Wayne
28. **El Paso, Texas** El Paso County
29. **Fargo-Moorehead, N.D., Minn.** Cass, N.D. Clay, Minn.
30. **Fresno, Calif.** Fresno County
31. **Grand Rapids, Mich.** Kent, Ottowa
32. **Great Falls, Mont.** Cascade
33. **Hartford-New Britain-Bristol, Conn.** Hartford, Middlesex & Tolland
34. **Honolulu, Hawaii** Honolulu County
35. **Houston, Texas** Harris, Brazoria, Fort Bend, Liberty, Montgomery, Waller Counties.
36. **Indianapolis, Indiana** Boone, Hamilton, Hancock, Hendricks, Johnson, Marion, Morgan, Shelby.
37. **Kansas City, Mo., Kansas** Cass, Clay, Jackson, Platte, Ray, Missouri. Johnson, Wyandotte, Kan.
38. **Las Vegas, Nevada** Clark
39. **Little Rock-No. Little Rock, Ark.** Pulaski, Saline
40. **Los Angeles-Long Beach, Calif.** Los Angeles County
41. **Louisville, Ky.-Ind.** Bullitt, Jefferson and Oldham, Kentucky. Clark, Floyd, Ind.
42. **Manchester-Nashua, N.H.** Hillsborough County
43. **Memphis, Tenn; Ark; Miss.** Shelby, Tipton, Tenn. Crittenden, Ark. De Soto, Miss.
44. **Miami, Florida** Dade County
45. **Milwaukee, Wis.** Milwaukee, Ozaukee, Washington, Waukesha.
46. **Minneapolis-St. Paul, Minn.-Wis.** Anoka, Carver, Chisago, Dakota, Hennepin, Ramsey, Scott, Washington and Wright, Minn. St. Croix, Wisconsin
47. **Mobile, Alabama** Baldwin, Mobile
48. **Nashville-Davidson, Tenn.** Cheatham, Davidson, Dickson, Robertson, Rutherford, Sumner, Williamson, Wilson
49. **Nassau-Suffolk, N.Y.** Nassua, Suffolk
50. **Newark, N.J.** Essex, Morris, Somerset and Union.
51. **New Orleans, Louisiana** Jefferson, Orleans, St. Bernard, St. Tammany Parishes

52. **N.Y., N.Y., N.J.**   Bronx, Brooklyn, Queens, Richmond, N.Y. Counties; Putnam, Rockland and Westchester, N.Y. Bergen, N.J.

53. **Norfolk-Virginia Beach, Portsmouth Va.-N. Carolina**   The cities of Chesapeake, Norfolk, Portsmouth, Suffolk, Virginia Beach, Va. Currituck County, N.C.

54. **Oklahoma City, Okla.**   Canadian, Cleveland, McClain, Oklahoma and Pottawatomie

55. **Omaha, Nebraska-Iowa**   Douglas, Sarpy, Neb. Pottawattamie, Iowa

56. **Orlando, Fla.**   Orange, Osceola, Seminole

57. **Philadelphia, Penn.-N.J.**   Bucks, Chester, Delaware, Montgomery, Philadelphia, Pennsylvania. Burlington, Camden, Gloucester, N.J.

58. **Phoenix, Ariz.**   Maricopa

59. **Pittsburgh, Penn.-N.J.**   Allegheny, Beaver, Washington, Westmoreland.

60. **Portland, Maine**   Cumberland, Sagadahor Counties

61. **Portland, Ore.-Wash.**   Clackamas, Multnomah, Washington, Oregon. Clark, Washington.

62. **Providence-Warwick-Pawtucket, R.I.**   Bristol, Kent, Providence, Washington

63. **Raleigh-Durham, N. Carolina**   Durham, Orange and Wake

64. **Richmond, Va.**   Richmond City; Charles City, Chesterfield, Goochland, Hanover, Henrico, New Kent, Powhatan

65. **Rochester, N.Y.**   Livingston, Monroe, Ontario, Orleans, Wayne

66. **Sacramento, Calif.**   Placer, Sacramento, Yolo

67. **St. Louis. Mo.-Ill.**   St. Louis City, Franklin, Jefferson, St. Charles and St. Louis County, Missouri. Clinton, Madison, Monroe, St. Clair Counties, Ill.

68. **Salt Lake City-Ogden, Utah**   Davis, Salt Lake, Tooele, Weber

69. **San Antonio, Texas**   Bexar, Comal, Guadalupe

70. **San Diego, Calif.**   San Diego County

71. **San Francisco-Oakland, Calif.**   Alameda, Contra Costa, Marin, San Francisco, San Mateo

72. **Seattle-Everett, Wash.**   King, Snohomish

73. **Shreveport, Louisiana**   Bossier, Caddo, Webster Parishes

74. **Sioux Falls, S.D.**   Minnehaha County
75. **Tampa-St. Petersburg, Fla.**   Hillsborough, Pasco, Pinellas
76. **Tucson, Arizona**   Pima
77. **Tulsa, Oklahoma**   Creek, Mayes, Osage, Rogers, Tulsa, Wagoner
78. **Washington D.C.-Maryland-Va.**   District of Columbia; Alexandria, Fairfax, Falls Church, Manassas and Manassas Park Cities, Va. Arlington, Fairfax, Loudoun and Prince William Counties, Va. Charles, Montgomery and Prince George Counties, Maryland.
79. **Wichita, Kansas**   Butler, Sedgwick
80. **Wilmington, Del.-N.J.-Md.**   New Castle, Delaware. Salem, N.J. Cecil, Maryland
    No SMSA for:
    Casper, Wyoming
    Burlington, Vermont.

Appendix B

AIR POLLUTION

For as long as time itself air pollution has been present. Wind, rain, plant growth and snow all contributed to the natural balance of clean air and pollutants caused by volcanoes, forest fires and wind erosion. As man industrialized in the last half of the ninteenth century to the mass transportation and sophisticated manufacturing system today he has greatly affected the natural clean air system nature has provided. Approximately 90% of today's air pollution can be traced to that produced by man, his factories and automobiles being the largest contributors.

Increasing evidence is proving that air pollution is a major contributor to respiratory and lung diseases. If not the cause alone, the various individual components of air pollution can aggravate and intensify symptoms of heart disease, lung diseases and possibly some forms of cancer.

There are six types of air pollutants described by the Environmental Protection Agency. Their relationship to health disorders is the source of many studies. Those most affected by air pollution are the very young, the elderly and those with heart and lung diseases.

1. *Carbon Monxide:* this is a colorless, odorless, tasteless and poisonous gas. It is produced by incomplete combustion of carbon in fuel. It is the most produced pollutant in urban areas, three quarters of all carbon monoxide being emitted by automobiles.

    The effects of carbon monoxide are many. It causes headaches, dizziness and nausea. It can be absored into the bloodstream, reducing oxygen flow and causing the heart to work harder. People with angina pectoris are definitely affected by the carbon monoxide present in the air. Carbon monoxide has also been proven to reduce the ability to reason, impairing the thought processes.

2. *Sulfur oxides:* these are several chemical combinations caused by buring chemicals containing sulfur. They are acrid, corrosive, poisonous gases. Sulfur dioxide is the chief by-product. Coal burning, electric generating plants and industrial plants are the chief sources of production. About two thirds of the sulfur oxides are produced in urban settings. Crowded cities, factories, apartment buildings and cold winters are apt to produce the perfect setting for the sulfur oxides. These chemicals have been major contributors to air pollution emergencies linked to large increases in mortality rates (e.g., New York, 1966).

    Not only have sulfur oxides damaging effects on human health, irritating the upper respiratory tract, but their effect on plant life and other materials is alarming. It causes leaf damage, and can attack trees. It can corrode metals, ruin leather and books. It has been known to damage paint pigments and disintegrate hosiery.

3. *Particulates:* these can be liquid or solid, large enough to be seen by the human eye or too small for even an electron microscope to detect. They are mainly produced by stationary

fuel combustion furnaces and present themselves in industry, forest fires and volcanoes as soot and smoke. They can remain in the atmosphere for long time periods and be transported by wind hundreds of miles away from the original source.

Often these particulates alone are not the cause of a health hazard, but act as a catalyst for other chemical reactions. They can increase discomfort of lung illnesses, affect vision, corrode metals and cause grime on buildings, etc.

4. *Nitrogen Oxides:* these are gases produced when fuel is burned at very high temperatures. Internal combustion engines and stationary combustion furnaces are the major sources for their production. Nitrogen dioxide is the most important of the by-products. It has a yellow brown color and sweetish odor in some concentrations.

These gases have been known to harm vegetation, retarding its growth and damaging leaves. Ability to breathe is affected in normal children exposed to air with a high concentration of nitrogen dioxide as compared with children living in areas with low level nitrogen dioxide readings. Other studies have shown animals exposed to high NO_2 levels on a long term basis were effected in the ability for oxygen to be carried in the bloodstream. Eyes and nose may become irritated through exposure, a brown haze can permeate the air and metal can corrode in times of high concentration.

5. *Ozone/Oxidant:* these are sometimes referred to as photo chemical oxidants and are produced from chemical reactions in the atmosphere with sunlight. Organic substances and nitrogen oxides and hydrocarbons gather in the atmosphere, developing a secondary pollutant (or pollutants) we call smog. The main substance produced is called oxidant and is measured to determine the amount of smog being formed. Ozone is another name for oxidant. It has the same properties as oxygen but with an additional atom (O_3 instead of O_2). It will mix with the same chemicals as oxygen does but will produce a much different effect, or reaction.

Ozone produces a variety of symptoms—coughing, irritation of eyes, nose and throat, headaches and severe fatigue. Ozone can also affect athletic performance and aggravate normal lung functions. It can discolor the surface of leaves, shrubs and trees, crack rubber and damage fabrics.

6. *Hydrocarbons:* are formed by incomplete combustion of fuel and fuel waste, similar to the process causing carbon monoxide gas. They become major pollutants because they constitute the photochemical process producing smog. There are over a thousand identified chemical combinations and are dangerous mainly in high concentration. The two major categories are named *aromatics* and *olefins*.

The aromatics, those formed in the incomplete combustion process, are thought to be possible carcinogens. The oil industry, alcohol, ether, paint and lacquer thinner industries produce hydrocarbons through evaporation in the production process.

The olefins don't appear to have a general effect on the human, but there is evidence of a general reduction in plant growth and evidence of abnormal leaf and bud development.

SOURCES:
Clean Air: The Breath of Life, U.S. Environmental Protection Agency
The Continuing Campaign for Cleaner Air, Marvin Zeldin, Public Affairs Pamphlet No. 572, Public Affairs Committee, Inc., August, 1979

Appendix C

I. Not felt or, except rarely under especially favorable circumstances. Under certain conditions, at and outside the boundary of the area in which a great shock is felt: sometimes birds, animals, reported uneasy or disturbed; sometimes dizziness or nausea experienced; sometimes trees, structures, liquids, bodies of water, may sway—doors may swing very slowly.

II. Felt indoors by few, especially on upper floors, or by sensitive, or nervous persons. Also, as in grade I, but often more noticeably: sometimes hanging objects may swing, especially when delicately suspended; sometimes trees, structures, liquids, bodies of water, may sway, doors may swing, very slowly; sometimes birds, animals, reported uneasy or disturbed; sometimes dizziness or nausea experienced.

III. Felt indoors by several; motion usually rapid vibration. Sometimes not recognized to be an earthquake at first. Duration estimated

398

in some cases. Vibration like that due to passing of light, or lightly loaded trucks, or heavy trucks some distance away. Hanging objects may swing slightly. Movements may be appreciable on upper levels of tall structures. Rocks standing motor cars slightly.

IV. Felt indoors by many, outdoors by few. Awakened few, especially light sleepers. Frightened no one, unless apprehensive from previous experience. Vibration like that due to passing of heavy, or heavily loaded trucks. Sensation like heavy body striking building, or falling of heavy objects inside. Rattling of dishes, windows, doors; glassware and crockery clink and clash. Creaking of walls, frame, especially in the upper range of this grade.

V. Felt indoors by practically all, outdoors by many or most: Outdoors direction estimated. Awakened many, or most. Frightened few—slight excitement, a few ran outdoors. Buildings trembled throughout. Broke dishes, glassware, to some extent. Cracked windows—in some cases, but not generally. Overturned vases, small or unstable objects, in many instances, with occasional fall. Hanging objects, doors, swing generally or considerably. Knocked pictures against walls, or swung them out of place. Opened or closed doors, shutters, abruptly. Pendulum clocks stopped, started, or ran fast, or slow. Moved small objects, furnishings, the latter to slight extent. Spilled liquids in small amounts from well-filled open containers. Trees, bushes shook slightly.

VI. Felt by all, indoors and outdoors. Frightened many, excitement general, some alarm, many ran outdoors. Awakened all. Persons made to move unsteadily. Trees, bushes, shaken slightly to moderately. Liquid set in strong motion. Small bells rang—church, chapel, school, etc. Damage slight in poorly built buildings. Fall of plaster in small amount. Cracked plaster somewhat, especially fine cracks in chimneys in some instances. Broke dishes, glassware, in considerable quantity, also some windows. Fall of knickknacks, books, pictures. Overturned furniture in many instances. Moved furnishings of moderately heavy kind.

VII. Frightened all—general alarm, all ran outdoors. Some, or many, found it difficult to stand. Noticed by persons driving motor cars. Trees and bushes shaken moderately to strongly. Waves on ponds, lakes, and running water. Water turbid from mud stirred up. Incaving to some extent of sand or gravel steam banks. Rang large church bells, etc. Suspended objects made to quiver. Damage negligible in buildings of good design and construction, slight to moderate in well-built ordinary buildings, considerable in poorly built or badly designed buildings, adobe houses, old walls (especially where laid up without mortar), spires, etc. Cracked chimneys to considerable extent, walls to some extent. Fall of plaster in considerable to large amount, also some stucco. Broke numerous windows, furniture to some extent. Shook down loosened brickwork and tiles. Broke weak chimneys at the roofline (sometimes damaging roofs). Fall of cornices from towers and high buildings. Dislodged bricks and stones. Overturned heavy furniture, with damage from breaking. Damage considerable to concrete irrigation ditches.

VIII.   Fright general—alarm approaches panic. Disturbed persons driving motor cars. Trees shaken strongly—branches, trunks, broken off, especially palm trees. Ejected sand and mud in small amounts. Changes: temporary, permanent; in flow of springs and wells; dry wells renewed flow; in temperature of spring and well waters. Damage slight in structures (brick) built especially to withstand earthquakes. Considerable in ordinary substantial buildings, partial collapse: racked, tumbled down, wooden houses in some cases; threw out panel walls in frame structures, broke off decayed piling. Fall of walls. Cracked, broke, solid stone walls seriously. Wet ground to some extent, also ground on steep slopes. Twisting, fall, of chimneys, columns, monuments, also factory stacks, towers. Moved conspicuously, overturned, very heavy furniture.

IX.   Panic general. Cracked ground conspicuously. Damage considerable in (masonry) structures built especially to withstand earthquakes: threw out of plumb some wood-frame houses built especially to withstand earthquakes; great in substantial (masonry) buildings, some collapse in large part; or wholly shifted frame buildings off foundations, racked frames; serious to reservoirs; underground pipes sometimes broken.

X.   Cracked ground, especially when loose and wet, up to widths of several inches; fissures up to a yard in width ran parallel to canal and stream banks. Landslides considerable from river banks and steep coasts. Shifted sand and mud horizontally on beaches and flat land. Changed level of water in wells. Threw water on banks of canals, lakes, rivers, etc. Damage serious to dams, dikes, embankments. Severe to well-built wooden structures and bridges, some destroyed. Developed dangerous cracks in excellent brick walls. Destroyed most masonry and frame structures, also their foundations. Bent railroad rails slightly. Tore apart, or crushed endwise, pipelines buried in earth. Open cracks and broad wavy folds in cement pavements and asphalt road surfaces.

XI. Disturbances in ground many and widespread, varying with ground material. Broad fissures, earth slumps, and land slips in soft, wet ground. Ejected water in large amounts charged with sand and mud. Caused sea-waves ("tidal" waves) of significant magnitude. Damage severe to wood-frame structures, especially near shock centers. Great to dams, dikes, embankments, often for long distances. Few, if any (masonry), structures remained standing. Destroyed large well-built bridges by the wrecking of supporting piers, or pillars. Affected yielding wooden bridges less. Bent railroad rails greatly, and thrust them endwise. Put pipelines buried in earth completely out of service.

XII. Damage total—practically all works of construction damaged greatly or destroyed. Disturbances in ground great and varied, numerous shearing cracks. Landslides, falls of rock of significant character, slumping of river banks, etc., numerous and extensive. Wrenched loose, tore off, large rock masses. Fault slips in firm rock, with notable horizontal and vertical offset displacements. Water channels, surface and underground, disturbed and modified greatly. Dammed lakes, produced waterfalls, deflected rivers, etc. Waves seen on ground surfaces (actually seen, probably, in some cases). Distorted lines of sight and level. Threw objects upward into the air.

SOURCES
U.S. Dept. of Commerce
U.S. Dept. of Interior—Geological Survey
National Oceanic & Atmospheric Administration

The Best of the Business From Warner Books